MISS

ADVENTURES

A TALE OF IGNORING LIFE ADVICE WHILE BACKPACKING AROUND

SOUTH AMERICA

AMY BAKER

MISS-ADVENTURES

Summersdale Publishers Ltd
46 West Street
Chichester
West Sussex
PO19 1RP
UK

www.summersdale.com

Printed and bound by CPI Group (UK) Ltd, Croydon, CR0 4YY

ISBN: 978-1-84953-996-8

Substantial discounts on bulk quantities of Summersdale books are available to corporations, professional associations and other organisations. For details contact general enquiries: telephone: +44 (0) 1243 771107, fax: +44 (0) 1243 786300 or email: enquiries@summersdale.com.

CONTENTS

LIFE IS A SUCCESSION OF
LESSONS WHICH MUST BE
LIVED TO BE UNDERSTOOD.

Helen Keller

'To Mum, Dad, and the Beauts'

SOME UNWANTED ADVICE

'So Amy, I hear you're off travelling again?' my mum's friend Sally asked, pulling up a bar stool to join my table, her forehead creased with worry. 'Hello Sally,' I said. 'Yep – you heard right. I'm off to South America on Thursday. I can't wait!'

I was back in Sussex getting in some quality time with my parents before I jetted off. They were currently at the bar of their trusty local pub getting in another bottle of red. Up until Sally made her approach, I'd been sitting in front of the open fire, feet up, pleasantly engrossed in googling where to meet Argentina's most eligible bachelors.

'And do you suppose you'll meet many people of your own age over there?'

'I expect so. Thirty isn't old. Loads of people travel in their thirties.'

As a lifelong friend of my parents who's watched me grow up, it was no surprise to me that Sally was eager to chat through my plans. 'Do they really? I would have thought a job and a family would be taking priority.'

Not this again. I channelled a frustrated sigh through flared nostrils.

'Maybe for some.'

Sally took a sip of her wine, and looked me in the eye. After a moment, she started nodding slowly. 'I see. I see. Just getting it out of your system, is that it? Before you can settle down?'

I don't know whether it was the heat from the open fire, or the fact that this was around the fifteenth time I'd been asked this question, but I could feel my face getting redder. I bit my lip.

'Hmm… not really, I'm not entirely sure I'll ever manage that, Sally.' I finished off the remains of my glass in one big gulp.

'But being forced to go alone—'

Here we go…

'I'm not being forced to do anything Sally, I *want* to go alone! It's half the point.'

'Huh! Is that so?' Sally looked genuinely perplexed.

'Yeah – I get to completely please myself. It's going to be great. Plus, I'm good at making friends, and a couple of my mates from home will be there when I first arrive, so please don't worry, I'm not worried in the slightest.'

'Well, even so, please remember, Amy, there are a lot of dangerous people in this world. Be careful, won't you.' She reached forwards to squeeze my hand.

'Of course I will.'

Sally smiled sadly, picked up her glass of red wine, and stood up to leave. 'Oh, and just one last thing, dear, do *try* not to get raped.'

▲▲▲▲▲▲▲

Sally's bombshell wasn't the first piece of blatantly obvious, completely unnecessary advice I received in the run-up to my departure. From the minute I handed in my notice and started to tell people about my plans to travel solo round South America for as long as my money lasted, the 'guidance' came in thick and fast, from all angles:

'Did you get my email? No? Well, I sent you one of those YouTube videos of a daylight shooting in São Paulo... I don't want to scare you, darling, I just want you to be prepared for all eventualities.'

Concerned relative

'Amy, could you please put together some thoughts on that article and circulate for me. Oh and while I've got you, did you hear that women get kidnapped in Colombia almost every month? Rumour has it they cut their tits off! By Monday, please!'

Alarmed colleague

'You mustn't let your guard down for even a moment. I've heard that the most dangerous people target women's toilets over there. I can't say I'm surprised. It's when you're at your most vulnerable, isn't it?'

Overly familiar barista

▲▲▲▲▲▲▲▲

Almost everyone I knew, and everyone I met, seemed to believe I was unlikely to return. In their eyes, I was embarking on a voyage to certain death on a continent populated solely by machine-gun-wielding, coked-up drug barons, sex traffickers, hungry deadly animals and plain-clothed cannibals. Everyone, it seemed, bar me, was terrified.

Some of the advice I noted down, for amusement in moments of boredom. The rest I dismissed with little more than a smirk and an 'Okay Mary, sure, I promise I'll always go for the testes.' I'd travelled before. I knew the deal. I didn't need a guidebook or advice on how to survive. I had this.

My aim was simple – enjoy some time out, go with the flow, visit cool places, meet great people, and hopefully figure some 'stuff' out somewhere between Argentina and Colombia. I didn't see much point in pondering what that 'stuff' might be at this stage; I just knew to expect it.

To my surprise, I found myself mulling over the madcap advice I'd been bombarded with as I was preparing to down tools and shimmy my way to Heathrow Airport. Advice I had at first dismissed as pure nonsense, issued by those who'd never travelled further than Calais, began popping back into my head – perhaps I'd been foolish to smile and nod blankly instead of listening? Maybe I should be questioning my own judgement if these people were so convinced I needed their advice? Would I gain more from my time away (and avoid mistakes) if I listened rather than shrugging off their suggestions and hoping for the best? And if it would pay to listen to Penny down the chemist and Mikey in the post room, might it also be wise to seek life advice from those who've actually achieved significant success? You know, legendary writers, respected feminists, people who refused to die despite climbing all the world's mountains, and other such overachievers?

Nah. I decided to wing it.

▲▲▲▲▲▲▲▲

The fact was that I was sick and tired of advice… I'm a woman, which means I've spent 30-odd years trying to filter the advice zooming at my head from every mouth within a five-metre radius. Before I became this person who no longer cared for listening, I'd reached the end of a very frayed tether and was delighted to tumble into an abyss of finally not caring what other people thought. I'd had it with other people's musings, thoughts, fears and ambitions being recited to me over and over, making me believe that they should also be my musings, thoughts, fears and ambitions. My sound-cancelling copper helmet was firmly in place and I was ready to army-crawl away from anyone who even attempted to lob an opinion in my direction…

I'm being unfair. There was of course a short period at primary school when I didn't feel bombarded. When I knew what it was to feel happy, content and like I knew it all. But that was back when I couldn't fully understand words or walk for more than half an hour without needing a glass of squash and a nap. Back then I dressed as Spiderman, longed to be a lollipop lady, and believed that being able to lip-sync the *Grease* mega-mix perfectly would make me a superstar. Everything was so simple back when I didn't give a monkey's about anyone's opinion aside from that of Michelangelo from the *Teenage Mutant Ninja Turtles*.

Then of course I hit secondary school, I grew up a bit and started being told about all the things I needed to do, and have, in order to be happy. And then, inevitably, I started to *want* the things, because people in my class had them, and I didn't want to be the uncool loser that had to go without. Yeah, I wanted the latest trainers, a colourful new fascia for my phone every week and a boyfriend with Mark Owen's face and haircut, but even then, I was torn between wanting all of it, and suspecting getting it might not be the big deal everyone was making it out to be.

Throughout school and college, I was repeatedly told not to bother with sport, drama and art because I was 'fortunate' to be one of the 'academic ones', to choose a 'sensible career' and, to do that, I'd best 'forget about those wishy-washy subjects once and for all'. It was a shame, because I quite fancied the look of Film Studies, but if it clashed with Modern History, and if this fully-grown adult with a sensible cardigan and a name plaque on his door was telling me I should pursue academia, then I guessed that's what I should do. I chose to study Law and Criminology at university because I thought it would lead to everything I 'needed' – power, money and status. All I *actually* got was a degree that I don't remember a single word of, student debt and a lot of excess stomach fat.

I don't remember at exactly what age I first started being told that finding a boyfriend was vital to my happiness. It's just always been the case. I'm pretty sure the concept was introduced to me via, oh, I don't know, *every fairy tale ever*, but that certainly wasn't the only medium telling me to aim for a relationship above everything else. For as long as I can remember I've been told that everything would be okay once I found the right man, that 'what you need is a rich husband', that 'you'll calm down eventually – once you find The One', and that 'what you need is a good man to keep you in line'. So I looked, which was fine, because a lot of them *looked* great. Sadly, what I found were the possessive, the offensively boring, the ones with girlfriends, and a whole bunch of handsome dickheads who didn't want to act like they knew me. Rather than dwelling on these failures, I always brushed them off pretty sharpish. I didn't want to award any man sole responsibility for putting a smile on my face. I wanted to learn to be happy on my own. Don't get me wrong, I did think it would be nice to find a smiley, kind, honest man eventually who'd make it his business to memorise all my favourite cheeses, to know when I needed wine or how to cheer me up in any given scenario, but I wasn't going to waste time on men that weren't right, just so I could feel I was putting in due diligence to 'the hunt'. I'm not denying marriage looks great – the idea of a pricey frock and a five-tiered cake I could cut with a sword *does* appeal – but it's certainly never felt like the be-all and end-all.

As my mates and I settled into working life post university, I started to feel pressure to be 'successful' and became acutely aware that I 'needed' *all the things*. Everything you read, watch and hear is telling you that in order to be truly, truly happy, you need a glamorous, high-powered career, a gorgeous husband, suitcases full of cash and a property decorated with tasteful modern art, freshly cut flowers and off-white furniture. And even though I believed it was possible to be happy without them, or with different things entirely, when the world you're still figuring out is telling you it repeatedly, that's what you decide to go in search of…

I was told I'd be happy once I settled into a career. One problem – I didn't have a clue what I wanted to do. I decided to try Event Management as my first job out of university based on the fact that the pretty girl from school with the long eyelashes told me, 'it's basically the coolest job you can get', plus it sounded like it might involve free stuff. But that didn't hold my interest so my mid-twenties saw me making a lot of coffee, working in a sweet shop, suffering through a stint as a showbiz journalist, letting someone take photos of my legs in a basement for £50… you know, the usual. I eventually set my heart on writing, and after three years of shitty internships and badly paid work, I found a job on an editorial team. This was it! I'd made it – I was working hard, and taking home a regular salary. I could afford new socks, soup, and the cost of public transport. Good for me! I was writing and editing a publication… and yet, I felt absolutely no sense of satisfaction. When I expressed my irritation, I was told, 'it doesn't matter if you hate every minute of it as long as you're earning money', 'you're not supposed to like it', and, 'get used to it, it's just the way it is'.

But I didn't get used to it. It bothered me that I didn't feel excited or passionate about what I was doing. Were any of the people around me excited and passionate, or was that not actually how things worked? I really wanted it to be the way things worked, man. I wanted to have a job that I was eager to get to every day. Where I left each evening with a sense of satisfaction that I'd been tested, I'd learnt things and I'd produced work that I was proud of. Maybe to find that I just needed to progress that little bit further to win the promotion to Deputy Editor I'd been working towards – maybe then the clouds would part, I'd start caring about my job, and I'd finally stroll through the elaborate gilded gates of Content Town. I would have arrived. There would be a fireworks display and everything!

That didn't happen though, because despite working as acting Deputy Editor for six months, doing it well, getting results and jumping through each and every hoop my employers had outlined for me, I was told 'I wasn't ready', that 'I had a long way to go yet', and that 'I would just have to be patient'. Rather than giving me the promotion I'd done the work – and actually begged – for, they asked me to sign a new contract that featured zero perks other than a three-month notice period, which they said 'demonstrated their commitment to me as an employee'. It was right about then that I thought 'Fuck this.'

The fact was, I wasn't happy doing what I was doing in London. I didn't feel like the life that I was living was enough, and I knew that a relationship or a job weren't going to suddenly make me feel different. I'd been trying my best to follow people's advice, and it hadn't got me anywhere in terms of finding happiness. The contradiction between what I was constantly being told I should have and want (a home, a husband, an HR Manager) and what I actually wanted (to just feel satisfied) left me feeling confused, alienated and completely inadequate. I needed to do something. I needed to shake things up, so I made a decision – to travel on my own around South America. While I was fortunate enough to have the freedom, and the opportunity to do it, I was going to go somewhere I'd always fancied to see if I could gain a bit of insight into and understanding of myself, without outward influence. If I could firmly establish my own attitudes towards life, and make sense of things, perhaps I'd get the sense of direction I'd spent so long scrabbling about for. I didn't know what I wanted, but I knew that I wasn't going to find it in an office block in Hammersmith, in front of a computer that I wanted to smash into smithereens with a sledgehammer. That evening I wrote my resignation letter (and then danced around my lounge for a bit).

Of course, I was *told* I'd be better off staying… Just a couple of hours after handing my manager the letter I was summoned to a meeting room. I sat there clutching my sweaty hands in my lap, consciously avoiding the eyes of those in the accounts department I could see through the glass door shooting me curious glances. The meeting room was so tiny you could barely move for the chairs around the table, and the radiator was aggressively pumping out hot air, steaming up the windows. The resulting claustrophobia was doing a real number on my nerves.

I was dreading this impending discussion with the company founder, John. He's an intimidating man, in both stature and demeanour, even when you're in his good books. The kind of boss who always knows exactly what you're doing, even when you haven't spoken in days. I liked and respected John, but I also feared him a bit – he was very adept at bringing you around to his way of thinking while making you believe it had been your decision. I couldn't let that happen this time – my mind was made up. I had to stay strong.

After ten or so hot and bothered minutes, the door burst open and John's 6 ft 5 frame filled the door.

'Morning, Amy.'

'Oh hi, John!' I squawked.

He pulled out the chair opposite me, took a seat and silently surveyed my flushed face for a couple of seconds. I grimaced back at him, raised my eyebrows and pulled on my earlobes just for something to do with my hands.

He let out a big sigh, put on his half-moon glasses and slowly opened his black leather folder. From it he pulled my resignation letter and the contract he'd wanted me to sign, placing them side-by-side on the table before shooting me a stern look, clearly conveying his irritation that I was wasting his time like this.

'John, I just want to sa—'

He held up his hand to stop me, lifted the resignation letter and started to read it under his breath.

'Now let me get this straight,' he finally said, after what felt like six months of silence, 'you're going to leave *this* job to go to South America to *try* to be a travel writer?'

'To travel and write, yes.'

Another full-body sigh. John removed his glasses and rubbed his eyes.

'Amy, you do realise that trying to be a writer is like trying to be a rock star?'

'Well, I don't think that's strictly true,' I protested.

'This is utterly absurd! You have to know this is not a sensible move for you!'

I shuffled around in my seat, finally opting to sit on my hands in a bid to cease fidgeting. *Come on, Amy, don't let him get in your head.*

'Maybe not, John, but it's what I want to do, and I think it's right for me right now.'

'You do know there's no money in travel writing?'

I shook my head. 'It's not the money that matters to me.'

'Even still, I saw Simon Calder, the Travel Editor from *The Independent*, buying his coffee in Pret the other day – PRET! Hardly the glamourous life you're imagining, is it? You need to be *realistic*.'

'I like Pret coffee,' I shrugged, 'I'd gladly buy all my coffee in there if it meant I could travel to all the places Simon Calder has.'

'Even still, this is a foolish, hasty decision. Chances are you won't be able to find a job when you come back, have you even thought about that?'

I hadn't.

'I've worked in this business a long time, Amy, and I know that you'll come to regret this, mark my words.'

I knew in that moment that I couldn't carry on listening to these kinds of reasons for not doing what I wanted. If I did, I'd never do anything. I finally looked up and met his eye.

'I'm going to do it anyway.'

And I did.

ARGENTINA

WHERE I LEARNT...

- That repeatedly answering *'sí'* to every question your taxi driver asks is not how you reach your intended destination.

- That it *is* possible to eat three steaks in one day.

- That spider bites are a real and inconvenient outcome of being barefoot in tropical locations.

- That interrupting an Argentinian man during a football match is akin to spitting on his firstborn.

- That Argentinians still like Jamiroquai... a lot.

RISKING MY LIFE IN PURSUIT OF PESOS

FRIENDLY ADVICE:
'Over here you know who looks dangerous. Over there, you're going to have to relearn who's safe and who might slit your throat... and quickly!'

Martin, IT department

EXPERT ADVICE:
'The best decisions aren't made with your mind, but with your instincts.'

Lionel Messi
(He's Argentinian. He knows how things work out there.)

I touched down in Buenos Aires on a sunny afternoon, excited and ready for adventure, but badly in need of cash. I'd done enough reading to know that tourists are advised to arrive in Argentina with US dollars, so that's what I'd done. However, as currency strategy isn't nearly as exciting as reading up on where to find the city's best red wine, that was as far as my research into currency exchange went. I figured I'd work out the rest when the time was right.

That moment came just a short while later while enjoying my inaugural beer in South America. I was with Leggers, a dear friend hailing from Virginia, USA that I'd been friends with for five glorious years. Leggers now lived in London and had generously given up ten of her precious holiday days to chaperone me through this initial period where she'd guessed (somewhat accurately) I might do brainless things like walk into the path of oncoming traffic, smile at men who carry flick knives and try to hug street puppies. There are only a handful of people in life whose word I unquestioningly (and unstroppily) take as gospel, and Leggers is one of those people. We were just clinking our bottles together and taking in the view of the sun-kissed rooftops of Buenos Aires from our hostel roof terrace when some posh British twit named Charlie plopped himself down next to us, completely uninvited, and dropped the unsettling bombshell about how backpackers go about getting their hands on pesos in Argentina.

'So, you ladies came armed with dollars, right?' Charlie flicked his sandy hair out of his eyes, and took a noisy slug on his beer.

'We did.'

'And you know how things work? Or were you hoping you'd meet someone like me who'd be able to bring you up to speed?'

I shrugged. 'We just figured we'd ask at reception.'

'No need, no need. I've got you ladies. Here's how it goes down in BA, Argentina…'

Sigh.

Leggers and I sat and listened as Charlie explained that the days of turning to a cash machine, or the humble bureau de change, are long gone. They are of course both still viable options, as are the usual currency desks found at airports, but if you want to get the most amount of pesos for your US dollars, you need to slap on your game face, and steel yourself for a visit to The Blue Market – Argentina's illegal currency marketplace.

The system sprang up a few years ago, when in a bid to reduce inflation and instil confidence in the national currency (the peso) the Argentinian government decided to impose strict restrictions banning Argentinians (and anyone else) from buying US dollars. However Argentinians rely heavily on dollars, and are therefore prepared to do whatever it takes to get their hands on them, so the restrictions actually ended up creating The Blue Market instead.

What this means in practice is that if you're brave enough to carry lots of US dollars, and to engage with a number of choice characters, you can acquire a far higher number of pesos for your dollars than you would at your bog-standard cash machine. See it as an initiation to prove you have the balls to be in town.

At first I thought Charlie must have been having a laugh. That he was playing a game with the two women perched awkwardly on stools before him who had so obviously just arrived. We didn't yet resemble the slightly grubby backpackers that surrounded us on the balcony: our fingernails were clean, our hair was brushed and we both wore unstained clothing – we stood out like a pair of goths at a One Direction concert. I didn't believe (or like) him. How could it be that taking huge wads of US dollars and visiting a dangerous part of town was the way things actually operated? This was a developed country, for Christ's sake. If it weren't for all the people speaking Spanish, I could very well be in Paris!

'I see what you're saying, Charlie… but is it really worth the hassle? Surely some people choose to just get their money by more traditional means.' I spoke in a tone that implied I didn't care one bit. Annoyingly, the panic rash creeping its way up my neck made it glaringly obvious that my cool demeanour was nothing more than above-average amateur dramatics.

'Well yeah… sure you can,' guffawed this 'seasoned' traveller, who appeared to have given up shoes (and knowing that guffawing makes people hate you), 'but you'll get half the amount you would if you went to Florida Street. Plus, it's an experience dudes… a story… and it's all about the stories.'

Leggers and I looked at each other in horror, both at being called 'dude' by this teenager, and by the fact it appeared we were required to actively go in search of potentially intimidating people to conduct financial deals with. It wouldn't be much of a story to recall if we were DEAD!

'Righty-ho then,' I said, for perhaps the first time in my life. 'Looks like we'll be taking a trip to Florida Street.'

Our fake nonchalance was fooling no one, but there was zero chance we were going to let this floppy-haired twerp from Windsor intimidate us. I knew there'd be times I'd be tested on this trip, I just hadn't expected the first challenge to come so soon… before I'd even had the chance to get naively sunburnt.

We could have held our hands up, admitted weakling status and gone to the cash point, but I needed to be realistic. Because of how hastily I'd decided to leave London, I hadn't had much chance to save for the trip. This meant I had a wholly unsatisfactory amount of cash, which I needed to make last as long as possible. Now that I'd discovered a way to stretch that measly stockpile a little further, it was just too good an opportunity to miss. Yes, the way we would have to go about it filled me with dread, *but* putting our lives in jeopardy seemed as good a way as any to get the ol' adventures rolling. After all, I'd come away to challenge myself, and to gain life experience – if this was the way people acquired cash in Argentina, it was the way that I should probably acquire cash in Argentina. I couldn't shun my first challenge – that would be no way to commence proceedings. Plus, I had Leggers by my side, someone taller than me whose hand I could hold. She was a tough cookie – she'd once lived in New York City! I knew I'd be able to rely on her to remain focused when the pressure of doing sums under the gaze of strangers with blatant disregard for the law became too intense.

▲▲▲▲▲▲▲▲

The next morning, armed with close to $1,000 in cash and completely insufficient upper body strength, Leggers and I headed down to reception at the hostel to seek some final advice from someone less condescending as to how we should proceed.

I'd compiled quite the selection of questions overnight:

Would we be able to tell who was trading money?

How would we know who was trying to
take us for a ride and who wasn't?

Should we pretend to be Argentinian?

What would happen if we got busted
pretending to be Argentinian?

Was there anywhere en route where we
could acquire a deadly weapon?

Which deadly weapon would I even be
comfortable operating? *Taser... definitely taser.*

The hostel receptionist barely had to look at us to see that we were nervy about something. Maybe because we stood fidgeting in front of him, scaring that morning's influx of new arrivals with our deathly pale faces and our uncharacteristically high-pitched voices when we enquired as to whether he might have a sec. He instructed us to sit, gave us a solemn look to imply listening was imperative and then began counting off the following points on his cigarette-stained fingers.

'Okay, first things first ladies, don't accept less than twelve pesos to the dollar. Just don't accept it. Walk away. Find someone else. Next, take big denomination notes and make sure that the traders know that you have them. Everyone here wants the big notes, the fifties, the hundreds, and they'll give you a better rate if you have them. Got it?'

We nodded.

This was far from splendid news considering my handbag was stuffed full of the 10s and 20s of a true pauper.

'This bit is important,' he continued. 'No matter how much they insist, never go anywhere with them. NEVER. Don't believe them if they tell you that they have a shop or an office around the corner. They might be telling the truth; chances are they are not. Do NOT follow them anywhere.'

Another pause and more meaningful stares at me and Leggers.

'Lastly, check every. Single. Note. These guys like to try to slip in the odd fake. Take your time. Check them all. Don't let them rush you. Okay?'

After a few long seconds of us staring at him willing him to offer more information, his silence made it apparent we'd received all the golden nuggets of wisdom we were going to get that morning.

'Coooooooool,' I said, standing up, clapping my hands a couple of times, rolling my neck and shaking my limbs to show I was 'pumped' about what we were about to do. Inside I felt as though I'd recently swallowed a whole bag of marbles, such was the lump in my throat, and the weight in my stomach.

'You'll be fine,' he smiled, all sweetness and light now the warnings on how to avoid being lured to certain death were over. He hurriedly ushered us towards the front door of the hostel, clearly keen to remove the two startled lady-babies from the reception area.

'It's that way,' he pointed out the door, gave us an encouraging shove into the morning sunshine and closed the door firmly on us.

It was a scorcher of a morning on the streets of Buenos Aires, already 30 degrees despite only being 10 a.m. As we'd arrived relatively late the day before, our wander to Florida Street was our first real exploration of the city. At first glance it didn't appear too dissimilar to most big European cities – there were lots of five- or six-storey off-white concrete buildings with attractive wrought iron balconies at every window, busy roads with three or four lanes of traffic, walls plastered with graffiti or gig and club night posters, steam from coffee machines billowing from the open windows of cafes – its familiarity relaxed me, and despite the task at hand, I was delighted to be here. This time three days ago I'd been fighting a losing battle against torrential downpours and sadistic bus drivers intent on soaking all pedestrians foolish enough to be on foot. Now, I was grinning from ear to ear, holding my arms and face aloft as I walked along like a possessed scarecrow in a bid to best absorb the sun I'd been so excited to see.

It was only a ten-minute walk from our hostel on Avenida 9 de Julio to Florida Street, and as there were no big sights along the way, I instead took it upon myself to keep our spirits lifted.

'Florida Street. Flo-ri-da Street,' I sang. 'What a lovely sounding place Leggers, don't you think? A place called Florida Street can't be scary, that would be unfairly misleading.'

Leggers looked at me, bemused.

'Sounds almost as friendly as Sesame Street if you ask me!' I chirped, clutching at straws.

'Yeah, sure mate, and I expect Big Bird's already there, handing out hundred dollar bills and Haribo,' retorted Leggers, justifiably trying to bring me back down to earth.

Having always been adept at deluding my own brain with idiotic reassurances, I decided to stop bothering Leggers with inane chit-chat about puppets (not for the first time) and instead set to summoning up an image of a Florida Street I could get on board with. In this case, a sunny street where smiling elderly gentlemen in white boater hats beckon you over to reveal treasure chests full of pesos (and rubies). I imagined laughing people do-si-do-ing around, eating blue candyfloss, offering each other encouraging thumbs ups while happily scattering handfuls of cash up into the air. Based entirely on this unfaltering ability to fool myself into thinking everything will be okay, I perked up considerably. What were we even worrying about again? It was sunny, we were in an incredible city – all would be fine. It was time to toughen up, unclench my bum cheeks and finally hug the adorable street puppy that'd been following us for the last couple of blocks. The fear was quick to resurface the minute we turned left into Florida Street and established there were no boater hats in sight. Not one. The street was narrow, pedestrianised and lined with 'shops' called things like 'Jizz' which appeared to sell only plastic handbags, imaginatively displayed undergarments and lighters with tits on them. The glaring sunshine that refused to cut you a break elsewhere in the city was nowhere to be seen. It was shady in every sense of the word. The natty rose-tinted spectacles I'd been sporting mere moments before were gone, and in their place I wore a bright red pair... freshly spilled blood colour, you could say. It seemed in every direction we turned people were lurking ominously in alleyway entrances... or scoping out people to rob newly acquired plastic handbags from.

Let's get this over with.

Leggers and I took a team deep breath and set out along that 150-m stretch of terror, taking in the scene before us with wide eyes. Although there was the odd deserted money exchange shop front, it seemed that most of the people there with the intent of trading US dollars for pesos with tourists had no affiliation to anywhere that looked 'legit'. There were fedora-wearing, toothpick-chewing *porteños* (Buenos Aires locals) faux-nonchalantly leaning loafered feet up against grubby walls, whispering *'cambio, cambio'* ('change, change') at passing tourists. There were skinny teenagers sporting high-waisted jeans, slicked back hair, suspicious amounts of gold jewellery and so few teeth they were forced to hiss rather than talk, and suited and booted older gentlemen trying to get your attention through unsettling amounts of winking and waving.

'Look for ones with kind eyes,' I whispered to Leggers.

A good idea in theory – far less helpful when you're reluctant to establish eye contact.

'I think we should go for a woman,' Leggers sensibly proposed.

With 'Plan A' agreed upon, we proceeded as would any self-respecting tourist... by stopping dead in our tracks in the middle of the busy pedestrian street, while spinning unpredictably this way and that trying to identify suitable candidates.

Things did not look good. The only women in sight were the ones lurking closest to the darkest alleyways, with the snarliest faces and broadest shoulders. One was sporting a bum bag so unnecessarily large that the only logical explanation to me at that moment was that it concealed a weapon. (In hindsight, clearly cash.)

'Scratch that. These women look terrifying. Let's just start asking for rates,' I said, amping up the fake bravado.

I whirled around and immediately came face to chest with an enormous dude in a red tracksuit and eighties-style head-sweatband. I couldn't help myself – I instinctively looked him up and down, and nodded my approval at his old-school fashion statement.

'*Cambio?*' I stammered, remembering I was here to get cash, not to dish out compliments.

He nodded.

'Twelve… I… I mean… *doce?*'

His booming laughter hit me like a shock wave. He shook his colossal head just once and turned away, still laughing.

'*Para grande dollars?*' I urged feebly to his back. He ignored me. *And to think I'd been compelled to high five his fashion choices. This dude didn't deserve my fashion praise let alone my US dollars!*

We shuffled onwards, sticking close, clutching our handbags like a pair of nervous grannies. Occasionally we'd break away from the hushed reassurances we were offering each other to speak to scary characters but making a decision was proving tough. We seemed to have a problem with just about everyone.

AMY: 'Not him. I don't like the way he's eating that banana.'

LEGGERS: 'She looks all right. Wait… nope… she's got a neck tattoo. Keep walking.'

AMY: 'No way, not her. I can see the tops of her nipples, I won't be able to concentrate.'

LEGGERS: 'Did he just signal something to that parked car? Yep, I'm sure he did. Retreat!'

AMY: 'Do you think he's *trying* to look like a really mean vampire?'
LEGGERS: 'Oh god, they've all got rat tails! That's it. I'm done! I think we should just go to the cash point.'
AMY: 'A hundred per cent agreed. Let's get two gigantic beers and never speak of this.'

Just as we were about to give up and retire shakily to the nearest place serving alcohol, I spotted something…

'Wait… that guy, that guy! He's wearing a gilet. Leggers, no one dangerous would dream of wearing a gilet!'

We ventured closer, emboldened by the fact that he was tending to a flower-stall-cum-news-stand. This had to be our man – not only was he dressed for a family camping trip, he also cared for current affairs, and nature! His affection for carnations was a clear indicator, in our eyes, of someone who couldn't possibly want to rob us of our teeth at knifepoint. Winner.

We knew it was important not to let our guard down based purely on this chap's unthreatening fashion statement. We'd come this far after all. Just because he was a chilly person didn't mean that he wouldn't occasionally give in to severe bloodlust. It was essential we remembered that.

The minute he turned around, all those sensible intentions flew out the window.

Standing before us was an exact Argentine replica of Paul Baker: my dad, beloved by both Leggers and I in equal measure. We whirled round to look at each other, grinning from ear to ear about locating my dad in South America! He even had the exact same twinkle in his eye that my dad gets when he's managed to pocket a handful of biscuits in the short time it takes Mum to pop to the garage.

'*Cambio señoritas?*' he asked, flashing us a familiar grin.

'*Sí, sí!*' we nodded, grinning like a pair of idiots.

He beckoned us over and we followed him into his tiny news stand with zero protest. I couldn't wait to get inside. I half expected Argentinian Momma Baker to be in there brandishing a half-empty packet of Hobnobs in mock-outrage. Instead we found a man with slicked-back hair and multiple chunky gold necklaces sitting behind a table piled high with cash.

'*Buenos días, chicas!*' He smiled, revealing an impressive set of gold teeth. *Yeah, he seemed friendly enough – anyone who liked gold and cash that much had to be trustworthy, right?*

When Argentine Dad chuckled good-naturedly at our proposed rate, shook his head and instead offered us ten pesos to the dollar, we caved in without protest. The fear had knackered us out. We were alive, the rate offered was still better than what you'd get at a cash machine AND we got to meet my dad's doppelganger... definitely an experience worth paying slightly over the odds for if you ask me.

I leaned over to Leggers as her money was being counted into a big pile in front of her. 'Remember to check every note.'

'Ha. Don't worry, I will – we have to follow at least one of that receptionist's tips.'

Leggers and I stood in that little news shed, slowly and carefully examining each and every note. He may have had a lovely smile, but we wanted to make sure Argentine Paul Baker and his gold-loving mate weren't trying to pull a fast one. Plus, I've never held that much cash in my hands before so I was relishing the opportunity to fan myself with it. Once we were satisfied that every note was real, we stuffed our handbags with our newly acquired booty and fled that shady street as fast as our flip-flopped feet could carry us.

To our relief we didn't have to venture far before we found a cafe with tables in the sunshine, perfect for refreshing our dry mouths with an icy cold celebratory Quilmes. The cafe was located on Plaza de Mayo, one of the city's most famous tourist attractions, and home to Casa Rosada — the flamingo-coloured presidential mansion, where Madonna once did an al fresco concert telling the Argentinian population to stop getting so emotional… funny really seeing as we could have done with that exact same pep talk half an hour ago.

WINNER = *THE EXPERT*

'The best decisions aren't made with your mind, but with your instincts.'
Lionel Messi

Lionel has an unfair advantage here. As an Argentinian himself, I wouldn't be surprised if he honed those impressive dribbling skills dodging the choice characters up and down Florida Street. Perhaps it was even the spot where he learnt to trust his instincts for the first time. I like to think that's the case, and that he too would have cannily turned down the opportunity to trade currency with a man eating his banana like a corn on the cob.

LESSONS LEARNT

I'll hold my hands up and admit I was a tad overdramatic that day on Florida Street. One of the reasons I wanted to travel was to have experiences like this — those that put me a billion miles from my comfort zone, but that I knew deep down I could handle as long as I obtained the facts, took a few deep breaths and didn't mind embarrassing myself a little. It was glaringly obvious from day one that it wouldn't be possible to ignore *all* advice while travelling. I had to remove the copper helmet I'd been wearing prior to departure, or at least position it so my ears were no longer covered. There was going to be so much information I didn't know – I needed to learn to seek it, hear it, and then do the best I could with it, given the circumstances. Things don't operate the same in every country. That's what compelled me to buy a ticket in the first place – I wanted to see and experience those exact things. Yeah, Leggers and I could have shirked how things operated in favour of doing what we'd always done, but then we would have missed out on an interesting experience, the chance to meet some of Buenos Aires' most curious characters and the all-important extra cash – and then who'd have been the mug?

I may have convinced myself that everyone was out to hurt us that day. It's safe to say they weren't – they were just doing their job. While we were quivering, sweating and trying our best to count in Spanish, they weren't plotting the 101 ways they'd like to maim us; they were probably just thinking, 'Come on, love, hurry it along. I need a piss, and I want a fag before Mateo comes back with my mid-morning sausage roll'… or, you know, something similar.

We proceeded as we should have done. We listened to our options for obtaining cash, made a choice to take a particular route, and then went and sought the facts from someone in the know about how to go about it. We used our eyes and ears to find someone we felt the most comfortable with. It was a reminder to apply the same vigilance I would in my hometown to my new setting. In London I wouldn't close my eyes, unplug my brain and get in a taxi with someone sporting gold-plated knuckledusters, a tool belt full of drill bits and a T-shirt saying, 'Do you like pain?'

so why would I just because I was on a new continent? I was on a holiday from the 9–5, not from rational thinking, and as long as I could remember that as I travelled, I was sure I'd be fine.

GETTING MY EYE IN

FRIENDLY ADVICE:

'Remember, if you don't like it, you can always come home.'

Paul Baker, my dad (the real one)

EXPERT ADVICE:

'The key is to learn from failures and then to keep going.'

Ranulph Fiennes
(Explorer of unknown lands)

Buenos Aires. Day three. My favourite lady at my side, a wedge of newly acquired bargain cash burning a hole in my shorts and no real game plan aside from Boss It. Having handled the first task that presented itself with *slightly* too much whinging, panicking and over-exaggeration, I indulged myself for a moment over my hostel breakfast by wondering what the next challenge to present itself might be. Would it be struggling to communicate something essential due to my shoddy grasp of Spanish? Would it be eating something I shouldn't? Perhaps it might be starting a passionate romance with a handsome *gaucho* (Argentinian cowboy) with a gait suggesting that wild horses weren't the only thing he was capable of riding into the ground? Who knew? But I was ready to find out.

I'd arrived in Buenos Aires without a care in the world. Thinking: cool man – time to see what this is all about. I hadn't considered the best way to get from the airport to my hostel. I hadn't considered the logistics of meeting Leggers in the city. I hadn't thought to wear something that would be comfortable in the heat. I was just so psyched to get out of the UK that I could only think five minutes ahead.

First I was excited to see what inflight movies there would be. Then to see what food I'd get. I was excited to speak my first few sentences in Spanish. Although that went terribly – rather than saying *'gracias'* to the two smiling flight attendants bidding us farewell as we filed off at Madrid airport, when the time came to express my gratitude, I'd just exhaled at them creepily because I couldn't form the word *'gracias'* in my saliva-filled mouth. Then, as I'm not a quitter, I sought out someone Spanish to help me locate the gate for my connecting flight in what felt like the world's most enormous, confusing airport, but the man at the 'information' desk clearly didn't understand my sentence structure, so we both just garbled vague things at each other for five minutes before he walked out of the booth, never to return. I stole his pen in protest and then followed someone I recognised from Heathrow at a discreet distance as I knew he was en route to BA too. Talk about handling solo travel like a pro.

I found Leggers and the hostel with ease, and my pulse had returned to its resting rate, when up popped Charlie to share his wisdom about Florida Street. That experience had been the rousing slap around the chops I needed to realise I was going to be faced with daily decisions and challenges, and as I wouldn't have Leggers around at all times as a glorious, fun-loving buffer, I needed to get in the swing of things sharpish. I wasn't going to be able to saunter around thinking I knew how everything operated.

I was in Buenos Aires, not Bognor Regis. Our first success gave me confidence – I was strutting along, high on life, thinking that no challenge would be too big, no onward move too difficult.

Add that confidence to the fact that a new place is always my favourite place to be, and when in such a location my positivity towards my new surroundings radiates off me. I want to go everywhere, look at everything, taste it all. I want to drink everything, eat everything, chat to everyone. I feel like everything is possible and worth my time. As a result of this sunny outlook, everything has its merits. Bins look interesting. Alleyways look glamourous. Seeing rats on the street is charming, rather than downright awful.

So, on day three I took this overly optimistic attitude, popped it in my knapsack and headed out to see what Buenos Aires had to offer…

▲▲▲▲▲▲▲▲

Our plan was to explore the city via a bike tour, taking in some of the city centre attractions before heading down to La Boca, potentially the most notorious part of town, known for its colourful streets, tango displays and – away from the tourist drag – its crime rates.

We met our tour guide and the rest of our group in a bike shed in the centre of town. There were seven Americans, including Leggers, and me. We were assigned bright green bikes, and off we went. We pedalled past Plaza de Mayo and Casa Rosada again – which were nice to see again now that my brain wasn't shaking from having to deal with cash around strangers. We cycled into the Puerto Madero part of town to sample what our guide, Nata, believed to be the best *choripán* (chorizo sandwich) in the city. He was on to something – the otherwise nondescript El Parrillon food truck not only offered generous amounts of chorizo crammed into crusty white baguettes, but their salsa and chilli sauce selection was extensive, spicy and delicious. I love a bike ride, and it felt great to be in the sunshine with Leggers, riding around, with a belly full of delicious spicy treats. With every spin of my wheels, I could feel myself unwinding even further. I may have been on another continent where I still had a lot to learn about how things worked, but the sun was shining and this was exactly where I wanted to be.

Just before we entered La Boca, Nata pulled us over to issue a few instructions.

'Right, we're now entering a more risky part of town so I ask you to put away any valuables, and to listen to any instructions I call out. Not everyone will want to rob you, but if someone spots a chance, they will take it.'

Our group nodded sombrely, and quickly relocated SLR cameras from around necks and in baskets into backpacks.

'There's no need to worry. La Boca does have some dangerous parts, but if we stay together, everything will be fine.'

Our first stop in La Boca was its major tourist street, Caminito, a location made famous after local artist, Benito Quinquela Martín decided to paint the corrugated iron walls of the street's buildings in vibrant clashing colours – squares of blue, yellow, pink, and orange framed clashing balconies decorated with international flags and statues of South American heroes, including Che Guevara and Eva Perón. The location of the barrio (neighbourhood) at the mouth of the Riachuelo, BA's river, is what gave the area its name, as *'boca'* means 'mouth' in Spanish. As the barrio used to consist solely of shipyards and the houses of the European settlers from Italy, Spain, France and Germany that worked there, most of the houses you see are built from cast-off shipping materials – corrugated iron, sheet metal and so on. Alongside the paint job, Martín erected a few makeshift stages for music and dance performances, and soon the artistic community of Buenos Aires flocked to this part of town, enticed by the cheap rent and the arty community. Today, Caminito is alive with crowds of tourists reclining in the sunshine watching tango displays, snapping up fridge magnets, brightly coloured paintings and Boca Juniors football shirts or having their photos taken with Diego Maradona lookalikes.

After an hour or so of exploration and souvenir-buying we hopped back on our bikes to head to La Bombonera – Boca Juniors' world-famous football stadium.

Nata had some more instructions for us: 'Now friends, please remember to keep those valuables out of sight at all times. As I said, you should be fine, but we're not going to take any chances.'

Maybe it was just his grasp of English – which was far superior to our grasp of Spanish – but his instructions certainly made me a little edgy.

Pushing off, we rounded a corner away from the touristy crowds and pedalled into a housing estate en route to La Bombonera. It was clear straight away that something was going on. There was a party atmosphere, music was blasting, there were people boozing on the streets, hanging out in large crowds grouped around TV sets pulled into front yards through windows. People were grilling meat, drinking more beers and generally having a good time. They all had one obvious thing in common – they were all supporting Boca Juniors. I could deduce this from the fact that everyone was wearing the blue kit of their beloved local team. Those that weren't socialising were walking in the same direction, some of them shirtless, swinging their blue shirts in circles around their heads, singing songs, cheering. I enjoyed it at first. People were smiling at us. I could smell weed. I could hear good music. I was riding a bike. What wasn't to enjoy?

But then, as was to be expected, the nearer we got to the stadium, the more the procession grew as people trickled into the main flow from side street after side street. The beer drinkers were rowdier, people started gesturing at us, shouting things, and a few bottles were getting lobbed close enough to make us sit up a little straighter in our saddles.

I pedalled up beside Nata, who had started to look a little bit pale. 'So… I take it there's a game going on today?'

'Yes, yes. I completely forgot. Silly me! Today is an important day in Argentina – it's the Superclásico derby. Boca Juniors are playing River Plate, the team from the north of the city. They don't like each other all that much.'

'Oh right. Should we err… give it a miss… maybe?' A bottle smashed a metre to the left of me.

'No, no… it's fine. We came to see the stadium. Let's take a look and then we can leave. Just do me a favour and pedal a little faster.'

Right you are.

We carried on cycling, calling out 'sorry' and 'thank you' to those we nearly ran over in the chaos. Soon we rounded a corner and came to a stop in front of La Bombonera – the enormous yellow-and-blue 49,000-capacity stadium, named as such due to its resemblance to a chocolate box. From our vantage point, we could hear the almighty roar of the crowds inside, fireworks going off, drums and horns being played with gusto, and the singing and chanting of those approaching the stadium. You could feel the noise and the footfall running through you. Right before us was a group of around 20 men, some of which were diligently tuning brass instruments. *How lovely,* I thought. *A brass band – how very civil!* Clearly my fellow cyclists thought the same: bags were being unzipped, iPhones were being unsheathed. *Perhaps they'll play a song.* As I twisted round to seize my camera from my backpack, I clocked Nata's face – it had lost all colour, and he was wringing his handlebars with considerable vigour.

'*Vamos, amigos,*' (come on) he whispered urgently, jabbing a thumb back in the direction he clearly wanted us to cycle, '*vamos, vamos.*'

He didn't have to tell Leggers and I twice. Nata was already off, and we were hot on his heels. Just as we were about to turn the corner, I chanced a peek over my shoulder and saw that the brass band and their gang of instrument-free hangers on had clocked us and were advancing in our direction, lobbing bottles and jeering. Those with instruments chose that moment to start playing – which certainly startled me into looking where I was going.

Once we'd speed-pedalled for 15 minutes, Nata stopped and explained that these men were not a merry band of music makers akin to The Barmy Army. They were Boca Juniors' most notorious gang of hooligans, with quite the reputation for being unwelcoming to gangs of tourists with absolutely no awareness of their surroundings. That day I learnt that not everyone wants to befriend me. And I also learnt that not every man wielding a tuba necessarily likes cardigans, tepid baths and being in bed before *Newsnight…* some of them like violence.

▲▲▲▲▲▲▲▲

Keen to pack as much into our itinerary as possible, that same evening Leggers and I were heading to a tango show/lesson where our food and booze dreams were set to come true courtesy of an all-you-can-eat buffet and bottomless beverages. Having wildly underestimated how large Buenos Aires is, how bloody hot it gets and how poor we are at cycling we found ourselves a little jaded prior to our first night out on the tiles. Add in the surge of fear we'd experienced on our cycle tour, and we needed something to kick-start the festivities. There was only one thing for it... we'd have to energise with the devil of all drinks – vodka Red Bull. Sometimes you've just got to do what you've got to do to get back in the game. We had a buffet to devour, and a dance floor to take by storm – we couldn't let trivialities as piddly as jet lag and heat exhaustion thwart our plans.

One problem: Red Bull doesn't agree with me. Every time I've dabbled I become instantly and alarmingly aware of the taurine sprinting around my system punching all my white blood cells in the face. It makes me feel light-headed... and then sick. As I hadn't drunk it since 2003, I'd conveniently forgotten this, and was therefore delighted by how peppy it was making me feel. I felt like I wanted to high five everyone in my vicinity, and then choreograph a dance routine for us all to perform later in the hostel bar.

Combine the Red Bull with our collective determination to maximise fun, and we were in trouble. We were on new soil, work was a distant memory and we would be saying goodbye to each other in just a few days... it was inevitable that we were going to get overexcited – the pee-in-the-street, hold-strangers'-hands, come-home-without-something-essential kind of overexcited. The problem with overexcitement is how tricky it is to manage. It's virtually impossible to keep a lid on things when you're too busy downing every drink and thinking you're hilarious.

We were hanging out on the roof terrace of our hostel again, basking in the evening sunshine, our fourth vodka Red Bull freshly poured, when I suddenly remembered that our only opportunity to see La Bomba del Tiempo – a live drumming concert – was that night. Jacked up on glucose, we made a quick decision to chop the all-you-can-eat buffet and our opportunity to learn The Dance of Love, and to instead hotfoot it to the drum party.

'It seems like the better choice to me. I wanna hear drums,' Leggers agreed.

'I hope they're loud.'

Our knowledge of Buenos Aires was such that when I pointed a slightly blurred eye at a map, the venue for the concert seemed to be only around the corner. We could have caught a bus, we could have hailed a cab.

'It's not far, let's run it,' I proposed.

'Oh hells yeah.' Leggers and I have a history of drunk running. While living in Perth, Western Australia, where we met, taxis were few and far between come closing time, so we often ran home together, just so we could reach our snacks faster.

So that's what we did. Well, first we downed our drinks, and then we worked ourselves up into an early evening state of dehydration and unnoticed hunger with a cheeky, nostalgic 7-km run.

We were very early.

There had been absolutely no need to jog it – the open-air bar area of the Konex centre had maybe 50 people in it, and we were 40 minutes early.

'We should probably get a drink in then.'

We sensibly recognised the need to remain hydrated and headed to the bar – by a sheer stroke of luck, the bar had a 2-4-1 offer on vodka Red Bull.

'Shall I just buy us four so we can save valuable queuing time?' I suggested to Leggers, as we waited for less than five minutes to be served.

'You're *so* sneaky. I love it,' she replied, nodding more than was strictly necessary to convey she was in agreement. When our drinks were placed in front of us, I didn't register that they were pint-sized. Probably because all the sugar had rendered me temporarily blind. It seemed like a sensible amount, especially given the fact that I was very thirsty, and that despite the run, I still felt like I had enough energy to sprint to the moon.

'Ooooh – let's spice things up with a fernet,' Leggers suggested. I liked everything that she was saying. I let her know that by stroking her face and ordering the shots.

Fernet, Argentina's favourite liquor, isn't nice. The bitter combination of liquorice and mouthwash made me want to scratch it off my tongue. Fortunately we had the Red Bull and vodka there to wash away its memory.

After we'd stopped panting, and our eyes had stopped watering from the shots, we took a moment to marvel at how spectacular we felt. We high fived our impromptu running tour of the Abasto neighbourhood – yet another part of town ticked off our list like absolute travel pros. Perhaps tomorrow we should run everywhere? Then we could eat all the street-side meat we wanted without fear of not looking our best in shorts. We had so many good ideas in that 40-minute window – it's such a shame I can't remember all of them, or I'm sure we'd both be millionaires by now.

Soon enough, it was show time. Time was passing very quickly. As we danced our way towards the main arena, we were stopped by a bouncer who told us it was a drink-free environment. What a misery.

'Best see 'em off then, Leggers. Can't waste them – I'm on a budget.'

'Typical Baker! Gotta get your money's worth.'

By now, Leggers and I had entered the bulletproof stage; the point where you don't even consider there could be consequences to your actions. When you've completely forgotten that hangovers are a thing that you're highly susceptible to, and when you have so much enthusiasm towards every drink offered that it might as well contain an elixir of eternal youth – no one is getting in-between that drink and your mouth. You'll fight them if you have to.

When your heart rate is already considerably elevated from out-of-character early evening runs and more sugar than you've probably ingested in a year and a half, listening to 15 people banging drums in an industrial warehouse made of metal is going to do little to calm you down. In fact, it's going to jack you up. Right up. I was throwing limbs in all directions with enough strength to do some real damage. I couldn't help it. I needed to move everything.

In addition to the whirlpool of caffeinated trouble sloshing around in my otherwise empty stomach, I could smell weed. Strong and alien-smelling, but weed nonetheless. I turned to Leggers when I first caught a whiff and declared, 'Do NOT let me smoke any of that!'

Leggers nodded sagely and gave me a thumbs up which showed that she was proud of my responsible decision, before stomping and fist pumping in a circle a few times, taking in the sights and sounds of the noisy warehouse. When she looked back, there I was, under a minute later, arm round a stranger, smoking his criminally strong joint.

I'd like to tell you that I remember the rest of the evening, but here is where it gets very bitty. I remember moving my body a lot to the sound of those drums. I remember more weed, more fernet, and maybe a couple more beers. I remember giving a word-perfect Spanish rundown of my life story to the lethargic taxi driver who transported us back to the hostel. Once there I remember talking far too close to a lot of strangers' faces, and potentially performing parts of the dance routine I'd thought up on the roof earlier in the evening. Oh, and I think there was vomit. Yeah, I'm sure there was.

I awoke myself the next morning with a huge all-body groan and looked across at Leggers, who was clutching her head in agony.

'Dude, we need to check out immediately.'

'I completely agree.'

Neither of us knew what had happened, but the feeling that we'd overstayed our welcome was very much mutual.

As I vomited up my stomach lining pre-hailing our escape taxi it occurred to me that this was not why I came away – to get so boozed that my brain wasn't capable of forming memories. It was all very well having a few drinks, especially when they cost £2 for some of the most joyous wines that my gullet had ever sampled, but drinking myself into a stupor was something I'd done back in Brixton – when I'd drink to forget how bored I was Monday to Friday. I didn't want to waste what money I had on booze, just to not remember what I'd done. As is to be expected, South American alcohol has the exact same effect as UK alcohol. I needed to remember that nothing positive comes from replacing all my body's fluids with poison.

▲▲▲▲▲▲▲▲

Buenos Aires was fantastic, but it was time to switch towns. We headed out to Iguazu Falls for a couple of nights. I'd heard it was impressive, but I hadn't quite expected to walk into the actual Garden of Eden. The waterfalls were spectacular, and you only needed to look at them for a second to understand fully why they are one of the seven 'new' wonders of nature. For one, there are butterflies absolutely everywhere; two, as far as you can see there are walls of waterfalls, with colourful birds divebombing the spray; and three, there's a tiny green train that removes your need to walk around in tropical heat. Our two days in Iguazu passed without incident – we navigated our way to the airport like pros, chatting in Spanish, tipping like champions. Perhaps now we were finally in the swing of things – we knew what to expect and no challenge or setback could distract us from enjoying our time together.

Our third and final stop was Mendoza, a city about halfway up Argentina's western border with Chile, just down the road from where all the Malbec is made… so perhaps we should just scrap its earth-given name and call it as we see it… heaven. As Leggers and I share a love of all grape products (bar fernet – definitely bar fernet) it seemed fitting to spend our last few days together cycling around and drinking wine… responsibly of course.

'Do you think we should have booked a hostel?' Leggers asked as we pulled on our backpacks at baggage claim and made our way outside into the sunshine.

'Nah – it's a popular place, and pretty big by the sounds of things. There'll be loads of places to choose from. Plus, my mate Matty recommended somewhere – he wrote it down in my guidebook, hang on.'

I put down my backpack and started to rummage through the now very messy contents. Typically, the guidebook was right at the very bottom. I needed to become better at packing my bag in an orderly fashion.

'Hold this.' I handed Leggers a beach towel, a bag of dirty clothes and a cagoule over my shoulder, practically climbing inside the bag to reach the guidebook. 'Aha.' I flipped through until I came to the page I'd earmarked. In red pen, Matty had written the name of the hostel, and it looked like it was in a great location, slap bang in the middle of town, right by the city's main park. Bloody lovely.

We hopped in a cab and gave them the name of the hostel. The driver pivoted in his seat. *'De verdad?'* (Really?) he asked.

'Sí, sí,' I grinned back. I trusted Matty; I was sure the hostel he had suggested would be fine. As we headed towards town, I thought back to the conversation we'd had over a pint prior to my departure. I'd gone to the pub wielding my guidebook so he could note down any tips he might have.

'If you go to Mendoza, you have to stay here,' Matty said, circling the name of a hostel in red. 'The dude who runs it is called Pineapple Rasta Max.'

'Excellent.'

'Yeah – he had a football made out of plastic bags and he laughed at me when I fell off a horse. *Such* a dude.'

'Cool. Sounds perfect. I'll be sure to check it out.'

As soon as the cab pulled up outside, I realised that heeding Matty's advice may have been an error. The qualities he listed were hardly characteristics of a world-class establishment, and now the place looked deserted, and our taxi driver seemed most reluctant to let us out. Most hostels in South America can be identified by a trail of backpackers spilling out of every door, staring at phones or sharing beers, but here there was not one person in sight. We wandered past a half-empty swimming pool filled with stagnant water and an array of deceased moths, past a series of smashed windows and a pile of yellowing plastic furniture before entering a cobweb-strewn reception area. I wasn't sure which member of the Argentinian Addams Family was set to greet us, but my fingers were crossed for Uncle Fester.

'Holy fuck Aimz, this place looks awful,' Leggers pointed out.

She wasn't wrong. The room had been painted dark green, which made it feel incredibly dingy. There was a pool table, but the felt had been torn to shreds and there didn't appear to be any balls. There was a bin overspilling with crisp packets and other rubbish beside the reception desk, and the whole place smelt like stale beer with just a hint of mould.

'*Hola, señoritas!*' A man rose up from behind the reception desk, fag in mouth, beer in hand (not Fester). 'Do you have a booking?'

'Ermm… no…' we answered, scanning the reception area for other signs of life. 'Do we need one?'

Where was Pineapple Rasta Max? And where was his charmingly crafted football that couldn't cause shin bruises if it tried?

'How many nights would you like to stay?'

'I think we'd like to see the room first,' Leggers said sensibly.

'*Bueno.*'

We followed the man as he limped through the communal outside area, which I'm sure must have been lovely when it didn't resemble the recent site of a mass-suicide. It *was* a suntrap though – so, so far it had earnt itself one plus point.

The receptionist pushed open a flimsy door leading into a dorm with eight beds in it. Rather than being placed at respectable distances from each other, they were all clustered together in the centre of the room. There was a decorative spattering of abandoned clothing dotted around the beds, and I could see at least three used plasters. It also looked like there was debris of some kind… oh yes, there was a hole in the ceiling and the light fixture hung down from where it should have been, red and blue wires poking out of the hole it had once been fixed into. Splendid. To top off the unusual bed arrangement, the room was lined with a row of metal lockers… all of which looked like they had been on the receiving end of a good kicking. We were either currently looking at the worst dorm room in all of South America, or Tracey Emin was about to appear with a cry of, '*Ta-da! I'm on a tour of South America and you're my very first guests. I thought you'd never find me!*'

'Is this the only room you have?' I asked, ever the optimist. Perhaps this was just the art gallery portion of the hostel tour.

'Oh? Do I need to show you another?'

Leggers and I looked at each other in amazement. *Ermm, yes, mate – this one looks like it's been decorated by a particularly violent tornado.*

'That would be *great*,' Leggers replied, while we both plastered forced grins on our faces.

We followed him out of the Hell Room to the room next door. This was no better – there was one double bed with a huge dent in the middle and some kind of black stain on the carpet below. Oil or blood? *Oil or blood?*

Leggers and I looked at each other again. She was shaking her head at me, and her usually smiling mouth was set in a thin, serious line. We nodded in agreement.

'No thank you, sir. We won't be taking up any more of your time,' Leggers declared, before about-turning and marching back to reception.

We would not be sticking around in Murder Town just to be polite. There were no other guests there, and all signs pointed to the last guests never being allowed to leave. We couldn't be handing over our passports and expecting to get sleep in a place so nightmare-inducing. Matty was clearly deranged, or maybe things had just gone to the dogs after Pineapple Rasta Max packed up his plastic bags and rode his disobedient horse out of town. I like sleeping, and there was no chance that I would have done anything in that bed other than stare at the ceiling, willing morning to come. I'd say there was a 90 per cent chance it was haunted, or housing some kind of supervirus. I swore in that minute to actually consider where I'd be staying moving forwards. If I'd arrived in town late at night, my only choice may have been to sleep in that hellhole, and that wasn't a risk I wanted to take.

'I know you hate it, Aimz, but I reckon TripAdvisor might actually be essential moving forwards.'

'I completely agree.'

▲▲▲▲▲▲▲▲

Once we'd found a hostel that didn't look like the Bates Motel, we asked the receptionist to recommend a fun activity to fill a couple of hours. Smiling, she whipped out a map and pointed with considerable enthusiasm at General San Martín Park – and more specifically, its viewing point. Much like most backpackers, I am a fan of a viewing point – they help you get your bearings, it's exercise, you get good snaps and, should you do nothing else that day, you can rest easy knowing you've enjoyed the best view in town.

'Yes! Let's walk to the viewing point, Leggers. Doesn't that sound lovely?'

'It certainly does.'

We walked out into the midday heat with adventure in our hearts and a spring in our step, and a few minutes later we arrived at the park. I don't know whether there were some renovations going on, but rather than the tree-lined boulevards and fluffy-duck-heavy lakes we'd been hoping for, we found ourselves walking along the hard shoulder of a major road. As articulated lorries hurtled by we found ourselves sidestepping sharp rocks, broken bottles and a whole lot of dog shit. We'd also forgotten our sun tan lotion – and the road, unsurprisingly, offered little shade. There was no part of this particular adventure that was proving enjoyable.

I'm not sure if the passers-by were trying to alert us to the fact that it's highly illegal to walk so close to a major road with all their honking, or whether they knew we were en route to the viewing point and wanted to warn us that it was not worth this dangerous assault course. Dodging empty beer cans became a fun little game to play to keep us moving, and to distract us from the fact that our feet were being torn to shreds.

No matter the dire straits Leggers and I have got ourselves into over the years, we've always had a kind word to offer each other to make the other smile during hopeless times – some of the pep talks that I've received from Leggers would go down in history if I were to put them on YouTube – but that day, on that treacherous roadside, we had not one word of encouragement for each other. We just kept our heads down and kept walking, knowing that if we walked fast enough, soon it would come to an end.

All we were rewarded with at the end of that walk was a half-empty lake full of litter. I think the park must have been having a fallow year from needing to be a presentable public space. Or maybe we were just in the wrong bit. Whichever it was, I knew that I'd perhaps think twice before setting out for a walk in the midday sun, in brand new flip-flops, with no water, just to look at a view.

▲▲▲▲▲▲▲▲

The day finally came when my holiday with Leggers was over. She was heading back to Buenos Aires to fly back to the UK, and I was catching a 16-hour bus to Santiago in Chile to catch a flight to Bolivia. The holiday segment of my trip was done and dusted, it was time to start backpacking.

A lot had happened in those ten days… We'd encountered overconfident rodents who wanted to steal our picnics directly from our handbags at whatever costs… but we'd also ridden a boat into the spray of the world's biggest waterfall.

We had wasted time and money watching a band called Los Fingers, just because we were enticed by the mix of heavy metal guitar and bagpipes we heard from the street... but if we hadn't, maybe we would have always wondered about that combination.

We had been pursued by hooligans, and received a hundred tiny stone bruises to the soles of our feet, but we'd also danced a lot, and shared a lot of long, boozy dinners consisting of steaks the size of my face, smothered in pepper sauce that must have been crafted by a team of chefs taking some time off from their day job as angels.

We'd certainly made some mistakes, but we'd also learnt some valuable lessons that would, with some luck, stand me in good stead for my onward journey to Bolivia.

WINNER = *THE EXPERT*

'The key is to learn from failures and then to keep going.'
Ranulph Fiennes

I wasn't going to give up at this early stage – yeah, there were a few moments that were hairy, but it wasn't enough to make me flee home. Instead, these ten days served to wake me up to having to be more aware, and to the importance of considering my safety, planning ahead, reading hostel reviews and not taking people's suggestions as gospel, especially when their reasons for giving them are vague, and not actual indicators of quality. If I was compelled to, I could craft my own football out of plastic bags – I didn't need to choose a hostel based entirely on seeing something so underwhelming.

As Sir Fiennes so eloquently states, I needed to learn from what happened over the course of those ten days so that I could move forwards with a tad more savvy... and that's what I would do.

LESSONS LEARNT

When you're somewhere familiar, you walk around on autopilot, instinctively knowing how to conduct yourself because you do it day in, day out. These few days woke me up to the fact that I knew nothing about my surroundings, and therefore needed to pay full attention. I of course wanted to relax and enjoy myself, and relish in new experiences rather than fear them, but I also needed to engage my brain, notice what was going on around me, and make informed decisions.

When I first got on that plane I hadn't wanted to listen to anyone. Then, acquiring our dollars quickly schooled me in the importance of heeding the advice of people with actual knowledge of how things operate. These initial misadventures showed me the importance of being subjective with the advice I received. There were going to be a lot of people along the way telling me their opinions on attractions and hostels: I needed to listen and then make my decisions based on what I already knew about myself, and what I was in the process of learning. I was done with blindly following people's advice to the letter – it was time to start actually interpreting it in terms of what it meant to me.

BOLIVIA

WHERE I LEARNT...

- That it's perfectly safe to swim in crocodile-infested waters if dolphins are there.

- That the best toilet you can expect on a Bolivian bus is behind a pile of bricks at the side of a motorway.

- That nothing is sexier to Bolivian men than a meaty calf on a woman.

- That egg sellers are the market-stall holders you should watch out for.

- That a red-wine hangover can be cured in less than ten seconds with canned oxygen.

- That most things, including houses, can be made out of salt.

- That sometimes deck chairs work as car seats if secured right.

ACCEPTING DEFEAT IN THE AMAZON RAINFOREST

FRIENDLY ADVICE:

'Do me a favour, Amy, try not to fall in love with everyone you meet. I can see it now, bone through your nose, baby on each tit.'

Vinnie, line manager

EXPERT ADVICE:

'Be mad.'

Salvador Dalí
(Very few qualms with being himself)

Starting my trip in Argentina had been a wonderful way to break myself in to travelling gently. It was sunny, everything was delicious and I had a best mate with me who I could laugh off all our schoolboy errors with. Even still, it hadn't been the assault on the senses I'd expected from South America. That came when I arrived in Bolivia.

My first glimpses of La Paz, Bolivia's largest city, were from the window of a plane – and even then, it still made me gawp a little. One minute I'd been pressing my forehead against the glass, worrying that my tiny, propeller-driven plane was flying a tad too close to the mountain range below and that I was about to become embroiled in some kind of mountaintop survival story aka that football team in the sixties that ended up eating each other, and the next – boom – there was La Paz, nestled in a vast bowl-shaped valley created by its river, the Choqueyapu.

From my vantage point overhead, La Paz looked enormous, sunny and every shade of orange and yellow. To the side I could see the three peaks of Illimani Mountain, the highest in the Cordillera Real range that I'd just been flying over. To be that close to mountaintops, you need to be pretty high up. La Paz is nestled at 3,650 m above sea level, making it a hotly tipped contender for 'hardest city to breathe in' – well, at least until your lungs adjust to the thin air associated with being at altitude. I'd been warned that I would notice this drop in air pressure the minute the plane doors opened, but even though I braced myself, the only evidence of the drop was the shampoo that exploded all over my hand luggage – ensuring everything would smell faintly of Herbal Essences for the next couple of weeks.

'DUDE! OVER HERE! AMY!' I heard her before I could see her. Ruth is one of my oldest friends, and favourite people: she's loud, excitable and very, very Welsh. She's also used to using her voice to command classrooms of unruly teenagers, so the thin glass partition that separated us did little to mask her excitement at our reunion.

Ruth and her boyfriend, Henry, had spent the last two years working like dogs in their jobs as geography teachers in Tottenham, subsisting on a diet of beans on toast in order to save as much as possible for their travels. When the time came, they sold everything they owned, packed up and departed London to travel the world. By the time I met them, they were six months into their 18-month trip, and had journeyed through the USA and much of South America already.

I grinned, jumped up and down on the spot, waved energetically through the glass, grabbed my backpack and practically sprinted into her arms.

'AWESOME!' Ruth bellowed in her thick Swansea accent, 'YOU'RE FINALLY HERE!' alarming the otherwise peaceful crowd waiting to pick up their loved ones.

'All right, Henry!' I pulled away from Ruth's embrace to greet him.

'Good to see you, mate!' Henry said as he gave me a hug. He's the polar-opposite of Ruth: the calmest, most placid man you've ever met. A rat could leap from the gutter and attach itself to his jugular, and he'd probably just shrug. They complement each other perfectly.

I hugged Henry and stood back to take a look at them, all scruffy and tanned, wrists loaded with bracelets from every country they'd visited. 'You guys both look annoyingly tanned and thin.'

'I've had a parasite since Colombia, mate,' Ruth revealed. 'It's not ideal.'

'Yeesh.'

Ruth grabbed my backpack from me and strode out of the airport doors. She hailed a cab in perfect Spanish and we were soon zooming out of El Alto Airport and into the Bolivian traffic.

The airport is located on the upper lip of the river valley, which means that the drive back into town mostly involves coasting down steep, windy streets. The suburbs get progressively nicer the further into the valley you descend. Apparently the richest suburbs lie right at the very bottom of the valley, where temperatures are sometimes as much as five degrees warmer than the parts of town heading up the mountain.

As we neared the centre of town, it was the volume of people that struck me first. The streets seemed a thousand times more crowded than in Argentina, and buses, cars and vans hurtled between traffic lights and stop signs, not at all shy to create additional lanes, or to blast their horns repeatedly despite it having zero effect on getting people or vehicles to move out of the way. Bolivian pedestrians didn't appear to fear these speeding hunks of metal; they were nonchalantly weaving in and out of fast-moving traffic, trying to flog everything from bags of nuts and dried beans to bottles of water, hot coffee and newspapers. There were fun forces at work to help manage the traffic – I spotted people dressed as furry zebras, trying their best to direct the traffic and help people cross the roads without incurring serious injury.

Also dodging traffic, as well as lining the pavements flogging various colourful wares, were many indigenous women, known as *cholitas*. These are the ladies famous for their thick pleated skirts, woollen shawls, heavy jewellery and of course the tiny bowler hats they precariously perch on their heads.

'They're all wearing them at different angles!' I noticed.

'Yeah, apparently if they're straight, it means they're taken, and wonky means they're single or widowed,' answered Ruth.

'What about the ones wearing them on the backs of their heads?'

'That means things are "complicated".'

'That's way better than updating your Facebook status!' I laughed.

Legend has it that these hats were brought to Bolivia by two British men, who had a huge batch made up to flog to British railway workers who were working in Bolivia at the time. When they cracked open the shipment, it was immediately obvious the hats were way too small for the men's heads, so rather than throw them out, they cooked up some tale about them being all the rage with European women, and they sold like hotcakes.

Maybe it was being with Ruth and Henry, maybe it was La Paz's hustle and bustle and crazy location, or maybe it was the fact that I was light-headed from the lack of oxygen, but I was excited to see what else Bolivia had to offer.

▲▲▲▲▲▲▲

An hour or so later, after we were checked into our hostel and I'd scraped shampoo from between the pages of my passport, Ruth, Henry and I congregated in the hostel bar to have a good catch up. These guys are the most organised couple I know – they think about logistics, weather conditions and budgets before they think about coffee in the morning. Therefore it came as no shock when before I'd even taken a sip of my beer, they revealed a solid itinerary had been outlined for our three weeks together.

'So, Aimz,' Ruth said, immediately getting down to business, 'we've booked our flights to the Amazon. We leave tomorrow!'

'Wow! Really?'

'Yep. We did think about waiting a day or two, but it's getting close to rainy season, and the longer you leave it, the harder it is to fly in. We really need to go ASAP, or else we might not be able to get there, or back again!'

I'd never planned to visit the Amazon rainforest. I thought it might happen, but it was hardly top ten. I'd sensibly filled those coveted spots with the places I planned on sunbathing at for six hours at a stretch. However, Ruth and Henry seemed excited, and they told me that if I wanted to do it Bolivia was the cheapest place to do so out of all the countries on my route. Plus, I couldn't really come all the way to South America and not go into the Amazon, could I? So, taking exactly the same approach I had done for each of my 30 years thus far, I shrugged and said, 'Yeah, sure.'

This was how I found myself in Rurrenabaque at the end of the second week of my trip. Rurrenabaque is a tropical town in the northern part of Bolivia where every restaurant has an ant problem, and where every shop does a roaring trade in insect repellent and plastic ponchos. Every backpacker we encountered was either excitedly preparing for their trip into the rainforest, to the Pampas (the lowlands of the Amazon basin known for its abundance of wildlife), or had just returned incredibly thirsty for beer and their beds. As Ruth and Henry had pointed out, we'd arrived just prior to rainy season. In just a few short weeks the grass runway our 12-seater plane skidded to a halt on would be nothing more than the boggy sports field that the arrivals hall looked like it was the shed for. There was of course the option to take the bus if planes weren't able to take off or land. However, that takes 24 hours and I'd heard the word 'sinkhole' bandied around in the vicinity of the bus station by deathly pale backpackers with tears in their eyes. So that was a firm no-no.

As I'd only visited cities so far, it was exciting to be in a place that felt a million miles from that. Rurrenabaque is located on the banks of the Beni River, and from any of the town's six or seven dusty streets you can see mountains covered in thick green vegetation in the distance, winking at you, hinting at what kind of sights you can expect to encounter once you head down the river.

The morning I met Arturo, I was in the office of the tour company we'd chosen to take us into the Amazon, perched on a stool carved out of a tree trunk, perturbed by the small dog with enormous nipples that was currently lying on my feet. Everyone but me was still in the kit room, loading up for the rainforest.

I'd finished, and was now preoccupied with wiping sweat from my upper lip and worrying about the unknowns ahead of me, chiefly the encountering of anything poisonous or hungry. I envisioned anaconda attacks at the watering hole (*do rainforests even have watering holes?*) and jungle cats approaching my tent in the dead of night – a single claw slowly slicing open my mosquito net and then my stomach. If this tiny lactating dog was making me anxious, what on earth did I think I was doing heading off to spend three days and two nights in one of the most inhospitable places on the planet? I needed some fresh air…

I wandered outside and was greeted by the sight of a local man of around 40 years decked head to toe in khaki, reclining on his motorcycle, lazily smoking a cigarette.

A woman heading out to the Pampas had also finished packing and had joined us outside. She took a seat beside me, saw where my eyes were trained, and called out, 'Hey! Are you our guide for the boat tour?'

The guy on the bike took a long toke on his cigarette before slowly sitting up.

'No, lady… Arturo only know jungle,' he said, turning from the woman and gazing into the distance.

My, my, my – what did we have here? A strong, silent type with a motorcycle, a deadly habit, and a penchant for speaking in the third person? My interests were piqued. This perfectly-timed distraction allowed me to cease speculating about the degree of pain associated with death by lethal toad venom, and to instead consider his waist-length black hair, jaguar-tooth necklace and forearms, which had surely been toned chopping down the mahogany trees they looked to be carved from.

Now that I knew Arturo would be escorting us into the rainforest, I was excited. Five minutes ago, when I'd been informed we'd be heading to camp aboard a flimsy motorised canoe clearly insufficiently robust to withstand a crocodile attack, I'd felt a hot wave of panic flush over me. Now, I sashayed towards it as though it were a luxury yacht.

Off we set, our tiny boat carving a path through the murky waters of the Amazon River. All around, thick, seemingly impenetrable jungle crowded the water's edge. Occasionally a squawking flock of brightly coloured parrots would appear from the trees for our delight, or we'd point at the birds of prey fiercely guarding their territories overhead. We passed by children from local tribes, splashing around in the water, who waved and chased our boat, and we cruised alongside wholly insubstantial rafts tasked with the seemingly impossible burden of transporting huge lorries downriver.

Although I was enjoying my first glimpses of a land so tropical it could well have been the back entrance to Jurassic Park, I admit the wonder I was experiencing was only half attributable to the view. The rest (probably 80 per cent) had to do with Arturo, who despite not being conventionally handsome was a whole lotta sexy. He sat at the front of the boat, his long hair blowing in the wind, lovingly sharpening his machete. It was impossible not to look. By the end of the journey I'd developed quite the headache from pointing my head in one direction while keeping my eyes swivelled back on this spicy spectacle.

Henry leaned over. 'Hey Amy, you like what you see, eh?' he smirked, and nodded in the direction of Arturo.

'What? No, no. I'm just trying to listen to what he's saying so I can test out my Spanish.'

'Sure, Aimz,' Ruth laughed. 'You're a *terrible* liar.'

When we arrived at camp we were greeted by a group of Danish tourists. They were defeated, dirty and desperate looking. Each one was dressed sensibly in the recommended rainforest outfit of lightly coloured linen, only theirs were completely mud-smeared. Most of the party were sunburnt or an odd shade of puce, no doubt caused by being slowly cooked by the oppressive heat that slapped us in the face the minute our boat stopped moving. One chap was sitting on an upturned bucket, head in hands, about 100 m away from the rest of group. He was shirtless, pink and sweaty, his little belly hanging over the waistband of his jeans, which seemed an odd choice of outfit given we were in an environment with 100 per cent humidity.

As we passed, I complimented his white wellies, and asked how he was doing.

'I do not like rainforest. I prefer pub.'

That was it. No smile, no eye contact, no humour, no 'well it was a great experience but I just can't wait for a shower'. Instead, he just stared into the middle distance, haunted, with the look of someone who'd awoken to find a giant spider fleeing his bunk bed, stopping only to call out, 'Don't worry, human, you won't feel a thing until next Wednesday'.

I realised he wasn't the only one looking haunted – every one of the Danes looked like they were teetering on the brink of meltdown. Conversation had ceased, and they barely looked at us. They just sat silent and motionless, a pile of filthy arms and legs in need of a meal, a good night's sleep and a cuddle from their mothers. What on earth had happened here? Was being here going to feel as bad as they looked? I certainly hoped not; I had Arturo to impress.

As soon as the Danes realised that our boat was their escape vessel, they scrambled onto it, piling in their belongings and exhausted bodies, before sailing into the sunset whooping in anticipation of cold beer. For us, it was time to find out where we would be sleeping.

Arturo guided us along a dirt path leading into the forest. I was on high alert so it was a huge relief that no spiders leapt at our faces and no dachshund-sized scorpions appeared from the undergrowth to block our passage. Upon arriving in a clearing, it became apparent that our whole group would be sleeping in a communal hut with only three sides. I'm not entirely sure why one side was left open – presumably to allow air to circulate. It was this open side that concerned me. There wasn't even a beaded curtain as a means of protection. Those jungle cats I was worrying about earlier would encounter no obstacle stalking in-between the beds, sniffing out the person with the most body fat. Looking around, I could see that meant me, so I immediately set about assessing where I'd be safest. Would it be against the wall, or would that be prime tarantula-egg territory and, while we're on the subject, should I check under my bed or would it be best to remain oblivious to any flesh-eating terror insects nesting mere centimetres from my face? By the time I'd finished faffing, all the beds were taken, and I was left with the one immediately in front of the entrance. Just perfect. I was doomed. I may as well have just marinated myself up and lay there awaiting certain death at the hands of whichever of the rainforest's meat eaters could get there fastest.

I didn't have long to ponder all the risks of my totally exposed bed before it was suggested that we have a swim: IN THE AMAZON RIVER! The home of crocodiles, piranhas and those fish that swim up your urethra and hook on to your insides the minute you let a bit of pee out. I'm not 100 per cent sure what they do once they're in there but I imagine it's akin to the plot of nineties classic *The Faculty*, and that's not something I'm interested in being involved in, even if a teenage Josh Hartnett were to appear. I felt particularly at risk – I honestly don't remember the last time I was in water without giving in to the need to pee.

I hadn't even blinked and Ruth and Henry were already half-naked.

'What you waiting for, Amy? It's boiling, come on!' Henry called.

I looked around sceptically, but the speed with which the rest of the group were shedding their clothes demonstrated their low fear levels when it came to wading into the unknown. I realised then that I was not prepared to be this group's chubby Danish dude sitting on a bucket dreaming of the pub. Not yet. If they were doing it then I was doing it. Ordinarily I would've frowned and firmly shaken my head at the suggestion I bathe in murky water housing god knows what. If someone were to suggest taking a dip in the Thames, or doing a few laps of the duck pond on Clapham Common, I'd have declared them barmy. Here it felt different – like something that *could* be fun. Plus, it was hot as hell.

I decided to focus on the two positives of taking this danger swim: one being that it would stave off the inevitable onset of body odour imminently due to overpower our group, and the other being that it would enable me to strut my funky stuff in my new bikini in front of the object of my affections; a good point which dramatically nose-dived mere moments later when I emerged from the shade and was momentarily blinded by the light reflecting off my milky white, Brit-in-November skin. I hadn't acquired a tan yet. I was a human mirror. For the record, a bikini covered in pineapples doesn't look quite so tropical on a girl the colour of a value loaf of bread.

Entering the river was problematic. There was no fancy pontoon to dive off or ladder to slowly slide down while looking seductively over my sunglasses. I took only two steps before one leg half sunk into the gloopy mud. The other was safe. This left my white bottom pointing in the direction of Arturo and the three other guides in a messy curtsey wholly inappropriate for lunch time. I hauled my leg out of the mud and, in doing so, tumbled backwards, and kneed myself in the eye socket. After 15 seconds or so of pain (and shame), I opened my eyes and saw that Arturo had sprung to my rescue. He grabbed my hand and hauled me up. I definitely would have enjoyed this display of strength more had I not been acutely aware that I resembled the victim of a Glastonbury Portaloo mishap. As I thanked him and rubbed my face, he kindly pointed out the drier route taken by everyone who'd listened to his instructions, rather than just doing what they wanted.

'Oi Aimz,' Ruth called from the water, 'you've er… got a little something… on your face.'

I looked down at my mud-covered body. 'Cheers for the heads up, mate; I hadn't noticed.' I shot her two muddy middle fingers.

'Your seduction tactics know no bounds, Baker!' Henry grinned, before diving under the water.

Dammit. I was going to have to try much harder if I wanted to impress this Jungle Adonis.

I had little time to dwell on being a human skid mark before we were whisked off on the next activity on our Itinerary of Death. The afternoon would be spent exploring the rainforest. Although initially a tad jumpy, I soon realised that deadly things didn't actually cover every surface of the rainforest. I was so pumped up on new-found confidence that when Arturo asked for volunteers to lick termites off a tree I was the first to shoot my hand up. Yes, it was great that something in the termites repelled mosquitos, but I wasn't driven by that – he wanted to see me lick something… alrighty then.

The task was not quite as easy as it sounded; the termites were Tic Tac-sized, fast-moving and intent on using your gum line as their own personal Scalextric track. It's difficult to look both alluring and nonplussed when you're trying to chomp wayward living creatures to death. Despite my gurning, I felt like this earnt me some cool points from Arturo. He evidently agreed as he saw fit to 'reward' me.

I felt a tap on my shoulder and turned round to find Arturo grinning at me. *Oh, hello.*

He beckoned me to follow him a short distance away from the group before revealing he was holding a nut (not quite the one I had in mind) roughly the same shape, size and colour as a walnut. Very gently, with just the tip of his machete, he popped it open and presented it to me on the palm of his hand. I leaned closer and saw there were four chambers, each filled with something white, puffy and... oh... pulsating.

Arturo scooped one out, popped it in his mouth and grinned. 'Tastes like coconut.'

I didn't believe him. At best it looked like it would taste like pus.

He held the nut out to me, smiling. My eyes were wide, and the corners of my mouth were pointing south, but I nodded that I would accept his 'gift' nonetheless. I couldn't refuse. This was my first challenge post entering the water. If I could avoid gagging, perhaps I could salvage my seduction.

I ate the worm.

It did not taste like coconut.

I can still remember it popping in my mouth.

As we explored the rainforest, through my terrible Spanish and the translation skills of more educated group members, we learnt about Arturo. This was a man who began life as a rainforest guide at the age of 11. He knew all there was to know about the environment he was born in, like how to stitch up human skin with the decapitated heads of Leafcutter ants, and how to extract deadly poisons from certain trees. In fact, after explaining this, he unsheathed his machete and launched himself at the tree. *Such calf strength!* The resulting laceration released a sizzling sap that gave off an acrid smoke as it burnt a trail down the trunk. Who knew trees could be so lethal? Not me! While we all stood well back, pinching our noses like sissies, Arturo casually collected it in his sap pouch, for later use, laughingly pointing out a large and deep scar he'd acquired in a previous sap pouch leak – as you do.

I was having trouble seeing through all the hearts bubbling out of my eyes. Arturo was by far the manliest man I'd ever encountered. I was used to the men of London. The only thing manly about them is their leg hair, and most of that was decimated years ago by the introduction of skinny jeans. I've known men to complain that clipping their toenails hurts. Arturo got bitten by a tarantula, was paralysed down one side for a week and laughed about it. You know how a dude from London would cope with that? He wouldn't. He'd cry himself to death.

After an afternoon of successful exploration, I congratulated myself on not once screaming out loud at things we encountered. I hoped we'd return to camp, sit around, drink some beers and listen as Arturo fondly regaled the group with the tale of how I, 'Brave Amy', had eaten a worm while they were preoccupied with the piddly little termites. Instead, he informed us we'd shortly be heading off on a night walk: IN THE AMAZON RAINFOREST. This man was relentless. I could only think of one thing in the world worse than going on a night walk: staying at camp alone while everyone else went on a night walk.

By day the rainforest was bearable. Yes, it was hotter than the surface of Mercury, and the threat of jungle cats meant I was constantly ducking down and protecting my neck at even the slightest rustle in the bushes, but largely I could handle it. At night, I completely changed my mind. I wanted out. Everything I saw was writhing, wriggling, squirming and probably bearing fangs. Within just five metres of setting out we'd seen our first snake. It was a highly poisonous viper apparently, and well within slithering distance of our open-fronted bedroom, yet Arturo saw no cause for alarm. Initial enjoyment of proceedings was also hindered by the fact that it took me a whole minute to realise why all the rainforest's insects were flying kamikaze-style at my face. Turns out, head torches shouldn't be worn on your head at night in the rainforest unless being blinded by insect antennae appeals to you.

The first planned attraction of the night involved a series of path-spanning spider webs large enough to ensnare sizeable human meat. Only toddlers of course, but that's frightening enough. With every web we encountered, Arturo would hurry off into the darkness in search of insects to sacrifice to the hairy owners of these woven deathtraps. He'd return, show us his catch and then lob it cruelly to its death. I reckon I could have flogged pictures of everyone's horrified faces to a gargoyle manufacturer for considerable reward, had I not been preoccupied securing all my clothing's entry points. Most alarmingly, with every fist-sized monster that revealed itself Arturo would look disappointed and say, 'Pffft, *sólo un bebé*' (It's only a baby).

We ventured on, past banana-sized centipedes, glow-in-the-dark frogs and more snakes just chilling out on leaves no doubt pondering which tourist to sink their fangs into. Every time anything brushed past my body (which was a lot because it was pitch black, and we were in a rainforest) my heart leapt into my mouth, and I'd steel myself for attack. It was knackering.

Eventually we stopped moving forwards and cut away from the path, deeper into the undergrowth. Arturo signalled for us to be silent, waited until we had reassembled, and whispered, *'aquí es la tarántula'*. *Did he just say tarantula?* What kind of tour was this? I thought we'd at least get to look at some fucking stars! He solemnly held a finger to his lips and said, *'silencio, silencio, silencio'*. Sure thing, buddy! He wouldn't hear a peep from this lassie. Making noise that might alert enemies to our location was the last thing I was about to do.

Our group watched on as Arturo lit up a cigarette, and moved closer to a hole about three metres from where we were standing. He picked up a stick and began poking at the hole. Ruth and I clutched each other in terror, as spiders began trickling out, one by one, in a creepy conga line of legs and fangs. Arturo was quick to point out that these were just the 'babies'. They didn't look like babies. They looked like mobile-phone-sized nightmares. Calling something a baby implies it's cute. Cute things don't jump two metres with zero run-up, giving you no realistic chance of anticipating attack. Did you know that baby tarantulas are technically more dangerous because they haven't yet learnt to control their venom? Well, neither did I until Arturo told us, with a massive grin on his face as though it were good news. Now they were loose, and probably more than a little miffed.

I balled up the sleeves of my jacket to prevent a surprise finger attack, and watched from the tiny hole I'd left in the hood of my cagoule for seeing-purposes. Arturo set to work, taking drags from his cigarette and blowing the smoke into the holes from which the babies had scurried. After each exhalation, he'd block the hole he'd blown into with a stick or a rock. He was smoking her out.

After a few moments, to avoid the risk of suffocation, the tarantula decided to make her bid for freedom. We saw her front legs first, emerging high in surrender, like two furry drumsticks.

The cigarette smoke had placed her in some kind of trance. After a few pokes to reassure himself she was placid, Arturo picked her up. He just leaned down, grabbed her by her huge booty and walked towards us. I kid you not, this Mama Jama was the size of a frying pan. First he showed us her face full of eyes, then he flipped her over and showed us her fangs. Next he asked if any of us wanted to hold her, as if she was a cuddly toy rather than a deadly creature we'd just separated from her children, poisoned and then violated. Although this would have been the prime time to show Arturo I was fit to be his lady-wife, I could only stare at him open-mouthed before silently sidestepping behind Henry. Being roughly my height and build, and decidedly un-jumpy, Henry was by far my best option for a human shield.

While those around me kneeled and allowed Arturo to place the still-moving tarantula on their faces, I could do little more than hang my head like a sulky three-year-old and concentrate on not peeing my pants. In my defence, Ruth and Henry didn't do it either, *and* that spider could have woken up from her trance at any time. Maybe she was screwing around, making us think she was hypnotised when in actual fact she was just biding her time waiting for the right prey. Her fangs were 5 cm long and looked like they were carved out of ivory. I had my ears pierced once and didn't care for it. Plus, this environment was far from sterile, and I didn't know how good an animal hypnotist Arturo was. Of course, he appeared to be good at everything, but how do you begin to identify a reliable animal hypnotist when you've only that second learnt it's a thing? I just couldn't justify taking these kinds of chances to impress a man. No dude is worth being attacked by a Frisbee-sized tarantula, no matter how well defined his forearms.

Needless to say, sleep did not come easily that night. Having tucked in my mosquito net so tightly it was impossible to change positions, I lay there, staring out into the darkness, picturing that spider strategising her vengeance the minute she stirred from her trance. I envisioned her utilising some kind of pine cone conch to summon tarantula colonies from all corners of the Bolivian Amazon. In my head, they were to attack at dawn. I would ensure I was ready by not blinking for even a second. Perhaps if I were awake I could negotiate; save myself and maybe Ruth. Henry, being the perfect size he was, would just have to be the tragic yet necessary casualty.

Miraculously I managed to survive the night without losing my mind. We did, however, awaken to discover that today presented an additional challenge – it was hot. Really hot. Imagine being locked in a wardrobe constructed from leaky radiators populated solely by you and thirsty mosquitos. That was my reality. Although it was nearly rainy season, it hadn't rained for a week, which meant the ground was hot, the trees were hot, everything was roasting bloody hot. Perhaps you're familiar with the feeling of being somewhere as it keeps getting hotter and hotter, and more and more humid, until something needs to happen for the pressure to break and things to return to a liveable temperature? Well, the pressure gauge in that rainforest was well in the red zone and yet the rain still hadn't come. Shade offered little respite, and there was absolutely no means of controlling the sweat. Salty, stinky water was bucketing out of every pore.

Sleep-deprived, a little miserable and wondering what else we could possibly encounter that would justify us staying any longer, we set out for the day. Ruth and Henry seemed tired too but in far better spirits than I. I couldn't be bothered to ask what they thought we might encounter. It would only make my cheeks sweat.

Bounding with energy and with not a drip of sweat on him, Arturo excitedly led us into the rainforest. Apparently because we were such a 'brave group' we were going to head off the path into the undergrowth. This was where the real adventures happened, apparently. Jolly good.

'What's the seduction plan for today, beaut?' Ruth asked as I tucked in the baby pink office shirt I'd borrowed from the tour company, as I didn't have anything long-sleeved with me to protect me from the rainforest's many bloodsuckers.

'Do you really need to ask?' I laughed, shimmying a little while indicating my shirt and popping the collar to ensure mozzies couldn't target my neck.

'You can't fail! Maybe tone down the staring a tad though?' she suggested.

'It's not staring! It's *listening* attentively.'

'No normal human drools when they listen.'

'It's SWEAT!'

'I don't believe you.'

The morning involved an impromptu step aerobics class, such was the need to lift your feet to avoid them getting tangled in the undergrowth. It wasn't just the rainforest floor that was thick with vegetation; you were surrounded by every shade of green you've ever seen. There were clearings and pathways of course, but when you went off road, you constantly needed to sweep aside branches (housing who knows what), vines and leaves bigger than my entire body. There were flowers of all colours, overripe unknown fruits overhead and crushed underfoot, sunny patches where beams of light cut through the thick canopy overhead, illuminating your path and all the mozzies baying for your blood, and then there were dark patches, where everything was wet to the touch, and you suddenly got the shivers, sensing something was sizing you up for its next meal.

Although the predominant sound I could hear was ragged breathing, my own or that of my group, there were also a million other noises going on around us. Screeching birds, the rustle of the very slight breeze through the trees, the throaty calls of crickets and frogs (hopefully they were just crickets and frogs). The rainforest was both incredibly peaceful and completely alive all at once.

Despite hearing many of them, we didn't actually see any living creature all morning apart from a decomposing wild pig with a maggot-filled face. There were of course mosquitos, and as I had no energy to swat them away, I just gave in and let them feast upon my face and hands, the only parts of me left exposed.

My spirits were momentarily lifted when we stopped for a rest in a sunny clearing, next to a ravine covered in purple and red flowers. Ruth, Henry and I took the chance to lean against a fallen tree – until we saw it was crawling with fingernail-sized red ants. I just managed to prevent a straggler venturing up my sleeve, when Arturo took off his shirt and set about hacking down some bamboo branches for us to drink from. He caught me looking and gave me a playful wink. Rather than return it in a way that acknowledged that I liked what I saw, or that I at least knew I'd been clocked staring, I just went red and hid my face behind a convenient branch, like some kind of lovesick teenager.

'Do you think you could try to be a bit more creepy?' Ruth joked, sidling up behind me, and poking me in my ribs.

'I can't help it, mate,' I admitted. 'I'm not thinking straight. It's too hot, and so's he.'

'Shame the same can't be said for you right now.'

I looked down. My pink shirt was now completely see-through and plastered to my soaking-wet skin. Team that with my slicked back hair, red face and bad attitude and I resembled Gaston from *Beauty and the Beast* after a baby oil accident, only far less muscular.

'Ha! I don't know what you mean, I'll be his wife by morning, mark my words!'

'Best stay behind that branch then,' Henry winked.

We continued on for a while along what appeared to be no planned trajectory. We'd stop every now and then for Arturo to point out a plant that had antibiotic qualities, or that made a mean cup of tea, or that could send you on the hallucinogenic trip of a lifetime if you were to chop it up and sprinkle it on your lunch. Disappointingly, we weren't allowed to try that. Suddenly Arturo started whooping in excitement. We all whirled around in circles looking for what could possibly be causing this ecstatic reaction. Hopefully it would be Tarzan coming to whisk me away from this waking nightmare. Nope – the thing that got him all fired up was slithering away from us... an enormous brown boa constrictor with a circumference roughly the size of one of Dwayne 'The Rock' Johnson's thighs.

The snake wasn't happy. He'd just eaten. We could tell this because the outline of the poor creature he'd swallowed made him look like he'd eaten a box. Whatever it was must have been in there, gasping for air, wondering why everything had suddenly gone dark. The next thing we knew, Arturo leapt on the snake and wrestled it, as we stood looking on and wondering whether we should try to get photos or try to help. *As if that were even an option.* He was so delighted by the encounter that I started to wonder whether he just wanted to give the snake a hug. He laughed with delight the whole time he was holding him. After a few minutes, while we looked on in amazement and he smiled and repeatedly thanked Pachamama (Mother Earth), he warned us he was going to let go of the snake, with just one word: 'run'.

Fan-fucking-tastic.

The second he released the snake, we took off, leaping over bushes and scratching our faces on branches that we'd neglected to clear on our way through, until Arturo's manic laughing made us stop and look back. He'd been 'messing' with us. The snake wasn't following. Instead it was writhing around in distress. We crept back closer and, before our eyes, that 7-foot boa constrictor opened its colossal jaws and threw up his lunch. For anyone interested, it was a jungle bunny.

Finally, I understood the haunted look on the faces of the Danes who were departing when we arrived. Now I too had seen things that would haunt me. At that moment, if someone had led me to that upturned bucket, I would without protest, nay happily, have sat on it and allowed my paunch to hang over whichever trousers weren't completely soaked with my own bodily fluids. And I (like my white-wellied Danish mate), would just wait in defeated silence for the boat home, sulkily daydreaming about cushioned seats, bottled beer and bar snacks.

Alas, we had one more night to survive and it was to be spent fishing. Fortunately, Ruth, Henry and I had had the forethought to pack a litre of rum. After five minutes of trying to catch something, followed by five minutes trying to feign interest in other people fishing, I gave up and began making my way through the rum. Swigging greedy slugs from that bottle in a bid to achieve the levels of oblivion required for respite from the constant need to scratch, I unapologetically ogled Arturo. He was perched patiently on a rock about ten metres away, barely moving aside from tiny flicks of his wrist. He suddenly leapt from where he was crouching to haul an enormous fish out of the water, which he proceeded to smack to death on the rocks. I'd have been horrified had I not found it so sexy that I burst into a spontaneous round of applause. No one else joined in. Arturo performed a little bow in my direction… then laughed and told me I looked drunk.

I shrugged to indicate I knew I was guilty, dropping the near-empty bottle of rum in the process.

'Correctamundo,' I slurred.

On the final morning, I emerged from my mosquito-net oven red-eyed, hungover and crazy-haired. Overnight, I appeared to have contracted some sort of stomach complaint that had turned my guts to liquid. Not sure which end things were going to materialise from, I sprinted to the toilet. Surprised to find the lid closed, I hauled it open and prepared to vomit everywhere. What can only be described as a tidal wave of a billion flies poured forth from the depths of that putrid, long drop. I sprinted in the other direction, swatting madly at the cloud of filthy beasts trying to gain access to my ears, eyes, nose and mouth. I knew only too well what they'd just been feasting on, the knowledge of which was doing nothing for my dodgy tummy. I reached new levels of cool that morning, running through the middle of the breakfast area, shaking my head and holding my nose, waving my other hand in the air in a bid to deter those fetid creatures from laying their maggot eggs in my warm, welcoming ear canals.

I'd reached the riverbank before I realised the cloud had dispersed and I was safe. I turned around to see all of those who'd started their days far more calmly, watching me with amusement. Then I promptly threw up.

I had no fight left in me.

I was the exact same shade of puce as the Danes had been, back when I mocked them so.

My clothes were filthy.

I stank.

I had vomit in my hair.

And now, to add insult to injury, my gurgling stomach implied a bout of the shits was upon me. I hung my head and admitted defeat. I was broken. I needed my mum.

Arturo chose that moment to arrive with a gift (and a bottle of water). As a memento of our time in the rainforest he'd set to work making everyone rings carved from coconuts. He'd used his dagger to carve each delicate wooden ring with something unique to us. One guy got a boa constrictor, another a tarantula.

Me?

Just Arturo's name.

I will treasure that ring forever.

▲▲▲▲▲▲▲

On that last morning (after I'd got the taste of sick out of my mouth) we lazed around waiting for the boat.

'Are you going to miss Arturo, Amy?' Henry joked.

'Oh, sure, terribly!' I laughed. 'Although I'm not convinced we're destined to become lovers. At least I'll always have this ring.'

'I'm surprised you could even be bothered to think about men – all I can think about is how many bites I've got,' Ruth said, lifting up her leg a little to get full purchase on her scratching.

'You've got to admit he's sexy?' I asked. Ruth shook her head.

'No? Really? Henry?'

'Well, I do like a man who can handle a machete.'

'Who doesn't?'

I was so weary I could barely keep my eyes open. 'This trip was HARD. I'm absolutely ruined.'

'Really? I thought you handled it like a pro,' Ruth laughed. 'The rainforest is clearly your natural habitat.'

'A habitat I'm happy to be leaving. I don't think my body is designed to be at this temperature for long periods. My brain feels weird.'

'Yeah – we are going to sleep so well tonight,' said Henry, letting out a big yawn.

'Do you reckon this is one of the hardest things you two have done?' I asked.

'Hmmm… well, we've done a fair bit of rainforest trekking now, and yeah it's hard, but how cool is it to be here? We're geography teachers – this is completely awesome for us!' Henry said.

'Yeah man,' Ruth agreed, 'those trees that look like octopuses and move around are the best thing I've ever seen!' We all nodded in agreement – those trees had been cool.

'In all seriousness, though,' Ruth continued, 'even though you hurt right now and probably can't wait to leave, we've found it's been the harder challenges that have been most memorable for us. They're the ones we chat about the most, and laugh about. When else are you going to get the chance to visit places like this? You've got to throw yourself into it, mate, even if every second feels unpleasant.'

I nodded. Of course the teachers were right. In the Amazon my every sense was activated. I saw things that petrified, delighted, overwhelmed and baffled me, all while being the exact same temperature as the inside of a freshly toasted pitta bread. That's a lot for one human to take. Every single part of my body and mind was awake, every organ was in overdrive, and it was exhausting. But realistically, what had I been expecting – a casual stroll around the park with a Calippo? Maybe I needed to be more open to this stuff moving forwards. Maybe I needed to actually seek it out.

'Aimz, let me get a picture of how happy you are with Arturo's ring.' Henry pointed his camera at me.

'Yeah – and we must capture how at home you look in your new favourite habitat.'

From my reclining position leaning against a tree, I wearily raised the fist that was wearing my new jewellery into the air in victory, and as I did we finally heard a deafening peal of thunder indicating we were about to be rained on.

'Quick, quick, we go before the rain,' Arturo called from the riverbank where he'd been heroically loading our stuff into the boat.

On the journey home, as it poured with rain, I may have been tired, but I felt surprisingly exhilarated.

'We need to remember this moment, Ruth,' I said sleepily.

'What do you mean?'

'Everything around us. The view. How it smells. How we smell! How the rain feels on our skin. This is pretty awesome.'

'Sure is, dude – and you're only just getting started.'

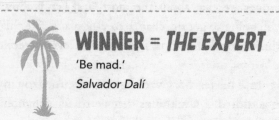

WINNER = *THE EXPERT*

'Be mad.'
Salvador Dalí

Vinnie – despite your utterly terrible, wildly racist and completely uninformed statement, you *maybe* had a point about the love part. I did need to learn not to fall in love with every person I met, especially happily married, 40-year-old men who spend the majority of their time in a place it would take me a whole lot of persuading to ever return to. I would however challenge you not to get a little doe-eyed over a man who tackles a 7-foot boa constrictor between his thighs and wins.

In the rainforest I had no choice but to give in to my intense emotions and 'be mad'. After all, I was in a place that was driving me stark raving bonkers. Lack of sleep and constant fear of attack isn't conducive to normal behaviour. Add severe sickness, diarrhoea and oppressive heat to that stinking pile of feelings, and things were only going to turn out one way – with me acting completely batty.

LESSONS LEARNT

Any hope of maintaining control in that rainforest was utterly futile. Frankly I shouldn't have bothered to even try. It was the most intense environment I'd ever been in. I hail from West Sussex, a land of Tories and gentle hills. Little surprise then that when faced with snakes, spiders, mosquitos and a swarm of aggressive sandflies intent on only biting my arse, I couldn't act as though everything was normal. It was as far from normal as I'd ever been in my life.

No matter how ingrained in me it is to constantly try to control my emotions, and my bodily functions, every single thing in that place was doing its darndest to make sure I gave in. I had no choice but to go with it and allow myself to be overcome by everything around me, including Arturo. As I morphed into a sweaty, uncomfortable ball of emotions covered in sick, I was forced to face up to the reality that it is not possible to be in control, and be everything you're expected to be, at all times. Trying to be brave, captivating, pretty, adventurous, educated and kind is exhausting enough in a temperate environment. In the rainforest, where all I wanted to do was claw at my itchy skin and noisily appeal to the heavens for some kind of Sympathy Rapture, I had no chance.

I had shrugged my way into the Amazon, and that was fine, because my intention when I left England was to go with the flow. However, now I'd seen how much an experience like this could challenge me, and change me, I wanted to make sure that my version of going with the flow now flowed towards the extraordinary. I couldn't just mosey around assuming I'd chance upon South America's finest. I had to conduct a bit of research, ask for tips and listen to people who'd come from the direction I was headed in. Ruth and Henry's sublime organisational skills introduced me to the concept of taking responsibility for seeing the things that interested me the most.

I also wanted to be able to relax into experiences like this rather than fight them with every fibre of my being. This was the first place in South America where I'd genuinely been knocked for six, in tiring, terrifying and terrific ways, but I didn't want it to be the last. I needed to be ready to accept any behaviour I exhibited in such moments – even if it involved another embarrassingly obvious crush, or another very public bout of vomiting. It taught me to no longer shy away from how I react to things, because if they're honest reactions, there's nothing to be ashamed of, or to cover up.

AN ENCOUNTER WITH THE WORLD'S MOST HANDSOME MAN

FRIENDLY ADVICE:

'Watch out for men with too much wooden jewellery, Amy. I know what you're like... you'll let them sucker you in with their yoga chat but essentially, they're unwashed... and you don't want to put your face anywhere near an unwashed penis, let me tell you.'

Carol, receptionist

EXPERT ADVICE:

'Do your thing and don't care if they like it.'

Tina Fey
(Comedian, writer, actress, producer, author
– and all-round women's hero)

We had one day after returning from the rainforest to recuperate in bed before we headed out on the second leg of our Amazon adventures with the tour company. This time we were heading into the Pampas. The three-day trip was largely boat-based, which meant we were able to enjoy the sights and sounds of the lowlands of the Amazon River without having to exert too much energy, which, after the rainforest, was just fine and dandy with me.

The Pampas is an incredible network of interconnecting rivers and tributaries called home by a large portion of South America's animal kingdom. Some of the waterways we journeyed down in our low-lying, motorised wooden boat were wide and spacious, and others were narrow and almost completely covered with a canopy of trees. Other channels were thick with reeds that reached well above our heads and were full of far too many spiderwebs for my liking. Cruising through those more foliage-heavy channels made me nervous, especially because it felt like there was potential for a lot of things to be lurking under the surface, or on top of the surface, or in the trees above. This concern only heightened after we saw our first few caimans, one of the most deadly animals in the Amazon region, heating their cold blood in the sunshine, or weaving through the water towards us to get a better look.

Despite occasional waves of fear, I was mostly preoccupied with monitoring my developing tan and looking at all the cool stuff around us. In comparison with the rainforest, this was positively luxury. All I needed to improve the experience was a cocktail and perhaps Mick Dundee and his big knife on standby, just in case any of those caimans decided to get a little frisky.

We saw giant capybaras – the world's largest rodent – so now I can say I've ticked that off the bucket list. They look cuddly, but highly suspicious, like you'd really have to get to know them before they'd let you give them a cuddle. We cruised past turtles surfing along on the river's current on the back of floating logs, and punky looking hoatzin birds lined up on branches, possibly discussing last night's gig. We raced alongside troops of howler monkeys gliding through the trees – and then, we saw the star attraction…

I'd come on this trip to the Pampas with optimism in my heart. Optimism that my animal dreams would come true and I would get to see a sloth in the wild, just doing its thing, being completely awesome and impressively lazy all at once. I've wanted to meet a sloth, any sloth, since the day I discovered that they existed – and then watched all the YouTube videos possible about them. I knew that chances were slim, and I didn't want to get my hopes up, but nonetheless, I kept my eyes trained on the treetops 96 per cent of the time. It was late in the afternoon when our captain took a little side stream, and we found ourselves very slowly floating through thick reeds and stagnant water, into an area that could be best described as a mozzie orgy. We were instantly set upon by swarms of the bloodsuckers, but as we all panicked and started donning cagoules and creating clouds of jungle-strength deet, our guide offered an explanation for why we were there.

'Sloth, sloth!'

I no longer cared that the backs of my arms were being gnawed into oblivion: above us hung a sloth. Not just any sloth, a stunt sloth – this fuzzy little dude was hanging upside down by his feet, watching us, while very calmly cleaning his own nails. I swear he was smiling directly at me. I couldn't have asked for a better sloth viewing. Every time I feel a little stressed, I picture that guy – giving off levels of casual we should all aspire to.

Of course, because we were still technically in the rainforest, there were parts of the Pampas that still served to terrify. Crocodiles were everywhere, basking on riverbanks, making sure we were aware of both their presence and the fact that they're roughly the same size and width as the wobbly boat we were travelling in. Just one look told me that if they wanted to, they could destroy our vehicle with one chomp of their jaws. I was particularly alarmed when we passed by five or six particularly mean-looking crocs, and then, no more than 500 m further on, our 'captain' told us we'd reached the part of the river where we could swim with pink river dolphins.

'But what about those gigantic crocodiles we *just saw* back there?' I asked, justifiably sceptical.

A couple of members of our group were already splashing around in the water.

Idiots.

'No worries. Dolphins scare the crocodiles away,' our captain reassured us, before pulling his hat further down on his head to seize his chance for a nap, while we risked our necks. I did not trust him.

Ruth and Henry were already in the water, of course. For two incredibly practical people, their perception of danger seemed *way* off to me.

'Amy! Come on, dude! DOLPHINS!' Ruth cried, splashing her hands in the water to alert all river dwellers to her presence.

I sat in the boat with my arms tightly folded across my chest, the only remaining passenger still utilising her brain. What could possibly come next? Hugging some bull sharks? Seeking out a jaguar to wrestle? I was definitely approaching my limit of dangerous animal encounters.

Our captain hadn't been lying about the dolphins, though. They were definitely there – people were squealing in delight at their pink fins breaching the water.

'Come on, Amy. Toughen up! You'll only regret it if you don't do it,' Henry called.

I shed my clothes and warily lowered myself into the water. Death by crocodile has been a deeply ingrained fear of mine since my brother told me he had one living in his bedroom to stop me sneaking in to play on his Super Nintendo as a kid.

Those prehistoric-looking motherfuckers still chill my blood to Arctic temperatures.

I began to swim over to where the group were hanging out – the last thing I wanted was to be picked off by a croc just because I was the only numbnuts out on a limb. As I panic-swam towards where my terrified brain perceived safety to be, something heavy and very much alive bashed into my leg. I've never moved as fast in my life – I shot directly into the air, and sprinted across the surface of the water, back to the safety of the boat. I don't know how I did it – let's call it a jungle miracle. Let those suckers frolic around like loons when there could be mean crocodiles, who clearly, CLEARLY, won't be deterred by some piddly pink dolphins.

In addition to meeting a sloth, and seeing numerous extraordinary animals up close, there was always something around that made me obsessively check my shoes. Insects you couldn't dream up, with more legs than they must actually require, loitering in corners of rooms surrounded by cocoons that were definitely harbouring even worse, more-evolved versions of them. Our accommodation for our time in the Pampas was wooden huts raised up on stilts along the banks of the river. Each living area was connected by narrow wooden slatted walkways. As the river got higher, crocodiles would hang out under your huts, just looking at you, letting you know they were there, their shiny eyes just daring you to fall in. It was a good job we didn't have any rum at our disposal – I needed to be 100 per cent sure-footed.

We spent three days and two nights in the Pampas, and our last afternoon was to be spent hunting anaconda. That's right, you heard – anaconda. We sat around at dinner the night before discussing what we knew about these enormous jaguar/crocodile/human-murdering nightmare providers…

'I think they can grow to something like thirty feet in length,' Henry informed us. That's roughly half the length of a bowling lane, for those of you needing a point of reference.

'They weigh loads too, like five hundred pounds,' chipped in Kevin, a doctor from Chicago. That's 35 stone, to the rest of us.

'I believe they only really attack in water though,' Ruth reassured. 'They surround their prey – sometimes kids – and then coil round, drag them into the water, suffocate them and then swallow them whole.' *No thank you.*

I decided to take matters into my own hands and sidled up to our captain on the morning of 'the hunt', trying to persuade him that none of the group were that bothered about going in search of one of the rainforest's most terrifying beasts. Ruth, Henry and I had after all come face to face with his slightly smaller but similarly motivated cousin only days before, and that was more than enough slithering for this chica. We went anyway – because apparently it's *not* all about me – and I spent three hours panicking and getting horrifically sunburnt. There was not one anaconda sighting – well, until we were in the van transporting us back into town, and we pulled over because someone had found one on the side of the road, and was waving it at passing traffic. Oh, Bolivia!

My time spent in the rainforest and the Pampas was unbelievable. I spent 90 per cent of the time completely agog at what I was seeing. Coming from a city where you rarely see the horizon, and where you often don't even feel like you're living on a planet, it was an enormous hop, step and jump to find myself here – where every bush and tree seemed alive with life I hadn't known existed. To be that close to nature, and to see how much is happening out there that has nothing to do with humans gave me some important perspective about how insignificant I actually am. In a weird way,

I felt relieved – it was a lovely reminder not to get too wrapped up in trivialities.

When we finally boarded the plane that was jetting us back to La Paz, I was ready to be leaving the humidity, and satisfied that I'd got to hang out with enough creepy-crawlies to last me a while. In fact, I'd be quite happy to only see them in low-budget Hollywood movies from now on. Apart from the sloth of course: the world's population of sloths are welcome round my gaff any day of the week. Feel free to let them know.

▲▲▲▲▲▲▲▲

Our next adventure was a 4x4 tour around Salar de Uyuni, the world's largest salt flat, located 3,656 ft above sea level. Returning to altitude meant oxygen levels plunged, and temperatures immediately plummeted to a level where your skin didn't physically recoil when covered in fabric. The contrast in landscapes from the north to the south of Bolivia was enormous. We went from a place where everything seemed to be alive to the top of the world, where the only plants I saw were cacti. There were animals, of course: llamas, flamingos and cool Bolivian bunnies called vizcachas. I hand-fed one some cheese. It seems dairy-based products are admired by both man and beast.

On the salt flats you spend your days journeying between otherworldly sights, such as bright red and emerald-green lakes coloured by algae and metals in the water, which surprisingly didn't seem to deter passing flamingos from having a paddle. There are crazy rock formations dotted around everywhere that have been carved into weird and wonderful shapes by the force of the wind alone, whole towns built using salt and a geyser basin, full of bubbling grey sulphur pools, that you do NOT want to slip into.

After the salt flats, Ruth and Henry decided their next stop would be the town of Potosí. Once there they'd journey deep into the ground at the famous silver mine, found in Cerro Rico, or 'Rich Mountain' as it was dubbed in the sixteenth century, due to the fact that it supplied almost 60 per cent of the world's silver.

I didn't fancy the mine. Call me old-fashioned but the idea of being miles underground with a considerable amount of unexploded dynamite made me want to turn and run in the other direction, which I kind of did. I decided to miss out Potosí and instead head to the next town, Sucre – Bolivia's capital city, where the country's Declaration of Independence was signed back in 1825. Ruth and Henry would join me there in a couple of days' time.

Ever mindful of my budget, I opted for the cheapest bus ticket out of town, setting off at 9 p.m. This meant hanging around in Uyuni station in torrential rain, long after it seemed the streetlights had gone off. I was confident that I'd prepared adequately for my first lone journey in Bolivia. I'd stocked up on snacks and crammed my backpack full of warm clothing. Bar the flight to the Amazon, we'd done all of our travelling around Bolivia on night buses. After a couple of particularly shivery journeys, I'd quickly learnt that travelling at night in Bolivia, over high mountain passes, often means temperatures inside your bus dropping so drastically you're given good reason to believe your nose may never feel the same again.

When I hopped aboard, excited to sleep, I found that rather than travelling beside just one human, I had to share the space with three: a teenager and his two younger brothers. This did not appeal to me one bit, especially as I was crammed against the window, and as the journey progressed, it got steadily colder and colder and I realised that my measly sleeping bag liner, hoodie and hat weren't going to cut the mustard. I curled up in a ball and tried to wrap the curtain around me to provide a little extra heat. Then one of the younger brothers, who could only have been about five and who had been staring at me for about 40 minutes, tapped me on the knee, lifted up the corner of their blanket and let me snuggle inside. I was so grateful I practically forced them to share all my snacks.

Despite the in-bus entertainment being the movie, *Highlander*, blasted in both English and Spanish throughout the night, I was soon cosy enough to get some sleep. Around two in the morning the driver shook me awake. The bus had stopped and people were starting to trickle off. He was holding a clipboard and pointing at my name on a list. Turns out the bus terminated in Potosí en route to Sucre and I was being turfed off here, along with the rest of the passengers. The driver led me outside, pointed at a man, and informed me that my onward journey would be in what appeared to be this stranger's personal vehicle.

'Erm… is there another bus I could catch?'

The driver shook his head. No.

'Will anyone else be in the car with us?'

He shook his head again. Nope.

'Is this man nice?' I pointed at the driver, who was simultaneously smoking a cigarette and eating a sandwich.

He shrugged, laughed and called something I didn't catch to my driver and then sauntered away.

If I didn't want to sleep on the icy cold streets of Potosí, it was clear I had no choice but to trust that this stranger would get me there safely. I spent the three-hour journey forcing myself to stay awake and trying to chat to my driver, Luis. At this stage my conversational Spanish only really stretched to colours, different foods and members of my family, but the pressure forced me to improvise, and Luis seemed to understand. It was a lesson – if a very tired one. Luis answered my questions, and smiled good-naturedly as I struggled to find my words. He also occupied himself by chewing coca leaves, chain-smoking and doing his best to dodge the stray dogs that seemed to think sleeping in the middle of a motorway was a good idea. Silly puppies.

We finally pulled into Sucre around five in the morning. I may have planned the snacks, and the mediocre warmth-providers, but I'd foolishly not thought to book any accommodation in advance. You would have thought I'd have learned my lesson back in Mendoza. When I'd travelled before, it had been around Asia where you can turn up anywhere and find a room without booking ahead. I really needed to shake myself out of that habit but in the meantime I hopped in the first cab I could find and asked the driver to take me to the nearest hostel. I was so deliriously tired from forcing myself to stay awake that I barely blinked when I noticed the driver's seat and passenger seat were plastic deck chairs secured (very steadily) with bungee cords.

When I arrived at the hostel I was ushered into a completely empty dorm room. Although I'd been on the road for less than a month, I knew what a rarity having a whole dorm room to yourself was. In most South American hostels I'd encountered so far you were either cruelly left to curl up with your backpack in reception until dawn (when you *might* finally be allowed to check in), or you had to tiptoe through a room of snoring strangers with only the light of your phone for guidance. It rested on your shoulders to negotiate a safe and silent path through a danger zone of rogue flip-flops with the potential to send you sprawling into a wall of metal lockers, or, more commonly, into the crotches of new acquaintances unlikely to take kindly to aggressive midnight cuddles. It's quite the physical and mental challenge when you've just spent ten hours on a bus.

I embraced my gloriously empty room for a whole day and a half before I remembered I'd left the UK to meet people, and see things. Sadly I couldn't stay in this little oasis of serenity moisturising my body, eating crisps and listening to Lady Gaga forever. I reluctantly checked out of my pleasure den and into a hostel the internet told me would facilitate human interaction. Once I'd loaded my valuables into my locker, I decided to go and interact with some humans up on the sunny roof terrace. Thus far, it had seemed South America had little to offer me man-wise. Aside from the Dutch man I'd snogged in La Paz largely because I liked the way he said 'let's drink beers', pickings had been annoyingly slim. This was irritating as I'd been under the impression that hot men would be lining the halls of each of my hostels, awaiting my arrival with refreshing glasses of coconut water, and thoughtful compliments. They weren't, and I was getting thirsty.

I'd be lying if I said I hadn't met men in my first few weeks, but in order to fancy them I had had to squint and rely on my ability to completely ignore everything they were saying. Although I'm practised in such techniques, I was determined not to continue to afford men such luxuries.

Like most 30-year-old women, I've got a couple of achievement badges on my relationship sash. The most noteworthy of these relationships dragged on for a few too many years, traversed continents and left me hesitant to pursue new men who seemingly ticked all my boxes. I hadn't felt ready to risk the chance of getting hurt again, so I erected some brick walls around my person, decorated them with a sprinkle of barbed wire and then only invited in dudes I knew there was no chance of me getting attached to.

I was interested in finally addressing this unfulfilling behavioural pattern, and did harbour a little hope that South America might be the place to do so. However, I was torn on the topic because on one hand, I wanted to seek real connections with interesting men whose brains I enjoyed as much as their faces, but on the other, I didn't want any distractions from focusing on myself, my writing and my enjoyment of the trip. I didn't want to get sucked in to pursuing romance rather than adventure, or to miss out on things because I was preoccupied pining over some fella I met in the last town who was heading in the opposite direction. I resolved that unless a guy appeared to be particularly special, I'd only allow myself to focus on the 'fun' part of the interaction.

Back on the roof terrace, I'd just cracked open a beer and got chatting to a boisterous 40-year-old Australian with lots of tribal tattoos and strong opinions about every subject raised, when out of the stairwell emerged a vision; a tall, dark, and *very* handsome vision.

I watched him approach, the opening chords of Bonnie Tyler's 'Holding Out for a Hero' immediately starting to play in my head. *Oh no*. A combination of the evening breeze and his powerful stride meant his long hair was billowing behind him like thick black smoke. A sheen of desire descended over my eyes making everything soft-focus. If this had been a film, he wouldn't have walked in, he would have swung onto the roof terrace through an open window with a rose between his teeth. Wait… he appeared to be heading straight for us. He was smiling, and waving at the Aussie. Oh, what teeth! So small and straight. Ergonomically designed for earlobe-nibbling. Thank goodness I'd moisturised.

The dashing stranger greeted the Aussie with a warm pat on the back, and then leaned down, held out his hand to me and introduced himself with a smile.

'Hello. I'm Daniel. And you are?'

I took his hand. '*I* am Amy Baker.' *Way to go, nerd.*

'How formal! Nice to meet you, Amy Baker.'

Daniel was from Portugal, and upon first impression he looked like a lot of things…

Like he'd dominate in a sword fight and utilise a bow and arrow with 100 per cent accuracy.

Like he'd make plucking stranded cats from trees his daily business purely because he wanted others to reap the benefits of his well-above-average height.

Like he'd spend weekends being the inspiration for nineties music videos by hanging out in low-slung trousers in rooms where open windows play havoc with the curtains.

Daniel was dreamy. So dreamy I didn't even mind the fact he was sporting the multiple wooden necklaces Carol had warned me about, what appeared to be clip-on sandals (they had clasps) and a maroon American Airlines complimentary blanket as a makeshift scarf.

From the get-go Daniel was all about putting his beautiful face close to mine, maintaining intense eye contact and touching me a lot as he spoke. I had to take a lot of deep, calming breaths in order to suppress my urge to reach out and touch his face. As well as heavily lashed chocolate-coloured eyes, he had some kind of mystical side-smile going on that made me want to give him all my money and agree to join whatever harem of women he must have waiting for him somewhere. I hadn't seen a man like him in South America, maybe not even in my life. I felt the need to excuse myself to go and write out multiple reminder notes to visit his hometown of Porto at the earliest opportunity. What other treasures lay undiscovered there? I didn't know. What I did know was I would pack nothing but condoms like Colin Frissell from *Love Actually* and just hope for the best.

To top off his dreamy appearance, Daniel was an artist, which automatically made him a good 20 per cent more desirable. Most women, at least those I know, fancy a little dabble in romantics with an artist at some stage in their lives. I mean, if they can be that skilled with a paintbrush or even a chisel, what are they capable of doing with the female body, eh? This intrigue also applies to hunky plumbers FYI. I'd dipped my toe into the world of artist-dating in my time, but my track record was dreadful. All of the 'artists' I've found myself buying pints for have either been overly concerned by conspiracy theories, trying to pass off shoplifting success stories as anti-establishment performance art or have spent the whole time moaning about their rent-paying sideline as a juggler at children's parties. Despite this appalling roster, intrigue was setting in. Maybe this artist was different?

If there was ever any doubt that I fancied Daniel (there wasn't), it vanished the minute he pulled out his sketchbook.

'Would you like to take a look at some of my drawings?' he asked, in his thick accent, looking through long eyelashes directly into my soul.

'I'd love that,' I blushed.

With every page, torn into shapes and decorated with scratchy handwritten sentences, that he presented to me, the desire within me grew. I think he could tell because once the sexy sketchbook presentation was complete, he seamlessly produced his camera from his shorts, momentarily, cleverly, making me aware of his dexterity and hand size. He then proceeded to show me what felt like 1,000 photographs he'd taken of sand in the Atacama Desert in Chile.

'Why have you taken so many?' I asked.

'I like the way the light at different times of day makes the sand look alive...' Blah blah blah, whatever. To me, someone who knows nothing about photography, it was nonsense. But it was sexy nonsense.

As he flicked through the photos, I forced myself to stop assessing his finger strength, and had a word with myself. This unbelievably attractive distraction was just what I didn't need, but exactly what I wanted all at the same time. A man so handsome, mysterious, tall and creative that he just had to be the Man Of My Dreams, surely?

It had taken a completely pathetic grand total of 40 minutes for me to revert from not wanting to be distracted by *any* man, to succumbing to the ingrained female programming that makes me question whether every hunk I encounter is destined to become my prince. Rather than implementing my new objective – to get to know him, to keep my head and to take my time establishing whether we actually had things in common – I'd automatically, and unconsciously, started daydreaming about our future together. Him painting in a sunny studio overlooking the Atlantic ocean in some ever-sunny corner of Portugal, me writing acclaimed novel after acclaimed novel in my neighbouring studio (because we understand the importance of space to our respective creative processes), stopping every now and then to ravish each other and hand-feed each other sardines. I'd ride a bike everywhere and always be barefoot. He'd paint only my naked form and make millions from it... and so on, and so on. Rational thought was in danger of ceasing altogether. I needed to pull myself together, concentrate on what he was saying rather than his kissable lips and stop pondering whether our babies would inherit his brown eyes or my green ones.

I didn't want to give in to this compulsion that had me constantly looking for someone to ride into the sunset with. When I'm not sitting opposite someone who could kill a weak-hearted person with just one wink, I suspect that sunset is utter bollocks. However, natural inclinations and years of conditioning unfortunately take their toll, which means there's a tiny irritating part of me who still believes that all will be glitter and rainbows the minute some dashing prince with a talking horse and a fat sidekick roll into town. I needed to fight these blasted natural instincts. The troublemakers.

This was my chance to prove to myself that I could remain emotionally removed from this encounter. That I could be attracted to a man, and his talents, without hoping for anything more. It was a chance to dip my toe back into the world of fraternising with men that weren't just physically attractive, but that had something to say that I was mildly interested in, without expectations. I made a decision. I wanted to remain my priority *but* I fancied him, and definitely wanted to see him clothes-free. Therefore, I would concentrate solely on the seduction. I didn't have time for anything else.

I may have made my mind up, but it appeared Daniel wanted to make it as tricky for me as possible. He seemed keen to actually get to know me.

'So, Amy, tell me about what you write?' Daniel had been downstairs to get us two more beers. The sun was starting to go down on the roof terrace, and many of our fellow backpackers had trickled off for dinner. The Aussie had disappeared too. It was only when Daniel went in search of refreshments that I even noticed. Who knows when he left... most likely at some point during the sand presentation.

'Observational humour, mostly,' I shrugged.

'Humour. Interesting. I should have known. Where do you think that humour comes from?'

'What do you mean?'

'Well, do you think you're naturally funny? Does it flow easily? Or do you use humour rather than honesty because you're scared of being serious?'

Well that went from sexy to heavy in the space of ten seconds.

This was the first thing that threw me about Daniel – well, apart from the fact that he looked like a brown-eyed Danny Zuko. Right away it was clear that he was the complete opposite of me when it came to discussing his creative side. Daniel's pride in his work was plain to see. There wasn't even a flicker of the self-doubt that plagued me every time anyone spoke to me about writing.

I'll admit, Daniel intimidated me a little. Not because he looked like he had fingers made for playing the shit out of a sitar, but because he was so sure of himself, and the thing he was passionate about. His art. He appeared to fully understand what made him want to create, and from the minute he heard I was a writer, he wanted to talk to me about my reasons for doing the same.

'When did you first start writing?'

'Ermm… I guess I've always written. It helps me to make sense of things in my head, but I've only started taking it seriously in the last couple of years.'

'I can't remember a time when I wasn't making art.'

'Oh yeah?'

'Maybe it's because I started so young that I can't remember my life before it. Do you ever write anything more serious?'

'Only for work. Everything I write for myself is pretty jokey.'

'How about poetry?'

'Only in friends' birthday cards!'

This would all be a lot simpler if he could just accept I was a writer, find it both charming and arousing in equal measure, and then get back to talking about something less personal. But nope. He wanted to chat about the thing that made me the most socially awkward. Daniel didn't want to talk about literature, or travel, or the plight of Macaulay Culkin – all things I could have spoken about with eloquence, and a quick wit. Instead he wanted to discuss what inspired us to be creative. The truth was I'd never thought to consider the answers to these questions, and my ignorance made me feel really bloody awkward.

'When was the first time you felt compelled to pick up a pen?'

'Do you write differently depending on different moods?'

'What form do you hope your magnum opus might take?'

These were all excellent questions, which I knew I should answer at some stage, but for some reason, I found the attention unbearable. Maybe it was because I was still mulling over my ex-boss John's comments about wanting to be a writer being like wanting to be a rock star, and wondering whether I was kidding myself. Maybe it was because I'd been 'trying to be a writer' for four years and I still hadn't really got anywhere. But around this time, whenever I told someone I was a writer, I would regret revealing it a second later. Inevitably my answer would spark questions like, 'oh, who do you write for?' or, 'where can I read it?' by which stage I'd have shrunk to half my size under their scrutiny. I was terrified I'd be revealed. That someone listening on the sidelines would spring from their chair, point at me dramatically and announce, 'Amy Baker, you're no writer!' I wanted people to think I was a writer, but I didn't yet believe it myself.

To regain control of this situation, I needed to start deferring the attention away from me, and back to him at every opportunity – it would be easier that way.

At this point Daniel suggested getting dinner. I nodded acceptance, coolly said I'd meet him downstairs in ten, and then sprinted to the bathroom to make sure I didn't have anything in my hair.

We decided to walk the short distance to the restaurant. Sucre's climate is milder than elsewhere in Bolivia, giving every day a spring-like feel, and as the sun hadn't yet set we didn't have to wrap up too warm. The city itself is a beautiful spot full of brilliantly white buildings decorated with terracotta roofs, and it was lovely to wander past some of the most historically significant buildings with such a stone-cold fox beside me. I didn't know where to look. We took in Plaza 25 de Mayo and Casa de Libertad where the declaration was signed, and then headed to Florin cafe – a popular spot with backpackers, for Mexican food and cheap mojitos.

So, after a month on the road and far too few encounters with eligible bachelors, I'd finally met the kind of man I'd envisioned meeting when I went travelling. The 'deep' type. The type who has interests outside of sinking beers, punching his friends in the balls and watching team sports. If you'd sat me down at the beginning of my trip and asked me to draw my dream man, it would have been a very shoddily-drawn version of Daniel. Here he was, sitting before me, asking me questions and touching me intermittently, yet I was steadfastly trying to remain removed from the situation because I didn't want to get sucked in. The questions were coming thick and fast.

'Tell me about your favourite piece of work.' *I'm not sure I even have one.*

'How do you feel when you've finished something you're proud of?' *God – have I ever even written something I'm proud of? Oh yeah – there was that article a while back about the joy of International Cat Day.*

'How do you think you'd feel if you couldn't write ever again?' *Probably relieved at this point.*

Catching myself trying to come up with sufficiently fanciful-sounding responses to his questions, I realised once again that I needed to pull myself together and resume my seduction plan. I wasn't going to let a situation like this interfere with my personal journey, or knock my growing confidence. I'd encountered handsome men before and hadn't been rendered completely useless. Today would not be the day to let myself start. I was capable of stuff. I too had notebooks full of pointless scribbles. Just because this guy looked like a sexy pirate, and could detect subtle differences between grains of sand like some kind of utterly useless X-Man, it didn't mean I should forget who I was and the tactics I'd learnt over the years.

Fortunately Daniel, like most men, responded to flattery, and was easily distracted by questions about himself. There was a lot to talk about. He'd been travelling for a while, and for the last month or so had been living in the desert (hence the pictures) training in some kind of new-fangled yoga involving chairs (to this day I've still got no idea what that means). He'd been living with, and learning from, a spiritual healer who'd hinted that Daniel might be destined to pursue a similar path. It was admirable, all this learning about oneself. Quite humbling really, considering that in the last place I'd stayed the overriding nationality was British, and the only thing I'd learnt was that imported, overpriced Strongbow tasted just the same as in the UK. I'd liked the rainforest despite it being hard, but this guy had really stepped it up a notch. Where does one even go to find a healer to train under? Did this mean that I was doing this wrong? Maybe I should be trying harder to have more unusual experiences?

I was annoyed that I was allowing myself to be drawn in. I thought I was more headstrong. Yes, he was undeniably gorgeous, but if I closed my eyes for a second and just listened, I already knew he was far from my ideal man. He was way too serious for me – he'd never have been happy watching YouTube videos of Japanese cats with me on a daily basis had it progressed any further. I needed to see this opportunity for what it was – a chance to get naked with a dude whose middle name might very well be 'swashbuckling'.

While he crinkled his brow as he spoke in a thoughtful and completely adorable way, I was having a battle in my head. It was as though there were three of me sitting around that table, sipping on cocktails, all contemplating what my next move should be. I'd been rendered completely incapable of not overthinking this situation – and my fellow Amys were doing very little to help me relax.

There was Romantic Amy: clutching her hands to her cheeks, face flushed and completely rapturous at the idea that this beautiful Portuguese artist could be The One. She wanted to impress him with answers to his questions that she didn't even know she had inside her. She wanted to be his muse. She was deluded.

Then there was Sensible Amy: she was the one telling me that Daniel was far too serious, that his looks weren't the be-all and end-all and that sometimes what you think you want and what you actually want are completely different. I loved the idea of him being a deep artist – but I'm not deep. I'm as far from a serious person as it's possible to be. Sensible Amy was telling me that pursuing him romantically was pointless and that I should instead try to gain some knowledge of myself from this meeting. She recognised that Daniel was an interesting person who might ask me questions that I could benefit from answering. Therefore she wanted me to throw water on the fire in my loins and actively engage with what he had to say.

Then of course there was Randy Amy: the loudest (and drunkest) of the bunch, who was standing on the table, hands on her hips, gyrating in Daniel's direction, encouraging me to say whatever I needed to say to improve my chances of sealing the deal. Whispering breathlessly in my ear to imagine the satisfaction I'd feel the next day when I could high five myself about successfully copping a feel of this Portuguese work of art.

'He's not right for you,' she giggled. 'Just do what you've gotta do to get it done, pat yourself on the back and email your mates at work a picture of him first thing in the morning! They NEED to see this.'

Randy Amy was pulling into the lead.

▲▲▲▲▲▲▲

After dinner was done, Daniel suggested we return to the hostel so he could read my 'Life Numbers'. Although by now I hoped this was a euphemism for the lines of my thighs, I suspected he meant what he said. I mean, why couldn't reading my future be the next in the long list of skills he'd been acquiring along the way? In-between his macro-photography and perfecting the art of downward dogging off an office chair of course. I mean, he already had the cloak...

Speaking of which, back on the hostel roof he poured me some stale red wine, set fire to a tiny fragrant branch, and wrapped himself in his airline-issued shroud. Things were getting interesting.

For those of you who aren't familiar with the ancient art of numerology or who have dismissed it as utter twaddle, allow me to explain the limited amount that I now know. You have a Life Number and a Destiny Number, and you calculate these using your date of birth. Once you've worked out these numbers, you can read all about the path your life is likely to take. Mr and Mrs Numerology (*definitely* their correct names) have somehow worked out all the character traits you will possess just because you have a particular Life or Destiny Number. Prior to my trip I'd been sitting firmly in the utter twaddle camp. Funny that as soon as I was being told that I'm 'fiery', 'unpredictable' and 'sexy' by some American Airlines-sponsored hunk, I started believing in it wholeheartedly.

As I fidgeted in my seat trying to assume the right position to render myself irresistible, some home truths were laid down for Amy Baker. If I hadn't been so mesmerised by his face and preoccupied with determining the correct amount of subtle hair flicks through a method of erratic trial and error, perhaps I'd have actually listened. Instead, I half-listened, made a mental note to google it all later and returned to imagining us being naked together right there on that roof terrace with only his tiny blanket to hide our modesty.

Here's how the 'reading' went down in my noisy head…

WHAT DANIEL WAS SAYING: 'Amy, if you desire something and you're willing to work for it, you'll achieve enormous success.'

WHAT I WAS THINKING: *I wonder what that means in terms of my future. Maybe I need to work harder, to try harder, to put myself out there more, to just keep going?*

WHAT I WAS FEELING: *I know what I desire… that face, those lips, those sexy teeth.*

WHAT DANIEL WAS SAYING: 'You have a tendency to get caught up in the daily routine, and this means you miss opportunities that come along. You must find a way of relaxing your mind, otherwise good ideas will live and die in your head.'

WHAT I WAS THINKING: *I really must look in to meditation. Maybe that's something worthwhile I can pursue here. Maybe Daniel knows somewhere good. I should ask him for his contact.*

WHAT I WAS FEELING: *Wanna hear my good idea? How about I climb inside that blanket and rub myself against you for a bit? Okay don't worry, forget about it.*

WHAT DANIEL WAS SAYING: 'You are multi-talented.'
WHAT I WAS THINKING: *Yes I am. Now if only I could apply myself and hone that talent, I might be onto something.*
WHAT I WAS FEELING: *You bet I am, soldier* (hair flick).

WHAT DANIEL WAS SAYING: 'You have many interests. You're independent, free-thinking, fast-moving and attractive.'
WHAT I WAS THINKING: *I am all those things and more, and they are things to be proud of.*
WHAT I WAS FEELING: *He just called me pretty!*

WHAT DANIEL WAS SAYING: 'You're talented but scared to put yourself out there. You shouldn't be scared; your efforts will be received well.'
WHAT I WAS THINKING: *But putting myself out there terrifies me. What if people don't like it? What if I put myself out there, and then realise that I don't have the talent I thought I had?*
WHAT I WAS FEELING: *I'll receive YOUR efforts well.*

WHAT DANIEL WAS SAYING: 'You resent restrictions, and responsibilities. Some would say you're reckless.'
WHAT I WAS THINKING: *And that right there is why I've never achieved anything. I need to grow up.*
WHAT I WAS FEELING: *By 'reckless' you mean sexy, yeah?*

WHAT DANIEL WAS SAYING: 'You turn and run every time the going gets tough. Some of your most valuable life lessons could be learnt from sticking around, and learning from those situations.'

WHAT I WAS THINKING: *He's right. I never see anything through. I get things 80 per cent done then completely change my mind. I'm flaky.*

WHAT I WAS FEELING: *Wanna get out of here, baby?*

WHAT DANIEL WAS SAYING: 'Patience is something you need to work on. You often act and speak with haste and impatience.'

WHAT I WAS THINKING: *Right again. This numerology stuff is interesting.*

WHAT I WAS FEELING: *For the love of god, man, kiss me, kiss me. KISS ME!*

And then, thankfully, he did.

▲▲▲▲▲▲▲

I woke up in the morning with a smile on my face, and sent that essential email to my workmates. The sense of satisfaction only stuck around for a couple of minutes. I immediately regretted deciding to remain removed from the encounter. When faced with my first chance to engage with someone on a deeper level for the first time in a couple of years, I'd shirked it in favour of instant gratification. I knew Daniel wasn't right for me – but he could have been a self-aware stepping-stone towards me rediscovering how to interact with guys that challenged me a little.

I'd really ballsed this encounter up in terms of managing my own feelings and emotions. I'd allowed myself to be bowled over by his looks, for one – which just aren't the be-all and end-all.

Then, I'd been closed off and unemotional, thinking that that would be the safest way to proceed – and that was false. This wasn't how I wanted future interactions with men to go. Sure, it was important to see it for what it was, but it didn't mean I should make a decision at the very start of the interaction and then erect protective barriers instantly. That hadn't got me anywhere so far, and it only left me thinking about Daniel for longer than I should have done – and that was exactly what I hadn't wanted.

It took a week or so for me to finally laugh at how abysmally I'd handled my first romantic liaison. I was back in La Paz for Christmas, wandering through a hidden courtyard of my hostel when I smelt a familiar smell – the odour of the same branch Daniel had been burning when he read my Life Numbers. I looked into the shadows, and there he was again, wrapped in the same blanket… reading to another enraptured chick from his numerology book. It was then that I realised why I was so pissed off with myself for how I'd acted – because I'd let myself feel grateful to be in his presence. After all, just because he looked like an airbrushed photograph, didn't mean he wasn't on the same journey we all are. The confusing journey towards working out how best to connect with people.

WINNER = *THE EXPERT*

'Do your thing and don't care if they like it.'
Tina Fey

Although Carol from reception presents a very valid point about an unclean penis, a love of yoga and wooden jewellery cannot be assumed a 100-per-cent-accurate indicator of poor personal hygiene. I will remain wary though, as Carol clearly experienced something traumatic and I don't want her to have suffered for nothing. I suggest you remain vigilant also.

Tina Fey's advice wins here. I elected to care that he liked me, and chose to be intimidated by his appearance and his belief in his creative talents. He asked me questions wanting to find out more – it was me who felt he wouldn't be interested in what I had to say. Rather than give him the straight answers he'd afforded me and believe what I had to say was of interest, I garbled vague responses I hoped would sound interesting, and then asked him to show me his photos again. I made jokes about having no talent, and then asked him about his influences. I didn't proudly do my thing. Instead, I established a dynamic between us in which his things were more important. I should have been way more confident about who I was, and what I had to say.

LESSONS LEARNT

I wanted to grow up and develop a better attitude towards members of the opposite sex. Yep, I'd blown the first chance to learn from a romantic encounter or to at least trial some different behaviour – but that didn't mean I'd lost my chance to do it moving forwards. I wanted to learn to be open, honest and unapologetic about my feelings. This was the first time on my trip when I recognised the opportunity ahead of me for personal growth. It made me understand that if I wanted to grow, I needed to be open to encounters that made me question my motives for doing the things I do, and behaving the way I behave. I'd been so quick to blame poor or unwanted advice for why things hadn't worked out for me thus far – and I'd already learnt that that was because I'd followed advice blindly, or not taken it subjectively, as I should have done. Until now, I'd been too stubborn to look at my own behavioural patterns and bad habits. I was searching for a sense of satisfaction, and I'd taken an important step by coming away to look for it – now I needed to continue to use every opportunity that cropped up as a chance to learn and grow. After all, that's why I had come. South America was the perfect place to start addressing patterns that weren't working out for me. I couldn't continue to behave as I always had done if I wanted to see change. I needed to try different things, and different approaches, and see where they took me.

This encounter was a turning point. It showed me the importance of being present in interactions, and being confident in what I had to say. I wouldn't learn anything if I was constantly changing myself to fit in with those I met, or by deflecting attention. It reminded me not to become preoccupied with how other people were behaving, or to concentrate so hard on what others are doing that I can't concentrate on myself.

Despite all the emotions and insecurities that meeting Daniel brought up, I'll remember him fondly. He unwittingly reminded me to be proud of where I am in life, wherever that may be. He believed those photos and scribbles were interesting so strongly that I believed it too. I needed to learn to believe the things I had to say were equally as interesting. Daniel reminded me of the importance of being present in the moment. Rather than being preoccupied with racing towards the climax of our dalliance, or a future imagined by other people that you think, but don't know, will bring you happiness, I should really be enjoying what's happening right now. Daniel was pleasing to the eye, it was most enjoyable being naked with him *and* he was the first person to introduce me to quinoa. Now, if that wasn't a moment to relish every second of, I don't know what is.

THE WORST THREE DAYS OF MY LIFE

FRIENDLY ADVICE:
'You should definitely climb Huayna Potosí, mate. It's the best thing I did in all of South America.'

Laura Kinzett, great friend

EXPERT ADVICE:
'Mountains are not fair or unfair, they are just dangerous.'

Reinhold Messner
(Climbed every mountain in the world, excellent head of hair.)

I wanted to lie down and die. To throw my hands to the heavens, stumble to my shaky, bruised knees, and lie there, face down, sobbing and hoping that now I had surrendered, the end would come quickly.

But I'm getting ahead of myself...

T-MINUS TWO DAYS UNTIL CLIMB

It was Boxing Day in La Paz, and while nursing considerable hangovers, Ruth, Henry and I were in the process of debating our penultimate move as a threesome. We knew two things for sure: that we were going to celebrate New Year here in La Paz, and that as soon as we had done that we were Chile-bound on the very next bus, to a beach that we thought would be a lovely place to spend our last few days together. From there we would be saying goodbye – Ruth and Henry would be heading south to the wilds of Patagonia and then on to New Zealand, and I'd be heading north, in search of heat on the beaches of Peru, Ecuador and Colombia. Our three weeks had been fun-filled, and it had shown me the types of challenges I should go in search of. It had also provided me with more training I needed to head off alone, so now I was raring to go. I was ready for the solo adventures ahead of me, and to carve my own path. So far, South America was everything I'd hoped it would be, and I was excited to see what would happen when I was completely in charge.

In the meantime, we had five days to kill, and the idea of spending one more day or night in the dingy bar of our Irish-run hostel was doing little for our cabin fever.

'You know,' I said, in-between scoffing mouthfuls of baked beans, 'we could climb that mountain that Kinzett suggested. She said it was the highlight of her whole trip.'

Henry and Ruth, also eating baked beans, paused to consider this option.

'You mean Huayna Potosí? I've heard it's seriously hard, mate… do you reckon we'd actually be able do it?' Ruth said, glancing in my direction as she scooped another mouthful.

I shrugged, 'Sure we can. If Kinzett did it, we can absolutely do it. Plus we've been in La Paz for ages, we're used to the altitude and I've heard that's half the battle.'

It'd been a couple of weeks now since I'd boo-hooed my way around the Amazon rainforest. This meant that the only memories left (aside from those of Arturo's forearms) were the ones where I remembered how great I'd felt afterwards and how incredible the wildlife was. I'd blanked out the utter terror I'd felt coming face to face with a humongous spider and a snake almost the same length as a London bus. It had conveniently slipped my mind how uncomfortable I'd been for 24 hours a day for three days. I'd blanked out how hard it was on my body and mind, and how it had tired me out so much so that when I finally fell asleep, I slept for 18 hours straight without peeing (turns out I was pretty dehydrated). All I was left with now was the wonderful sense of satisfaction I felt that I'd taken on a challenge and survived. I was hungry for more. Who cared what climbing a mountain involved – if Kinzett could do it, we could do it, end of story.

All jacked up on imported English breakfast foods, it was agreed. We rushed out and booked our spots immediately. Our climb up Huayna Potosí would begin on December 28.

T-MINUS ONE DAY UNTIL CLIMB

Having booked the climb so last minute, there was little we could do in terms of training. Instead we were advised to rest, hydrate and eat. Had I known those moments spent with a belly full of guilt-free pasta would be the most enjoyable part of climbing that mountain, I certainly wouldn't have scrimped on the cheese-covered garlic bread. Another life lesson right there: NEVER scrimp on the cheese-covered garlic bread!

DAY ONE

Oh, day one! How I long for the innocence of day one. Back before I really knew what pain was. Before the smoke-blackened penny had dropped and I understood the monumental mistake I'd made basing my plans solely on the opinion of Kinzett – a woman I'd conveniently forgotten 'enjoys' running marathons. That's right, she's one of those.

Around the time our dorm mates were collapsing into their beds in a fug of fruity vodka, we were sleepily piling into a minibus driven by the man who was to be our trusted guide for the next few days: Herman, a short but muscular local man with big brown eyes and a kind smile. Our first stop was to collect our kit from the storeroom of the tour company – a room chock-a-block with coat racks, ropes, boots and an array of tools I had no idea of the purpose of. The seriousness of what we were about to undertake hadn't yet hit home. Even as Herman dished out the ice axes and crampons, I thought little more than, 'Cool, daggers for shoes!' before flinging them in my kit bag, and hurrying back to the bus for a little more shut-eye.

It was an hour's drive from La Paz to base camp, but as we neared our destination, Herman woke us up to point out our chosen mountain. At 6,088 m, it is the sixth-highest peak in Bolivia's Cordillera Real mountain range. I opened one eye to show that I was invested in the experience. The fact that we couldn't see the peak, because it was *higher than the clouds*, failed to register as worrisome in my delusional brain. Much as I had on the day Robbie announced he was leaving Take That, I chose to go back to sleep and to pretend my world wasn't about to end.

Our first port of call was base camp: a drafty wooden hut full of lumpy bunk beds on the banks of a reservoir. The corridors of the hut were decorated with wonky framed photographs of climbers perched on mountain peaks with big smiles on their ice-burnt faces, and of groups of jubilant people, drinking beers, arms around each other, ergonomically designed walking poles held aloft in victory. Despite the icy breeze whistling through the gaps in the hut's wooden slats, the main communal area was lovely and toasty due to its large open fire. I could have hung out there quite happily for the duration of the day, warming my tootsies and tucking in to my emergency chocolate-covered cracker stash but, inconveniently, we had to go and practise 'mountain climbing' on a nearby glacier.

As Ruth and Henry had spent years talking about glaciers in their classrooms, they were excited to see it. I, on the other hand, wasn't entirely sure what a glacier was.

'It's a slow-moving mass of ice that's formed when snow remains in one place long enough to turn into solid ice,' Ruth informed me.

Ice? Oh! I hadn't expected that.

The afternoon that followed consisted of an extensive lesson in how to interact with said ice. We practised walking on the glacier with crampons, we learnt the many uses of an ice axe, and the importance of a helmet, and we repeatedly rehearsed sliding down increasingly steep icy slopes, to train in how to stop mid-slide by jamming our axes into the snow. Now, I can't be 100 per cent sure but, looking back, I perhaps should have spotted that our guides were preparing us for the possibility of encountering a lot of ice.

After we'd satisfied Herman that we were adept in what he hilariously kept referring to as the art of 'saving our lives', it was time for our next challenge: scaling a 15-m ice wall.

I sauntered over to Herman and nudged him playfully. 'Mate, we're not actually going to have to do this, are we?'

He stared at me for a moment, considered the question, and then gave a confused head movement, which I chose to interpret as 'no'. Good. That was settled. This was merely a fun first-day activity, and not something we needed to be prepared for – what a relief!

Nonetheless, I made sure to seat myself behind a rock, hoping that when my time came round, he might forget I was there.

I had little interest in the ice wall. This seemed a pointless exercise, seeing as we weren't actually going to have to do it, as Herman had just said. I watched male travellers with significant shoulder widths grunt and groan their way to the top. If they were struggling, I had zero chance of making it. I felt a bit sick, and my arms had all the strength of two freshly baked baguettes.

Despite my steely determination to stay out of Herman's line of sight and remain still long enough for the falling snow to disguise me as a sensibly dressed snowwoman, soon enough, my turn rolled around. Herman peered around the rock, grinned and beckoned me over. He hooked me up to the safety ropes, handed me two ice picks and gave me the nod. I launched myself at that ice wall like my life depended on it... for the first three or four swings of the axe. Then I was completely pooped. Despite giving it my best, and emitting a series of guttural sounds that I'd rather forget making, I only managed to claw my way up eight metres before fire ripped through my entire body and I had to lie down to recuperate on a conveniently placed ice ledge. Eight metres wasn't too bad, I thought to myself. I was quite proud of eight metres.

Once the day's activities were complete, we returned to base camp to refuel and get an early night. At least, that was the plan. Our guides piled our table high with bowls of soup, rice and potatoes, and platters of meat. There was fruit, bread, biscuits and cake, but all we could do was stare at it and wonder where on earth our appetites had buggered off to. Altitude had done me dirty. My ever-hungry stomach had shrunk to the measly size of a satsuma. I felt so queasy I could barely force a biscuit.

Noticing nobody was eating, Herman urged us to drink coca tea to relieve the nausea. Coca tea is a stimulating drink, popular in

South America, made with the leaves of the same plant as cocaine. This was the first piece of his advice that I decided to listen to. I downed mug after mug in an attempt to overhydrate the sickness and murder it. It worked for a brief period, but when the time came to go to bed, for the essential rest required by those about to scale a mountain, I was too het up to sleep. Instead I lay staring at the bunk above me, worrying obsessively about why I couldn't sleep, or come to think of it, breathe. It was as I lay there, eyes as big as DVDs, that the realisation finally dawned on me that the task ahead might be testing. If I couldn't breathe and felt sick lying down, how would I feel when I added walking to that equation? What on earth had I let myself in for?

DAY TWO

A surge of vomit keen to acquaint itself with my pillow woke me with a start, and had me sprinting to the bathroom. I'd advise against running at altitude where possible. No matter how hard you fight to regain your breath you'll still feel as though you're breathing through a duvet. Once I'd thrown up, coerced some vital oxygen back into my lungs and brushed my teeth, I dragged myself to join the others at the breakfast table. Unable to utter the words 'good morning', I managed a weak exhalation, which I hoped sufficed as my acknowledging their presence. Overnight, all conversational skills I'd once possessed had been obliterated, along with my appetite. I poured myself a coffee, piled in four sugars and used my remaining strength to drag the mug towards me.

Two cups in, our group remembered we'd packed altitude sickness tablets for this exact situation. Being the sensible, responsible humans they are, Ruth and Henry had read the information pack we'd been given when we signed up and had persuaded me that the 26-boliviano (£3) cost of the tablets was money well spent. Thank goodness I was well-versed in making all my key life decisions based on the actions of others! Apathy did have its perks. I scrabbled through my bag, discovered the desired booty and popped two tablets into my clammy and weak hand, and then offered the packet to Ruth and Henry.

'Wait, wait,' Herman barked from behind the kitchen counter. 'Before you take them, how bad do you *actually* feel?'

I lethargically turned my bloodshot eyes towards him and arched an eyebrow, in the hope it would convey that if he didn't hush his pretty little mouth and let me take my meds there was a real risk I'd have to spit pre-sick into my breakfast soup.

'I've certainly felt better Herman,' I eventually managed, patting my chest, and suppressing a little bile-induced burp.

'You've tried coca tea?'

'Considerable amounts, yes.'

You've got about five seconds to get to the point, buddy.

'Well,' he said, starting to walk out of the room, 'I think try another cup. Those tablets can make your eyeballs deflate.'

Pardon? My beloved eyeballs could what now? Since when had eyeball deflation been a medical side effect of anything? Was there some conspiracy in place to keep this atrocity a secret from the world? It felt like it. More pressingly, what were the odds of them 'flating' back up again? Did they even have that capacity?

Everyone around the table who had been discussing possibly taking the tablets fell silent. After 20 seconds or so spent picturing my eyeballs slipping from their cosy socket-homes to hang down my face like two bunches of rotting grapes, Henry shrugged (standard) and popped his tablets: even the possibility of eyeball deflation didn't faze him. His nonchalance inspired the rest of us, and we followed suit.

With the tablets sticking in my throat, I took a moment to appeal silently to the mountain gods: 'For the love of all that is holy, please don't let today be the day my eyeballs deflate. Please don't let me become *that* statistic.'

▲▲▲▲▲▲▲▲

Day two's game plan involved our group, which consisted of me, Ruth, Henry, a German dude, Herman and another Bolivian mountain guide, packing up all our kit, loading ourselves up like donkeys and setting out for the high camp at 5,200 m. To someone still wallowing in a muddy cesspit of denial, it sounded like a simple enough hike. We were already super high up. Realistically how much higher could we possibly have to go? The answer, of course, was much, much higher. Over the course of the following six hours, I battled with a fair few emotions…

The first to show up and slap me in the face was confusion. Where had all the oxygen gone? The initial part of the trail involved a staircase of huge concrete blocks that had been laid to help climbers quickly ascend to where the trail *actually* started. I'd thought base camp was bad, but oxygen levels were taking a marked dip every 50 or so steps. This proved problematic given that each of these steps was half a metre high, and we were laden with backpacks full of metal kit. The difficulty this early on quickly fouled my mood.

When every step you take leaves you gasping for air, you quickly tire of climbing higher and higher, especially when you know the situation is only going to get worse. As we walked, I found myself fantasising more and more intently about inhaling delicious oxygen once more. I longed to feel her life-giving capabilities flow through every inch of my body. I yearned for her to come forth and soothe my dry throat with her moisture. She failed to heed my call, of course. She was too busy hanging out at sea level, lounging around in the sun with a pina colada.

Fear was the next emotion to rear its unwelcome head. As the hours went by, the terrain became increasingly dangerous. Our path transformed from the concrete steps to slippery moss-covered boulders, to loose shingles, to icy rocks with a tendency to shift position dramatically as you trod on them. The outcome of every footstep was a surprise. The minute you adjusted to your new terrain it changed, and you'd find yourself skidding towards sheer rock faces, leaving clouds of dust and pebbles in your wake. At one stage the path hugging the mountain was so narrow I could see no sensible way to proceed other than to plop myself down and bum-shuffle towards my ever-patient group, like a giant baby, with exactly the same capacity for unexplained crying. I needed to keep my centre of gravity low. The rocks below seemed perfectly placed for impaling foolish tourists with poor balance. I wasn't going out like that. I'd sooner have my eyeballs deflate.

Confusion and fear were compounded by frequent bouts of panic. The panic when I remembered there were such things as mountain lions. The panic when I realised we were way too high for helicopters to come to our rescue. The panic when I was reminded that coffee and exercise equal bowel activity and we were miles from anything resembling a toilet. Herman was very reluctant to allow me to lag behind without an explanation that I was in no rush to give. Instead I chose to loiter behind the group every time they stormed ahead, hoping they'd catch on and give me a little peace to perform my ablutions. Alas, every time I thought I'd found a quiet corner, Herman's concerned face would peep around the corner and catch me pre-squat. I eventually gave up on the idea.

In any downtime, shame would show up to afford me a much-needed confidence boost. I'm not too fond of being rubbish at stuff and there was no escaping the fact that I was the weakest link in this chain of happy hikers. I was tripping, dawdling behind and gasping for air like I was breathing through a damp Christmas jumper. Herman barely took his eyes off me, and I didn't deal with the scrutiny well. I felt patronised, but rather than humbly accepting I was the least physically fit and resolving to show everyone I was trying my best, I decided to heighten tensions by adopting the role of 'sulky teenager in midst of monumental argument'. I huffed and puffed every step of the way, and I moaned to my teammates that I was 'bored of walking', as though I'd genuinely believed we'd be riding state-of-the-art mountain segways the whole way. I insisted on breathing breaks every 100 steps, and only perked up briefly when bribed with chocolate. I had successfully regressed to my 13-year-old self.

Just when I thought my shaky legs wouldn't carry me another step, the thick clouds cleared and there before us was high camp – a two-bedroom orange hut nestled within a circle of enormous grey boulders on the mountainside. We'd survived day two. The relief that we didn't have to walk any more, and that there was a toilet, made me momentarily as happy as a child holding a kitten. Momentarily.

I rushed inside that tin hut, flung my bag to the floor, donned all my warmest clothing and sat in the corner until the time came to feast upon a dinner of instant noodles and tinned frankfurters. I sighed. I'd paid for this opportunity. I'd parted with a considerable number of earth pounds to be put through an experience that was offensively exhausting, *and* I was now all too aware that the hardest bit was yet to come.

DAY THREE

At the strike of midnight, Herman started banging on a saucepan to signal it was time to wake up and get moving, which served to instantly remind me I was in a bad mood. We had to start walking at this hour to ensure we made it to the summit before the sun came up: it's colder at night, so the snow is frozen and easier to walk on, but the minute the sun comes up, the snow starts melting, which makes it an unstable certain-death luge, and in some instances, can cause avalanches. Strapped into our crampons (which provide you more purchase on the snow and ice) for the first time, we set off, leaving behind our cosy little hut, ropes connecting us at the waist, Herman at the front, the other guide bringing up the rear, head torches lighting the way.

It's important to look where you're going while on a mountain, and this task was made easier with the light from our head torches, and the fact that the ground was the whitest white you can imagine. The thickest snow you've ever seen. The kind that would send five-year-old you into a frenzy of delight based on the fact that you know there's zero chance you'll be making it to school if you can't even see the wheels of your mum's car. This wasn't a fun snow day though – no one around me was carrying a sledge; there would be no snowball fights. We had one task – move forwards.

The first three hours were spent walking up and down huge, sweeping, snowy valleys. Wading through knee-deep snow in iron shoes is tiring enough without having to tackle the equivalent of icy sand dunes. If you've ever tried to climb a sand dune you'll know what I mean. When establishing a firm footing is nigh impossible it doesn't matter how many times you pump your quads; you'll only progress slightly before you slide back the way you came. That's what climbing this mountain was like – for hours, and with no chance of getting a tan. We huffed and puffed our way up snow sand dune after snow sand dune, reaching each peak with hope in our hearts it'd be the last. Time and time again the sight of another deep valley of blindingly white snowy anguish dashed our hopes. Though they appeared manageable, these valleys, by some cruel frozen illusion, actually stretched for miles, and climbing out of each one was like scaling the side of an equilateral triangle. It was rubbish.

The constant uphill struggle had my smoker's lungs rattling in my heaving chest. My average step count before doubling over, gasping for air and asking Ruth for the 1,000th time why we were doing this, had decreased to 20. The fact that she didn't once scream in my face that this had been my stupid idea in the first place, proves beyond any shadow of a doubt she is a far better person than I. Perhaps containing her fury was keeping her warm.

I'll admit, I was verging on the hysterical and was resorting to aggressive hyperbolic statements with every onwards step.

AMY: 'This was your stupid idea in the first place.'
RUTH: 'Well… it actually was your suggestion, and we all agreed, but yep, sure. I'm awfully, terribly sorry.'

AMY: 'Everything hurts, even my teeth. Does your everything hurt?'
RUTH: 'I think that's the cold, do you want my jumper?'

AMY: 'We're going to die out here, I just know it.'
RUTH: 'Dude – you need to calm down.'

AMY: 'I hate life.'
RUTH: 'Here, eat this chocolate.'

We suddenly took a stop that I hadn't insisted on, and our two guides took a moment to converse. There was a lot of pointing at me, and then at Henry and the German.

Herman approached Ruth and I. 'The men will continue ahead to have the best chance of reaching the summit. I will stay with you.'

Bollocks! I was slowing them down so much that they'd decided the only option was to cut the dead weight – aka me. How humiliating.

As the lights of their torches slowly disappeared into the distance, I realised sadly that my weakness had deprived Ruth and Henry, love's young dream, of reaching the summit of a mountain together. I felt awful, and resolved to try my hardest to keep moving and stop repeating, 'Are we there yet?'

Spurred on by my newfound resolve, I tried to distract myself from the giant ice wave we were approaching by taking a moment to appreciate my surroundings. The stars above really did seem to be within touching distance, and there were bloody loads of them. My spirits lifted considerably as I gazed upwards at the beautiful sight. This enjoyment was short-lived however as the 'ahhh' that escaped my lips morphed into 'arrrgghhhhhh' as I felt the ice collapse beneath my feet.

My chest slammed into solid ground, and I realised I was lying half in and half out of a human-sized hole, two legs dangling in an abyss I could sense but didn't want to make direct eye contact with. *Was I about to die?*

Fortunately Herman and Ruth were there in a shot, hauling me out and to my feet. Ruth and I looked at the crevasse and back at each other in total shock. Sensing he was about to witness a display of over-the-top sentimentality from the two of us, Herman tugged at the ropes we were attached to, barking, 'Move, move. Sun mean avalanche!' They were just the words of encouragement I needed having just a second ago cheated death. *Thanks for the pep talk, Herman, you miserable brute.*

I decided I needed to channel this fresh anger towards Herman into energy to power myself forwards. Plotting elaborate acts of revenge against Kinzett was also proving helpful. Animosity was proving to be a strong driving force that day. How could Kinzett have knowingly recommended this to me, having known me for more than ten years? Didn't she know how much I liked sitting down? Was it that she actually disliked me with a passion and I just hadn't realised? My new technique of negative visualisation appeared to be increasing my stride length. I pictured Kinzett reclining smugly on a chaise longue of velvet pillows, nursing one of those glasses that holds a whole bottle of wine, schmoozing with fellow mountain climbers, and other physically-fit smart-arses. There she was, all comfy and jolly, laughing heartily at her cunning ruse, as I embarked on this god-awful death jaunt. She won't be laughing when I spike her gin and tonic with laxatives at her next important public event, will she now!

Although helpful, it was hard to stay jacked up on revenge plans when you're seriously worn out. Every time I spotted any sort of peak in the distance, I'd shout, 'Herman, please tell me that's it?' at which point he would laugh heartily, displaying the abundance of oxygen his lungs had somehow managed to source in this hostile environment, saying that no, we still had four hours to go. How could the number not be going down? Oh right, because I was *barely* moving.

Just when I didn't think it was possible to be any more miserable, we encountered our next obstacle: a 20-metre ice wall. I shook my head in disbelief – I'd been deceived! Herman looked at us, pointed at the wall and grinned. How could he smile at a time like this? He'd looked into my innocent green eyes back on day one, and told me (hadn't he?) there would be no ice walls, yet here we were standing at the foot of exactly that. Only this one was higher than the one I'd failed to climb back when my muscles weren't completely shot-to-shit by an uphill battle I was despising every living second of. I had no words to express my fury, so I clenched and unclenched my jaw at him a bit, and refused to make eye contact.

I'd hoped my steely demeanour and exaggerated nostril flaring would make Herman realise he was in the wrong. That he would apologise while wrapping me in a warm embrace, take my hand and guide me to the secret elevator all mountains must have to transport lazy billionaires to the summit. It was safe to say, however, that Herman didn't give a monkey's about my childish strop. As far as he was concerned, I'd paid to be here. His only job was to get me to the top, by any means necessary. Plus, he climbed this mountain twice weekly. This was his equivalent of a stroll in the park. He'd probably fallen into hundreds of crevasses just for a laugh, clawing his way to safety with finger strength alone. He doubtless spent his downtime finding new routes up each of the region's mountains, sporting only shorts, a T-shirt and the grin of a mad man. This ice wall was nothing to him. He could probably sprint it given enough of a run-up.

There was no way around it. We either had to take on this 20-m-high nightmare, or give up and turn back. I couldn't let Herman win – I could see his lack of confidence in me glistening in his eyes and I did not appreciate it. I am a strong woman and I will not be told I'm incapable of doing something by a man – that would go against everything that I stand for. I also couldn't let Ruth down. She was one of the most competitive people I knew, and if I stopped her summiting this mountain just because I was too much of a wuss to try to climb this wall, I wouldn't be able to forgive myself. It was about this time that I started wishing I'd actually listened when Herman was teaching us how to use the ice axe rather than messing around flinging handfuls of snow at Ruth's face and posing for photos with it, treating it as my new accessory, rather than the vital survival tool our guides were expressly demonstrating it to be. Well, well, well – didn't I just have egg on my freezing cold face.

'Are you okay?' Herman asked. His doubt in me might as well have been tattooed on his forehead, it was so obvious. It was probably a reasonable prediction given the fact that my eyes were brimming with tears, and I was muttering 'no, no, no' under my breath. Well, fuck him. I'd show him. I may have been acting like Justin Bieber's more precocious cousin, but I wasn't going to let him break me. He didn't believe in me? I'd just have to show him how wrong he was.

'Yeah, I'm fine! This looks GREAT.'

'See you at the top.'

Off Herman went, scrambling up that ice wall, stopping every now and then to grin back down at the two hopeful faces peering up at him, hoping with all our might that he wouldn't fall to his death, leaving us alone to perish on this terrifying mountain. He made it in less than five minutes. The smug bastard.

'Come on, Aimz. You've got this,' Ruth said.

I was to go next. I'd been in the middle of Herman and Ruth since the crevasse incident. This was clearly the spot designed for the person everyone was most worried about. I looked up at the frozen wall in front of me and took a deep breath. This was up there with the most frightening things I'd ever attempted. Yes, I'd flung myself off bungee jumps and from planes, but in those instances I'd been attached to hunky instructors called Baz or Spike. Here, the only thing I was attached to was an ice pick jammed into the ground at the top of the wall by a 5 ft 6 Bolivian man who apparently cared little for whether I lived or died.

I looked down at my solitary ice pick. When we'd climbed the 15-m wall back on day one – well, when I'd climbed 8 m of it – we'd had two ice picks at our disposal. Now we had just one. This worried me. Would it hold my weight? If I fell, I'd fall right on top of Ruth, who'd be coming up behind me. I didn't want to injure her. That was the last thing she deserved after putting up with me through this climb.

'Come on, Amy, it's not that high – you can do it.'

'If I die, tell my mum I love her and I'm sorry that I've never achieved anything in my life, okay.'

'Amy, don't be sil—'

'Just tell her, Ruth!'

'Sure. But you're not going to die. You can do this.'

I nodded solemnly. 'I love you. Thank you for being my friend. I've enjoyed every minute.'

Off I went. The technique was simple enough – kick foot daggers into wall as far as they go, swing ice axe into wall, haul yourself up as far as you could, and repeat. The only problem was that securing enough purchase on the wall with your foot daggers involved kicking quite hard into the ice, plus, you need considerable arm strength to haul yourself up anything. The combo was quite the full-body workout, and as I've mentioned, my arms might as well be made of plasticine.

'Come on, faster, faster,' the world's most sadistic Bolivian called from the top of the wall.

'Go fuck yourself, Herman,' I muttered under my breath.

'That's it, Baker! You're doing it. You're a warrior!'

I looked down at Ruth's smiling face and realised I'd travelled nearly ten metres – the hatred really was spurring me forwards. I quickly returned to looking only at the wall in front of me – ten metres is high.

I did show Herman. I showed him by hauling myself up that wall in the most dramatic fashion possible, howling the whole time that I was going to die. I showed him – for not giving me the freedom to be scared, tired or in need of a rest – by crying every single inch of the way, shouting that it was unfair we were being made to do this and telling him I hated him with every single painful swing of my ice axe.

Herman may have had to haul me up the last metre but I made it. It was an emotional 25 minutes.

'Yay, Ruth. You winner!' I managed, as she clambered over the top of the wall five minutes behind me like the champion she is.

We lethargically high fived and then lay there gasping for air.

Less than a minute later… 'We go now.' Herman was on his feet. 'Sun mean avalanche.' He pointed to the horizon, where the first signs of the sun were beginning to show. Off we went.

By this stage I was complaining very vocally with every step.

'This is the worst experience of my life.'

'I think I'll just stay here and let the mountain have its wicked way with me.'

'All mountain climbers are idiots.'

Ruth remained a supportive angel the whole way…

'I know it's hard, but think about the achievement, mate.'

'You don't want to die here, mate. You need to reach Colombia – the men there, just trust me.'

'Yeah, you're right – mountain climbers *are* idiots.'

I could also tell that Herman wasn't charmed by my inability to hide my emotions, but I wasn't in the mood to give a damn about what he thought of me. I had more pressing things with which to concern myself, like survival. With every goading tug on my waist-rope, the anger burned within me, spurring me forwards. I discovered there to be a particularly powerful type of resentment bred between a man who thinks an activity is tantamount to climbing into your attic, and a woman undertaking the hardest challenge of her life. Such resentment involves a lot of tutting, eye rolling and dramatic frowning – from both parties.

'You must move faster,' Herman called for the 986th time, tugging harder on the waist-rope.

Did he not understand that of course I'd like to travel faster, that I'd sprint the whole damn thing if it meant this torment could be over and I could return to normality with the aid of an enormous alcoholic beverage and an entire Victoria sponge cake. If it meant that I could brush the frost from my eyelashes and the snot from my nose and file this away under 'life experiences never to be repeated'. However, I couldn't move faster. My lungs were threatening to disintegrate and the little muscle I'd possessed before the start of this living nightmare had been atrophied away by overexertion and unfaltering negativity. Moving faster was impossible.

'Look!' Herman shouted, pointing in the direction of the mouth of a nearby ice cave, decorated with sparkling stalactites.

Herman, you shit. Why was he trying to stop me now? I'd just got into a rhythm fuelled by hate. Ordinarily, yes, I might have been intrigued by an ice cave, but couldn't he see that I was already utilising my neck muscles to look suitably downtrodden?

After five hours in icy purgatory, feeling as though I was making no progress and from which a murderous yeti attack would have been a welcome escape, the peak of Huayna Potosí finally appeared in the distance. We could just about make out Henry and his group at the top – the first of the day to reach the summit. The end was in sight. I had maybe 15 more minutes of toiling before I could turn to Herman and laugh in his stupid face for doubting Amy Baker's ability.

However, the final ten metres of the climb were the most terrifying by far. The summit can only be reached by conquering a steep path, over the side of which lay two sheer drops of a couple of hundred metres onto sharp rocks and boulders below. There was no way you'd survive the fall. Anyone who lost their footing at this stage would shatter into a hundred pieces. Losing your footing was a real possibility, the final path was so frighteningly narrow it needed to be tackled in single file, and when you factor in whistling winds, weary legs and the distraction at being so close to your goal, it is treacherous to say the least. Though those final ten metres were shaky and expletive-ridden, we made it to the top. *Take that, Herman, you sadistic bastard!*

Upon reaching the summit, Ruth and I hugged in celebration, standing together on top of the world. As she whipped out her Wales flag for photo ops, I thanked her over and over for spurring me on with her encouragement. That's when the tears really started. Not tears of joy at achieving such an incredible feat with one of my very best friends, nor at the incredible scene slowly revealing itself as the early morning rays illuminated the mountain range we'd just defeated. These were the bitter tears of realisation. We were at the top of a mountain – we still had to get all the way back down.

'Quick, quick,' Herman shouted. 'Sun mean avalanche. We go now.'

Goddammit Herman.

WINNER = *THE EXPERT*

'Mountains are not fair or unfair, they are just dangerous.'
Reinhold Messner

Although yeah, climbing a mountain was an achievement, and yeah, now I suppose I can wow whatever future offspring I might bear with the fact that their overweight, agoraphobic mother once scaled a mountain with an ice pick, it's safe to say Reinhold, the mountain master, secures the victory with his sound, fact-based advice.

While it might have been the biggest thing that I've achieved, it was definitely not the most enjoyable. I suffered every single step of the way. That mountain was dangerous. I should have considered my physical fitness and what the activity actually involved before I decided to tackle something clearly way, WAY beyond my ability.

LESSONS LEARNT

Some may say that anyone who attempts to climb a mountain with this kind of defeatist attitude is bound to fail... and they'd be right. My attitude stank like week-old chicken. I had no business being on that mountain. I didn't respect it. I hadn't fully comprehended how difficult it would be, or what we'd have to battle against. Had I realised, I wouldn't have been there. I would have been elsewhere, doing something fun, like eating a cheeseburger, or researching puppy hybrids. However, because a trusted friend had told me it was 'brill', and 'not to be missed', there I was, decked out in the ugliest kit imaginable, still damp with the sweat of past lunatics who'd also stupidly concluded climbing a mountain higher than Kilimanjaro constituted 'good holiday fun'.

It's safe to say I won't be partaking in any physically focused activity again without reading into it extensively beforehand. I mean, I did look it up, but somehow I found myself on Buzzfeed instead. Weird. I should have paid attention to what it involved rather than once again choosing to blindly follow the advice of someone else, someone in this instance who once came third in an event horrifyingly named 'Super Biathlon'. I learnt that just because an activity is one person's idea of fun, doesn't mean it's going to be another's. Especially if you're that other, and you prefer avoiding brushes with death, and activities that put every single fibre of your body under intense stress.

However, again, weeks later, when I'd finally regained full use of my leg muscles and was able to stop frowning, I reluctantly realised what the climb had taught me the hard way – that challenging myself and achieving something big involves a lot of work, and the mental capacity to never give up. It made me realise that I have impressive hidden reserves of strength to call upon when really challenged. Now I knew that, moving forwards, I had a choice – I could either listen to other people when they told me they didn't think I was capable of doing something or, I could dig in my heels, jut out my jaw and keep plodding forwards.

I couldn't have climbed that mountain without Ruth by my side, telling me I could do it, geeing me on, and giving me bites of her chocolate bars. It showed me that the support offered by loved ones is fundamental to achievement. Working towards a collective goal kept me on track, and the strength and comfort offered by a person I care about worked wonders when everything felt utterly hopeless.

This mountain taught me that I couldn't continue to go through life assuming that everything would go smoothly. I needed to give actual consideration to my decisions based upon my knowledge of myself. And, last but by no means least… no matter how twinkly the stars – I'm always going to remember to look where I'm fucking going.

PERU

WHERE I LEARNT...

- That toilets on the Inca Trail should be feared unless you have the thighs of a Russian dancer.

- That Machu Picchu *is* everything it's cracked up to be.

- That llamas can, and will, sneak up on you.

- That smoking is even deemed acceptable in vehicles aggressively leaking petrol.

- That people can successfully extract money from you using the power of baby goat alone.

THE REASON I HAD TO FLEE PERU

FRIENDLY ADVICE:

'I hear they eat rat over there! Did I hear that right, Derek? It's South America they eat rat, isn't it? You don't want to eat rat, Amy, no one does.'

Diane, family friend

EXPERT ADVICE:

'There are no regrets in life, just lessons.'

Jennifer Aniston
(Always immaculate, and a champion
of both diet and hydration)

After the horror of the mountain climb, Ruth, Henry and I finally said goodbye to Bolivia and headed back down to sea level, to the beach town of Iquique in northern Chile. Post mountain, all we desired were lazy days on golden beaches and relaxed evenings, barbequing meat and drinking cold beers.

Sadly our farewell holiday had to come to an end, and after a particularly tearful goodbye with Ruth, and a predictably unfussy 'see ya later' with Henry, I found myself facing my next steps completely alone for the first time. I had two mates flying out to meet me in Colombia in a couple of months, but I had to get there first. I did feel a little lost, and found myself looking over my shoulder a couple of times expecting to see Ruth or Henry rounding a corner hand-in-hand or wielding a guidebook, but I didn't have time to dwell, or even to enter into that way of thinking. I'd been gearing up for this since touching down in Argentina with Leggers, and after indirectly learning how to plan like a pro under the tutelage of Ruth and Henry, I was more than ready for this part of the trip.

Despite my optimism, I'll admit that I was pretty on edge throughout the 20-hour journey I had to make from Chile to Peru. I needed to hotfoot it straight to Cusco without delay in order to get there in time for my arranged trip on the Inca Trail, and as this wasn't a typical route trodden by backpackers due to its distance and indirect path, I had multiple stops and numerous bus terminals to contend with.

My first goal was to reach Arica, the last stop before the Chile–Peru border. Once there, I was directed into an enormous car park with hundreds of cars and vans parked bumper-to-bumper. A dozen men approached me, noisily jostling for my custom by trying to outbid each other to become my *collectivo* driver. These *collectivos* are the tried-and-tested way to cross the border, and are essentially taxis but the driver also assists you with filling in all border-crossing paperwork, before transporting you to the other side. I opted for a dude wearing a Bob Marley T-shirt who wasn't trying as hard as the rest.

I found myself travelling alongside a middle-aged Chilean lady with big, dyed red hair who was accompanying her two elderly parents into Peru to access cheaper medical treatment. I discovered this because, when forced to, I found that my Spanish actually wasn't too shabby. The daughter was astounded that I was travelling alone; '*muy fuerte*' (very strong), '*muy valiente*' (very brave), she repeated to me over and over again, while stroking my hair and enquiring sympathetically as to whether I missed my mother. She was right, I did. She was lovely, and it was just the dose of kindness and reassurance I needed at that time. I hugged her tightly and thanked her when we said farewell forever in the car park of Tacna bus station across the border in Peru.

The onward journey towards Cusco was spent sleeping and being hungry as I stupidly hadn't thought to change any money into Peruvian sol at the bus station prior to boarding. A mistake I wouldn't repeat! In another welcome dose of kindness from strangers, the lady sitting beside me on the bus noticed I hadn't eaten and insisted on plying me with chocolate biscuits.

I eventually arrived into Cusco 20 hours later, hungry and shattered but sleepily delighted at myself for successfully navigating my first journey using Spanish skills and savvy alone. I was the boss of me – in charge of my sleeping patterns, meal times, who I made friends with and how I spent my days. I was finally taking full responsibility for myself in all areas. Well, in all areas besides one…

▲▲▲▲▲▲▲▲

I'll admit that from the minute I arrived in South America, all prior consideration for my diet went out the window. No one was around to watch me any more, to shake their heads in warning as my hand crept towards Pret's finest high-calorie sandwich. I was in charge of my own dietary destiny, and I did not manage things sensibly.

In Argentina I gobbled down deep-fried pastries and put in heroic efforts to consume as much red meat as possible. It was here I was first introduced to the magic of the empanada – South America's version of the Cornish pasty, also stuffed with delicious meat, or veg. My particular favourite was the sweet potato variety, served with lashings of the hot sauce I would come to seek out at every dinner table I sat at throughout my trip. These tiny pockets of tasty pastry could be gone in three mouthfuls… which anyone with good sense knows means they don't count. Around 11 p.m. each night, when all sensible humans should be deep in the throes of digestion, I'd make like an Argentinian and take to the streets with one thing on my mind… meat. I'd find any restaurant with steak on the menu, and order it rare while calling for giant carafes of red wine like some kind of reincarnated Tudor. I forgot salad. I was happy to completely deny its existence until my tongue started to feel unusually large, and I had to give 'scurvy' a quick google. It was a false alarm, but rather than acknowledge my body's hints that I needed some nutrients that weren't animal-based, I got stuck back in.

I was in heaven. The wine was almost cheaper than water, and it was some of the finest I'd ever tasted – it would have been downright rude not to hydrate myself accordingly. Every Malbec, Cabernet Sauvignon, Pinot Noir, and Tempranillo I drank tasted better than the one before. Every sip was like a waterfall of kisses tumbling down my oesophagus with the sole purpose of warming both my belly and my heart. If I'd had the time and space, I would have purchased a paddling pool, filled it to the brim and just sat there in a deck chair, in the sunshine, sucking in red wine through the world's longest straw, gradually getting drunker and drunker.

Observers to this gluttony could well have believed I was part of some government-funded medical experiment to see how quickly an ordinarily healthy 30-year-old woman could contract gout. I didn't care. Even if it had have happened, I'd have just wiped the red wine from my greasy chin and laughed out loud at the devious crystals of sodium urate congregating around my joints like dehydrated office gossipers. I was happy to soothe any future pain with fond memories of iPad-sized steaks, and goblet after goblet of god's own Malbec.

In Bolivia, I switched from slabs of red meat to '*menús del día*' (daily set menus). Although standards slipped significantly, there was no denying Bolivian grub was an absolute bargain, and I love a bargain. These meals were made up of three courses and were served on plates so massive they'd make Harvester whither in humiliation. They cost no more than 20 bolívianos (£2.40) and if you timed it right you wouldn't need to eat anything else all day long. It was genius.

The Bolivians like to get the ball rolling with a big bowl of soup. Sometimes there would be meat in there, other times it would be exclusively gristle. If you were lucky and ordered well, you may even chance upon a couple of tiny chicken feet. This took some getting used to, and those first couple of stirs of your bowl were always a nervous moment...

Is that an eyeball? Nope, gristle.
What on earth?! Gristle.
That's a vein, I'm sure that's a vein. Tastes like gristle.
I didn't know chickens had scales. You do now (and you'll never forget).

Anyway, I bravely soldiered on.

With the main course, although it was pot luck as to what meat you'd receive, one thing you were always guaranteed was a good jaw workout. The rest of your plate would be piled high with boiled rice, a tasty tomato–potato combo and sometimes a boiled egg... as a bonus... often unpeeled. If you were a champion and made it to dessert you could expect pre-packaged neon jelly as a nice stomach settler. I ate it all. It wasn't what you'd consider traditionally delicious, but there was lots of it, and that's a thing I'm a fan of so I was more than happy. There were pieces of eggshell in my eyebrows and green food dye in the corners of my mouth, but I didn't care, I was committed to getting my money's worth.

Once I crossed the border into Peru, I happily ate questionable meat. There could have been dog, maybe even some rat (*yeah, whatever Diane*). Although the man cooking grizzly-looking rodent kebabs over a dirty oil barrel *did* smile and *tell* me they were guinea pig, a Peruvian delicacy, there's a good chance he may have been fibbing. I'm sure that any large rodent when skinned and impaled cruelly on a stick would look much the same and consist of similar stringy meat prone to instant disintegration the split-second it touches your tongue. Did it taste nice? Not really. Did I enjoy feeling like a motherfucking cave woman feasting upon her day's catch? Absolutely 100 per cent yes.

And then, I met ceviche.

I'd flirted with it in northern Chile, but it was when I hit the coast of Peru that I fully embraced this delicacy of raw fish cured in lime juice. It was delicious, spicy, fresh and, most importantly, good for me. Especially as it usually came served with salad, corn, avocado or yams. This was it – time for a change. Carbs and rat kebabs were out. Raw protein was in.

Over the course of the next month spent travelling north along Peru's coastline, I ate ceviche for lunch and dinner every day. I applauded myself for my sensible choices while delighting in how mysterious I must look because I was alone and dining upon local cuisine, like some kind of travel-hero. I treated myself to a fancy plate and a whole bottle of white wine in a fancy restaurant in the Barranco district of Lima to celebrate two weeks of successfully navigating alone. I perched on tiny chairs and spooned it hungrily into my mouth from plastic tubs at the fish market in Lima's infamous Chorrillos district, which I incidentally visited every day during my stay in town. I'd just hang out, pretending to be enjoying the view, when in actual fact I had my beady eyes set on the fishing boats out on the water, knowing that the catch I saw them hauling in would soon be chopped up and transformed into the Tupperware treat of my dreams. In Huanchaco, a surf town to the north of Lima close to Trujillo, I ventured out at sunset to scribble in my diary and dine upon the biggest bowls I'd ever seen, served with giant corn and lashings of red onion; completely negating my chances of meeting men, but I didn't care – I only had eyes for ceviche.

Admittedly after a couple of weeks of this thoughtless eating pattern my stools loosened somewhat, but I didn't feel any urgent cause for alarm: I was off my tits on lime juice and raw sea bass. Even when the thought occurred to me to eat something bland, it would only remain in my mercury-addled brain for a second before being completely obliterated by my overpowering lack of common sense and the dangerous levels of chilli in my system.

Skip to the end of the month, and the close calls were becoming a lot more frequent. There were frantic dashes back to the hostel from the beach. There were worried, wiggly waits outside toilet cubicles and nervous overnight journeys on buses lacking any facilities, driven by humans in possession of suitcase-sized bladders. It appeared all bus drivers were committed to aiding expansion of Peruvian potholes by driving through them at breakneck speed, showing very little regard for their vulnerable, overloaded undercarriage – and I'm only half talking about the bus. It's safe to say that this wasn't ideal for passengers needing to keep things clenched at all times.

Despite the ever-increasing urgency I was faced with, I maturely chose to ignore the problem completely. Lima and Huanchaco have their fair share of bars, and I had no intention of missing out just because things were bordering on the touch-and-go. I continued to drink every shot presented to me, convincing myself that alcohol would eventually cure my persistent stomach complaint… as though that's an actual possibility, and not just something idiots tell other idiots.

I was nearing the end of my month in Peru, and was set to spend my last three days in the resort town of Máncora on the northern coastline, just a few hours south of the border with Ecuador. By this time, I was feeling far from shipshape, but as Máncora is Peru's major party destination, I was determined to soldier on. By day people nurse hangovers on the sandy beach or, if they possess good balance, they may go for a surf. The minute the sun starts to set, the town begins to shake as every bar along the main drag collectively cranks up their eighties sound systems to the max. By night people congregate to drink double-shot-sized nightmares appropriately named 'Blood Bombs'. Then of course there's the terribly mediocre cocaine bought from tuk-tuk drivers who follow you up and down the street pestering you until you give in. I'm told the coke in Máncora is cut with baby laxative so as you can see, I was hardly in the spot for some much-needed R & R. That would just have to wait until Ecuador.

'Do you reckon it's normal to poo eleven times a day?' I blurted out to my mate, Izzy, who'd just innocently asked what I fancied for lunch. Izzy was from Yorkshire; I'd met her back in La Paz, and I'd been bumping into her at various spots all the way through Peru.

I was forced to finally speak up after realising I'd been considering the ocean as a logical location for my next well-overdue session of stomach cramping and bowel evacuation. That was an indicator of how weak I felt. I'd lost all good sense, along with the nutrients essential to a healthily functioning body.

'No, you idiot! I thought you were looking a bit thin. How long has this been going on for?'

Izzy sat there expectantly as I did some very lethargic mental calculation.

'Oh… erm… hmm… well… coming up to a month.'

The look on her face quickly transformed from one of sympathy to one of outright horror.

'Mate. What? How old are you?! Why haven't you done anything? You've probably got a parasite! I had one in Bolivia. It's really common. I felt dreadful and was shi…'

She carried on talking but I was no longer listening. I had ceased doing so the second the word 'parasite' came out of her mouth. Instead I stared into the middle distance, fighting waves of nausea while picturing a three-headed serpent with multiple rows of razor-sharp teeth sleeping soundly in my stomach. There he was, in my mind's eye, resting up for dinner time when he'd start shaking his maracas (probably made of gristle) in anticipation of the raw fish fiesta that was about to start all over again. I could taste every single piece of ceviche I'd shoved into my stupid mouth. I could feel the texture. I could smell it. Suddenly the gurgles my stomach had been making were no longer funny. They'd taken on a sinister turn, and could now be interpreted as the battle cries of my unwanted stomach dweller demanding to be fed or else suffer the consequences. And by 'consequences', I mean his fanged, 20-

eyed face bursting forth from my stomach (or worse!) to satiate its hunger with the blood and flesh of anyone unfortunate enough to be within biting distance.

What I should have done was spring from my beach towel as fast as my weak body would allow and head straight to the nearest doctor's office. At the very least, I should've consulted a pharmacist. Instead, like any brainless imbecile who hates confrontation, addressing issues and missing out on fun, I chose to ignore it again, and to go out drinking.

After another night on the Blood Bombs I woke up early, dehydrated and sweaty. I tried and failed to get back to sleep. My dorm was full of incredibly slim, chatty Argentinian girls who snored like they were channelling Diego Maradona. Rather than commit bloody murder, I decided to get out of my room and go in search of what had become my failsafe hangover cure… a litre of yogurt drink.

Ladies and gentlemen, raw fish and litres of dairy: the diet of champions!

Twenty minutes later, I tossed my peach yogurt drink into the bin. I felt like a new woman. I felt stronger, steadier on my feet – I was sure I could feel the 'calcium' rushing to my bones. I felt so great I realised it'd be nice to continue feeling like this. Today would be the day I addressed the fact that I was ill. Proud of myself for reaching such an adult decision, I decided to honour the occasion with a celebratory fart. A bottom fanfare if you will. I should probably mention that this was something I'd been refraining from doing since I departed Cusco almost four weeks previously, when I'd experienced the first few rumblings that something was up with my digestive department.

I have no idea why I chose that moment on that busy Peruvian street to break tradition but this turned into a celebration I wish to forget. That momentary lapse in concentration will go down in history as one of my most ill-thought-out decisions ever. I took a chance, and it backfired spectacularly… all over my pants.

By some grace of god, I had a contained situation. It was imperative I keep it that way. I stood frozen to the pavement, assessing the damage, doing the obligatory bit of laughy-crying behind my sunglasses. The good news was that the door to my hostel was just 100 m away. The bad news? Within that 100 m was a row of open-fronted cafes full of backpackers enjoying their breakfast. I realised in sheer horror that I recognised a few faces from my time in town, the worst being Anton, a Swedish boy I'd kissed the night before. At 22, this was a man so young he'd clearly never been exposed to such atrocities. Basically, he was a Swedish Bambi, and I was about to kill his mother and resign him to a lifetime of living with rabbits.

Anton was handsome, polite and very tactile. All attributes I'd admired the night before, but I knew that if I gave him the chance, he'd be at my side greeting me with kisses and an invitation to sit down before I could say 'poopy pants'. He was sitting there looking all angelic, his skin glowing in the morning sun, drinking some fruit concoction that would no doubt do wonders for his stamina. And there I was, loitering indecisively in the street with a dirty, dirty secret that he could never be allowed to find out. I couldn't believe that this was happening to me. Miraculously, I'd managed to convince this spritely hunk that I was a glamorous and very together 30-year-old as opposed to the type of skatty mess who'd persistently ignore a stomach complaint up until the point she sharted in public. I didn't want his illusion of me shattered – he'd never call me beautiful again, and that was just unacceptable.

I decided that although movement was problematic, it was my only option. Should there have been a rock within leaping distance for me to cower behind until Anton left, I'd have made that leap and suffered the consequences gladly. As I was on a street un-peppered by conveniently placed rocks I had no choice but to soldier on.

My choice of speed was essential: move too slowly, look like a creep, and attract the attention of everyone waiting to be fed. Move too fast and... well, that creepy walk could evolve into some kind of dirty protest. The result was akin to Kevin Spacey in *The Usual Suspects* mixed with a healthy dose of *Forrest Gump*... in the early years, before his leg braces were removed and we discovered he could run fast and play ping-pong like a hero.

Obviously, my strange behaviour drew the attention of Anton and his friends instantly. Waves were exchanged and I had no choice but to continue towards them, dragging my feet so as not to risk any catastrophic movement to my underwear.

I stuck to the very edge of the pavement. This meant I was around a metre further away than it's normal to be when you encounter friends. It was imperative to stay out of reaching distance. I may have had to walk past them but nothing in the world was going to make me stop and chat or hug, or even make eye contact.

As I drew up alongside them I did what any desperate person would do: I lied.

I nodded an oh-so-very nineties 'sup'-style greeting in the direction of their table, pointed at my foot and said, 'Surfing injury, I need to go ice this up,' and continued walking forwards as though I had an invisible ball and chain attached to my ankle.

I was completely dry and had nothing with me or on me that indicated I had come from the sea. Also, the previous evening, I'd drunkenly told Anton several times that I couldn't be bothered to surf because I 'just enjoy lying on the beach too much'.

I'll remember the baffled, and slightly hurt, expression on his perfectly smooth face forever.

WINNER = *FRIENDLY ADVICE*

'I hear they eat rat over there! Did I hear that right, Derek? It's South America they eat rat, isn't it? You don't want to eat rat, Amy, no one does.'
Diane, family friend

Although I can't be certain I actually ingested rat, when I look back, it's certainly a possibility. Saying that, the sticky situation I ended up in wasn't just down to the unidentifiable meat. It was the result of close to two months of rejecting all digestive common sense.

Jennifer Aniston speaks wise words; this was indeed a lesson. However, if I'd followed Diane's advice, perhaps I wouldn't have had anything to learn. I would have been happy to continue on in life not knowing the shame and embarrassment of soiling oneself in public. Diane knew that if I didn't pay close attention to what I ate, I'd regret it. And I did. Probably more than I regret anything, ever.

LESSONS LEARNT

It seems it pays to think before I put things in my body... who would have thought it? It also appears I can't continually ignore issues hoping they'll eventually remedy themselves. That's not how adults should behave.

I don't want to be the girl who shits herself in the street. When I'm on holiday I should be out there enjoying myself, not having to take to my bed for a shame nap before leaving town in the dead of night. I'd been so excited back before I left Ruth and Henry to make all my decisions myself, and then I only go and shit myself a month later. What an idiot! It was safe to say this was the wake-up call I needed to learn the importance of looking after myself, and nourishing myself sensibly. I wouldn't eat only Hobnobs, or only ham sandwiches, for a whole month, so why I thought it was okay to eat spicy fish in abundance, I have no idea. I was in a spiral of fish addiction and the only thing that could snap me out of it was far too close a call with complete public humiliation.

This taught me the importance of listening to my body. If its warning methods start dominating my every waking hour, I will recognise it as the time to do something about it. And, if I'm ever feeling a little under the weather I vow to *never* chance a danger fart… it's not worth it.

ECUADOR

WHERE I LEARNT...

- That the fountain of youth *does* exist, and the Americans are already onto it.

- That a volcano erupting in your vicinity sounds like someone firing a canon at your head.

- That cows like to follow humans.

- That Jeff 'Ja Rule' Atkins once starred in a film called *I'm In Love with a Church Girl*, and it's actually all right when viewed in Spanish.

- That sometimes donkey is the best mode of transport.

TWO UTTER WEIRDOS

FRIENDLY ADVICE:

'We're all inherently weird, Amy. It pays to be a little suspicious.'

Bobby, best friend

EXPERT ADVICE:

'If you judge people, you have no time to love them.'

Mother Teresa
(An actual saint)

I'd been travelling alone for six weeks now, through Peru and up into Ecuador, and I was thoroughly enjoying the experience. As I'd reassured Sally back in Sussex all those months ago, I was good at making friends, and more than happy to strike up conversation with anyone and everyone at any given opportunity. The rate with which you make friends when travelling alone is one of the best things about it, and although it's always sad to say goodbye, you know that as soon as you arrive in the next town there'll be a new group of mates awaiting you, and if there isn't it just means you get a little taste of the alone time you were after too.

While socialising presented little challenge, it did take me a little while to adjust to dorm-room living. I'm not really one for sharing personal space. Unless it's the touch of someone that I know and love, or have decided I want to get to know and 'love', I'd prefer people to remain at a safe distance, just in case they sneeze. Backpackers don't have this luxury. We have budgets, and ordinarily they're paltry. This makes bunking up with complete strangers night after night an unavoidable part of the process. Sometimes it's just a few; other times there are 19 of them, and they all stink.

For the most part, I found my dorm buddies to be people with similar ideas about how to conduct themselves in public, and in private. There's an unspoken rule that as you're all in it together, you'll be considerate enough to do all you can not to piss each other off, or disgust them too much. Having said that, we're all human... you can't be expected to hold in *every* fart.

Of course, there are the exceptions to the rule: those who think manners are for sissies, and who vow to do whatever they damn well please because they've paid 12 sol (£3) to be there too, goddammit, and they're intent on getting their money's worth by utilising every inch of your shared quarters for unsavoury activities involving narcotics and/or bodily fluids.

By this stage, I'd established that there are two major problems with hostels:

1. Outside of the shower cubicle, your standard hostel offers little in terms of privacy. This means people have no place to go to do the weird shit they'd normally do in their bedrooms. Some accept this; others can't help but let their gross habits ooze out into the public sphere. This can mean encountering such delights as

the rogue testicles of complete strangers lounging around in inappropriately tiny towels, underwear so soiled it justifies disposal by men in hazmat suits and more liberated pubic hair than it's normal to see in one human lifetime.

2. In hostels, people booze. People sometimes booze from breakfast time, or even sometimes from the day before. There's a complete collective disregard for public reputation, because if you do anything dreadful, you can pack up your shame along with your backpack and flee at first light à la Leggers and I back in Buenos Aires. Booze means people lose inhibitions, and when this happens, they often forget they're trying to hide being a grubby little pervert.

You meet a lot of people when you're constantly on the move. Ninety per cent of the time those you come across are normal, pleasant folk, just journeying to and fro much like you, wanting to see things, meet people, learn and enjoy a little downtime from normal life. Sadly, wherever high numbers of humans congregate, the odds of encountering a couple of utter weirdos increase significantly.

Although thankfully few and far between, these anomalies do pop up every so often, so it would be entirely negligent of me not to warn you that they exist. Most of the time they stay quiet until you're three or four beers in, which appears to be the threshold for feeling comfortable enough to drop a little strange-bomb. Usually this weirdness materialises in the form of a questionable opinion, accompanied with far too hearty a laugh. Or, more often than you might expect, it comes in the form of a wildly racist statement, which has everyone in hearing distance casually shuffling their stools in the opposite direction. In a worst-case scenario, they'll wait until the dead of night to go full weirdo, and then you might find yourself awoken from your slumber by some creep you said one word to shining his iPhone in your face at 4 a.m., gurning his face off, enquiring as to whether you fancy waking up to come and look at him naked.

▲▲▲▲▲▲▲▲

I'd been in Baños in Ecuador for a couple of days when I met Mal. He hailed from Gatwick. This fact alone should have really set the alarm bells ringing, given the fact that Gatwick is an airport, and not a town. Maybe there were flats for plane enthusiasts at the end of the runway, I didn't know. Maybe before he flew he'd been stuck in the airport departure lounge for a prolonged period à la Tom Hanks in *The Terminal*. Having learnt what I had about this chap, that would have probably been the safest place for him: an area where you aren't allowed any liquids over 200 ml, and where burly security guards block all exits.

Mal seemed all right at first. Just a typical English 'lad', complete with skinhead, polo shirt and chain-smoking habit. He spoke a little too loudly, and a bit too close to my face, but I've been known to mumble so I let it slide.

Our first conversation happened during the day, while everyone was out enjoying activities. My white-water rafting group had conveniently forgotten to pick me up, so I was hanging out alone in the hostel doing some reading when Mal rocked up. We progressed safely through the usual first questions: Where have you been? Where are you going? Where's been your favourite place? It was a normal run-of-the-mill intro conversation. It took a little bit of an odd turn when he started talking about why he'd started travelling in the first place...

'I *really* love travelling,' he said, taking a deep drag on his Marlboro Red, 'I 'ave ever since I had the best night of my life.'

'Oh yeah?' I asked, mildly interested. 'What made it the best night of your life?'

'I only went and fucked two birds di'nt I?' he said, unnecessarily acting out a thrust for me, just in case I didn't get the picture.

I blinked. 'Sorry?' At this point we'd been talking for less than five minutes.

'Yeah... mate... I was in Thailand at that Moon Party, and this well fit local chick came and said 'er and 'er mate were looking for a "friend", and ya know what I said?'

'What did you say?' *Forgive me, I was curious.*

'I said, too fucking right!' He nodded enthusiastically, 'Course I did, I've got a cock ain't I?'

Oh goodness. It seemed peculiar that this was the first thing he wanted me to know about himself. We weren't playing 'I Have Never'; we were eating cheese sandwiches.

'Good for you,' I managed.

'Cheers mate. It was brilliant. They were SO fit. And I gave it to 'em good, know what I mean?' He punched me playfully on the shoulder, and I tried not to gag. He continued, 'Ever since that night, all I've done is travel. I go 'ome, work at Gatwick, then I travel. I've been doing the same thing for three years now. It's all I'm ever gonna do. I fuckin' love it.'

'Clearly! That's... cool.'

Fortunately at that moment a minibus pulled up, and my smiling, normal mates came piling out.

'Okay, see you later,' I said, quickly standing up to leave.

'Yeah, cool mate. It's been good chattin'. We're from the same neck of the woods, we probably know loads of the same people.'

'Hmm… perhaps.'

'We should hit the town later, yeah?'

'Errr… maybe.' I nodded, completely baffled. 'Bye.' And then I vacated the area.

▲▲▲▲▲▲▲▲

Although brief, this conversation had me on high alert. There was something about Mal that didn't sit right with me; maybe it was the look in his eye, the way he talked about women – I don't know. What I did know was that I wanted to avoid him at all costs.

Largely I'm a trusting person, but I'd had a bad encounter back in Cusco, Peru, that meant my odd-bod sensors were now switched on at all times. I'm only mentioning this now because I'd chosen to completely blank it out for a while on account of it being utterly disgusting…

I was fresh off my first solo bus journey from Chile to Peru and had a couple of days to rest up before I set off on the Inca Trail. Rather than boozing, my plan was to stock up on sleep. Sadly, the only room left in the hostel had me bunking with nine men. It didn't matter that much: I had earplugs, an eye-mask and a total determination to sleep. I'd also been assured that eight out of the nine of them were leaving at 5 a.m., so even though they might wake me up as they left, I felt pretty chuffed I'd be able to get a nice long lie in before new arrivals checked in.

'*Buenos días!*' I called as I greeted the testosterone-heavy room, dumping my backpack on my bottom bunk.

Everyone smiled back, bar one – a chubby, dark-haired guy who looked at me for a couple of seconds from his top bunk before returning to the magazine he was reading. Whatever – by this stage, I'd learnt that I didn't have to connect with everyone I met. Plus, sleep was the prerogative, not socialising or practising my Spanish.

When 4.30 a.m. rolled around, eight of the nine got up, collected their bags and left. I rolled over briefly, but in general was incredibly impressed at their quiet efficiency. When I stirred, I noticed the one guy still there was the one that hadn't been much of a fan of eye contact when I'd first greeted the whole room. He was stirring too. Our bunk beds made up an L shape. I was on the bottom of the long bit, he was on the top of the tail.

I drifted back to sleep quickly after the guys left, only waking again when I felt him relocating into the bunk bed above me. It struck me as odd, but I'd seen people do weirder things in the pursuit of the comfiest dorm room location. *Perhaps his bunk is drafty*, I charitably thought to myself before hauling the covers over my head, and falling back to sleep.

The next thing I knew, the sound of heavy breathing started to permeate through my blanket and my wax earplugs. Something was afoot.

I cautiously removed an earplug, and even from the relative safety of being under my blanket, I was immediately exposed to the full extent of the breathing. It certainly wasn't snoring, or even overzealous mouth breathing; it was ragged, and unsettling… like the panting of a newly infected zombie.

Alarmed, I cleared my throat and made a real show of rolling over and huffing and puffing. I wanted him to know I suspected him of foul play, but that if he stopped whatever it was he was doing immediately, I would let it go. It was 5.30 a.m. – all I wanted to do was sleep.

Suspicious activity ceased for about ten minutes. I left out one earplug in order to monitor the situation but I soon grew drowsy again. It seemed as though my huffy rolling to and fro had had the effect I'd hoped – namely that he now understood he best not try his luck with this overly tired English rose.

… And then the bed started shaking.

I tried aggressively clearing my throat again.

It didn't stop.

I tried again.

It sped up.

I could hear the laboured breathing again. Upsettingly, it wasn't the only noise I could hear. There was some tell-tale wet slapping going on… that I still hear in my nightmares. I could no longer deny what was happening – this guy was enthusiastically pleasuring himself on the bunk bed directly above me.

'Erm… exactly what the fuck do you think you're doing, mate?' I said loudly.

The squelching stopped.

I spoke slowly, and with enough venom that even if his English wasn't excellent he would still know I was on the brink of losing my shit. 'I know what you're up to, and you need to stop it RIGHT NOW.'

Silence hung in the air for about 15 seconds, but then the little creep obviously couldn't hold it in any more, and started up again with gusto. He was going for it. He didn't care he'd been caught – he liked it.

I leapt from the bunk to a safe distance about two metres away. My eyes met his. They were as beady and black as you'd expect.

There was not even a glimpse of remorse on his flushed face. His mouth just hung open hideously.

I pointed a finger at him and said, 'YOU'RE A FUCKING DISGRACE.' And then I kicked the metal bed frame (a painful act I immediately regretted) and stormed down to reception in my cow-print pyjamas.

Needless to say, I was irate, and creeped out, and keen to encourage his castration with anything rusty and blunt at the earliest opportunity. I flew into reception in a flurry of swear words and angry arm gestures, marched right up to the night watchman and demanded he throw the creep out of the hostel immediately. If he did so efficiently, I'd be able go back to sleep. Maybe then I could awake several hours in the future and pretend this nauseating incident had been nothing more than an unsettling nightmare.

Unfortunately, the night watchman only spoke Spanish, and my language skills didn't stretch to 'wanking sex pest'.

I needed the security guard to know what had happened. I needed him to understand the gravity of the situation, and how much it wouldn't and shouldn't be tolerated.

Over and over I shouted the sentence, '*El hombre en mi dormitorio es MALO*' (The man in my room is bad), and to demonstrate I hadn't just come down to report a nightmare, I teamed this statement with a full range of hand actions, hip thrusts and some alarmingly accurate sound effects. The poor chap, who must have been about 60, eventually clocked on and went bright red before saying something into his walkie talkie and rushing up to my dorm.

Relieved that something was being done, I closed my eyes, gave a big sigh and sat down on the chair the guard had just vacated. A few moments later when I opened them again, I saw the faces of five bemused backpackers waiting in reception to check in who had clearly witnessed the whole angry charade.

At least they had the good grace to give me a sympathetic round of applause.

So yeah, that happened.

And understandably this now meant I was particularly sensitive to people who made me feel even a little on edge. I hadn't met anyone similar since Cusco, but for some reason, Mal got my haunches up. I was watching him.

▲▲▲▲▲▲▲

Another problem I'd identified with staying in hostels is that you're forced together. Sometimes this is great, like when you're the one needing to make friends fast. Other times, not so much, just like back in Baños when some skinhead, who bloody loves threesomes, popped his head up just as we were all heading out for the night, to ask if he could come too. No self-respecting backpacker could say no to this request; it would breach ALL of the codes. Backpackers are welcoming by nature.

There was a relatively big group heading out that night, but my satellite group consisted of me and another English girl called Sarah, an Aussie called Mark, two Irish chaps, Adrian and Pete, and now, Mal. The second I introduced him to Sarah, I saw his unblinking eyes lock on to a target. Sarah was a fair bit younger than the rest of us, and exuded youthful innocence.

In the first bar I clocked Mal cornering her, and chewing her ear off. God knows what he was saying – hopefully it didn't revolve around how much he bloody loves shagging. She seemed relatively relaxed about the whole thing, but made her excuses at the first opportunity and got chatting to Adrian. I could have been wrong, but it seemed to me like lusty looks were being exchanged, and that wasn't lost on Mal: he stood at the bar, nostrils flaring, taking angry slugs on his beer as he watched their flirty exchange.

The evening carried on, and we continued drinking. Sarah and Adrian continued chatting, and Mal continued watching. When the bar we were in closed, the DJ invited us all back to his house for a party. Well... I say a party – there was about ten of us dancing around his living room, all sharing a communal vodka and orange out of one giant cocktail glass. Which seemed perfectly normal at the time.

Despite enjoying the 'party' and the novelty vodka orange, I made a point of keeping an eye on Mal, and every time I did he was either talking to Sarah, or trying to get her to talk to him. The time had come to help a sister out...

I wandered over and spoke in his ear, 'Mal, mate. You've got to stop staring at Sarah. I'm pretty sure her and Adrian like each other. Just leave them to it. There are other females here.' I indicated the other ladies in the room, and gave him a friendly pat on the back.

He shook his head. 'I know she doesn't like him. She told me.'

'Did she?' *Course she didn't.* 'Are you sure? It kinda looks to me like she likes him.'

We looked back over to where they were standing just in time to see them start kissing.

Mal huffed, 'Fuck's sake!' He collapsed into an armchair, and that's where he stayed, aggressively hogging the communal cocktail and watching the snogging far too intently, until the time came to leave.

On the walk home, Mark, Pete and I were trailing behind Sarah and Adrian who were walking hand-in-hand. Mal hovered in-between our two groups, occasionally lunging forwards to grab Sarah's wrist, or to karate chop their hands apart. We were all telling him to relax, but Mal clearly couldn't hear, or was choosing not to. He was committing fully to his peculiar behaviour.

Back at the hostel we decided to grab another beer and hang out in the garden. Sarah and Adrian snuggled in a corner, upping the snogging ante. I really thought Mal would give in gracefully, especially as Sarah hadn't looked at his face for about an hour, was ignoring everything he said to her and clearly only had eyes for her Irish beau. Rather than retire to bed, however, Mal sat about one metre from where they were kissing, and offered a whispery, unsettling commentary…

'She likes *me*…'

'Leave 'er alone, you prick…'

'She's not enjoyin' it, I can tell…'

'Mate, you're doin' it wrong…'

Eventually Adrian and Sarah, tired of the weirdness, made their excuses and hurried off in the direction of the dorms. Less than a minute later, Mal trotted on behind.

'Well, that was fucking weird,' Mark remarked.

'Correct!' I agreed. 'I'm so glad I'm not in the same dorm as him. I pity whoever is.'

Roll on the next day: Mark, Pete and I were getting ourselves breakfast in the hostel kitchen when Sarah and Adrian arrived, both looking a little shaken.

'You will NEVER believe what happened last night!' Adrian exclaimed, spooning sugar into his coffee. Sarah just stared into the depths of her mug, forehead in hand.

'We were… well, you know, and suddenly something just felt off. Weird, ya know?'

We all leaned in, intrigued. *Oh, please no.*

'I looked around and that Mal dude was on the top bunk opposite with his iPhone out. HE WAS FILMING US!'

Sarah rubbed her eyes, shook her head and looked at us through her fingers, clearly utterly mortified. 'It was so fucking weird. I've never seen anything like it.'

'What did you do? What did you say?' our table urged.

Adrian rubbed Sarah's back and continued, 'Well, I obviously shouted at him to stop, didn't I? He did... for about thirty seconds, and then I saw the *flash* go!'

NO!

Sarah piped up then, 'So *obviously* we left the room then because I was *super* weirded out – but Adrian went back to get his fags and...'

'HE WAS ONLY ON THE FLOOR... SNIFFING THE FUCKING SHEETS.'

... So yeah, weird people travel too.

Best beware anyone claiming to be from 'Gatwick'.

WINNER = *FRIENDLY ADVICE*

'We're all inherently weird, Amy. It pays to be a little suspicious.'
Bobby, best friend

When Mother Teresa made her statement about judging people, I'm sure her intentions were pure. Maybe she could afford to be so forgiving because she lived a life free of such complete grot bags. Sadly, hers is not a realistic statement. Some people deserve to be judged because they do things that require judgement, things that could see them before an actual judge if they're not careful.

Bobby knew. He knows a weirdo when he sees one. His advice was realistic. For every 50 people who are kind and normal, there's one you need to watch out for, whether it's for their awful opinions, or for their disgusting actions. You can't go through life trusting everyone. You are not a Smurf.

LESSONS LEARNT

Although you can't go around suspecting everyone of being a weirdo, it pays to be a little guarded. The vast majority of unusual folk you meet will probably be harmless. Just because someone talks about their mother too much, or wears obscenely small Speedos, doesn't mean they are a threat. The difficulty comes when trying to distinguish the harmless odd bods from the ones that might try to expose their goolies, steal your knickers or watch you shower through a hole they've drilled in the communal showers.

This was yet another lesson in trusting my instincts, and a reminder to always pay attention to who was around me. From the minute that dorm-room deviant wanked his way into my nightmares, I realised that not all backpackers are harmless, some are just downright weird and as I was going to be in close quarters with them for a little while longer, I needed to keep one eye open. It also showed me that I won't be able to read everyone correctly right away – sometimes rotters will weasel their way through that net.

From these unsettling scenarios, and from sharing rooms with new people day-in-day-out, I quickly tuned in to when someone made me feel uncomfortable. It didn't happen often, but when it did I quickly removed myself from the situation, voiced my suspicions to friends if I thought they might encounter them too and told management if I thought it necessary. I wasn't too polite to speak up. I was paying for my bed – I wanted to sleep somewhere I could relax and feel safe. Speaking up meant they knew in no uncertain terms that their behaviour wouldn't be tolerated, and hopefully it would also stop them acting like savages around anyone else.

COLOMBIA

WHERE I LEARNT...

- That swimming in crocodile-infested waters is actually okay if you don't know you're doing it.

- That I cannot salsa dance.

- That jungle running during rainstorms is reckless.

- That Shaggy's greatest hits album is a triumph.

- That it is possible to source the morning-after pill at the top of a mountain if you know the right people.

- That if you spend long enough trying, you can learn to throw accurately with your weaker arm.

THE NIGHT OF THE SUPERSONIC WEED BROWNIES

FRIENDLY ADVICE:

'Don't ingest anything given to you by a stranger. People don't tend to give things away unless they're trying to incapacitate you, Amy.'

NHS nurse injecting me with the rabies vaccine

EXPERT ADVICE:

'Here's the key to understanding risk: it's largely a matter of opinion.'

Howard Marks
(Highly practised marijuana consumer)

Of all the countries I planned on visiting, Colombia was the one I'd been the most excited about, and it did not disappoint. Everything delighted me – the blazing sunshine, the tropical rain, the thick fog creeping its way down the sides of the imposing mountains that ringed the towns and cities I passed through on my way north. Landscapes of jungle, mountains, gorges, forests, endless skies and multi-coloured rivers, winding, misty mountain roads where markings appeared to be nothing more than a guide for the weaving, beeping, music-blasting cars, and where gangs of daredevils would sprint into traffic from the hard shoulder and attach themselves to moving lorries to hitch free rides into town.

Everything felt exciting and every spot was different and wonderful in its own right. From the small, peaceful whitewashed town of Popayán in the south, where the streets were romantically lit up at night by flickering candle-filled lanterns, to San Agustín, where people still got from A to B on horseback, rocking wide-brimmed cowboy hats and spurs. There were whole villages where every stall and shop specialised in the same product – I passed through Cheese Town, Petrol Town and Towel Town. There was Salento, with its impossibly tall palm trees reaching 60 m into the sky, where you shrugged and decided that hot chocolate mixed with cheese actually sounded quite nice, and where you congregated at night to drink beers and play tejo – a game where you fling metal discs at a sandpit rigged with dynamite. There were the big cities like Cali and Medellín with fascinating histories, and populations of people so welcoming, and so delighted to have you in town, that they'd invite you into their family homes, take you on tours of their favourite food stalls and salsa spots, and would patiently help correct your Spanish, before inexplicably being the ones to thank you – for giving Colombia a chance. Colombia was more exciting, more varied and more fun than any country I'd ever visited, and I felt happy and at home.

I was riding a 10-ft wave of self-confidence at this stage. I'd successfully navigated my way through three countries, and although it was exactly what the majority of people around me had done too, I was pretty darn smug about it. I had this travelling shit nailed, and felt as though any situation could crop up (bar strangers with a tendency for public masturbation) and I'd handle it with the same resting heart rate as that glorious fluff-ball of a sloth I'd encountered chilling out in the Bolivian Amazon.

Ever since I'd realised back when I was travelling with Ruth and Henry that I needed to stop just going with the flow, and instead take responsibility for my trip, I'd been doing exactly that. Thinking things through, writing articles and notes about what I was doing, being honest and open and remembering myself in encounters with dashing dudes. In my eyes, the progress I'd made was undeniable. I'd proven I could take control, and steer myself in a direction that found me here, in Colombia – a place I loved – feeling the happiest I'd ever felt in my life. Maybe now was the time to ease up on myself, and to just enjoy seeing what might crop up in my remaining weeks.

By the time this laissez-faire attitude had firmly returned, my backpack and I had reached the north of Colombia. This was the most anticipated part of my trip. Two of my best mates, Alana and Rachel, had flown in from London and we were set to mosey around Colombia's Caribbean coast together for a couple of weeks. A week or so into their visit we headed out to Costeño Beach – a surf camp in the middle of nowhere on the road to Palomino. This place was heaven on earth: a deserted tropical beach, open-fronted bamboo huts, hammocks rather than beds, the need for shoes a long distant memory. It wasn't just the setting that was enchanting; its inhabitants boasted just as much natural charm. Beards, bum cracks and lithe surfer bodies greeted you every which way you looked. When your eyes tired of squinting at those riding the waves, there was a volleyball court to point your face at for further indulgence and, should you tire of that, a skate ramp. It's worth noting that shirts were not compulsory in any of these arenas. This meant that although most of my body had entered deep relaxation mode, my neck was bloody exhausted from all its rigorous swivelling. As the cherry on top of a downright sexy cake, if your heart required a little downtime from fluttering, there were a number of animals to look at – which was ideal for relieving the overwhelming desire to stroke something.

Maybe now's the time to mention the fact that backpackers like weed. They do, you know. They bloody love it. They'd roll around in it if they could. If you happen to be that way inclined (and it's hard not to be when your only tasks most days are to float from beach to hammock to bar), you'll rarely struggle to find new chums to get high with. Just look for the hammock hogs. You'll be able to identify the stoner amongst them by their general lack of reading material, and the delight on their faces at the simple act of swinging while looking at the sky.

The night in question began innocently enough. We were hanging out in the communal area sampling the hostel's tremendous homemade hummus, enjoying a couple of beers, a couple of joints – who were we to refuse when offered such treats by hunky Swedish men? I clocked one of the guys who worked there popping open a Tupperware container, which looked to be full of individually cling-filmed chocolate treats. Already a little stoned, the smell of freshly baked goodness was like music to my nostrils. When further investigation revealed them to be weed brownies I was sold instantly. Enthusiastic eye contact and eyebrow wiggling between Rachel, Alana and I confirmed we all wanted in. I was up and over there in three excited steps, which, incidentally, would be the fastest I'd move for a good few hours.

'*Hola, señor,*' I chirped, slamming both my hands down on the wooden counter in excitement. 'I will take three of those tasty-looking treats off your hands, *por favor*.' By this late stage in my journey my Spanish had reached dizzying heights.

'Three? You sure?'

'Fuckin' *bueno*, my friend.'

The guy grinned, looked down into the container, and giving it what looked like considerable thought, plucked three brownies from different corners of the box.

'These are the perfect three for you. For beautiful girls I choose them special.'

I beamed and awarded him a double thumbs up. 'Cheers, mate.'

'One thing… they're strong.'

'Perfectamundo,' I exclaimed. 'They look great. Well done, you.' Snatching up my treasure, I gave him a wink and headed back to Rachel and Alana, shimmying my shoulders and biting my bottom lip, thinking I was the coolest dude ever. The girls were suitably delighted.

'Yo, Amy, they're strong all right. Go slow,' some faceless person shouted from somewhere.

I flung a cursory thumbs up over my head as an indication we'd heard their warning, but by then the wrappers were off. Those delicious bastards didn't stand a chance. We were three stoned women, the brownies were warm, gooey and chocolatey: resistance was futile.

Things got off to a tremendous start. The communal area was getting busier by the minute as more guests showed up to join the festivities. We sat there chatting, drinking our beers, enjoying the sights around us and happily accepting the joints being passed from all angles. Good music, good company, a belly full of all my favourite things – life was good…

… and then it started to kick in.

STAGE ONE – THE GIGGLES

I'd been sniggering to myself for a good couple of minutes before I realised I had absolutely no idea what I was sniggering at. Rachel and Alana were laughing too, but they were both looking in opposite directions so it didn't appear that I was missing out on a shared joke – at least not between them.

There were many things newly amusing me that could have caused the chuckling to commence: a joke, a funny word, other people's faces, our faces. However, the most amusing by far were the camp's rabble of dogs. They weren't up to anything special but I tell you what, the only way they could've been funnier was if they'd stood up on their hind legs and performed the Macarena. I think we'd all agree that would be something worth seeing. I certainly did: I entertained the thought for a whole one minute 45 seconds. When new friends questioned why I was giggling in the low, unsettling way I'd adopted, I just pointed at the puppy, hoping to convey my inner train of thought, namely: *Don't bother with me, near-stranger, I've been rendered useless. Check out that guy. He has paws!*

STAGE TWO – LOSING THE POWER OF SPEECH

Where only minutes before the surrounding crowd had all been people I wanted to get to know, right now the idea of holding a conversation with anyone other than my two equally stoned friends was completely out of the question. A few people we'd already met tried, but they received little more in return than a well-meaning but spectacularly useless:

'I've no idea what you just said?'

Or:

'Was I talking? I thought you were talking? Was I... were we... were you saying something, mate?'

Or:

'Okay... I think the last word I remember was "chicken".'

Having not yet lost all my manners, I made sure to pretend to be listening. I even threw out the odd knee-pat to demonstrate that rudeness wasn't my intention. That approach backfired when people were wearing interesting fabrics, or items with entertaining add-ons, like toggles. I unwittingly spent *an amount* of time zipping and unzipping the pocket of my neighbour's cargo shorts. The mesmerising way the chunky teeth of that beige zip fit together... so seamless... so smooth... that was sheer mechanical genius. Surely the person who designed that won an award? Surely they were Scandinavian – they're a neat people. It did cross my mind to ask whether anyone knew, but they were deep in conversation, and I didn't want to interrupt with a question of little relevance to what they were saying. It would only draw attention to the fact that I was fiddling with a near-stranger's shorts pocket. I had to feign at least a little cool – it was our first night there, after all. Instead I mumbled under my breath to no one in particular, 'Zips are fun.' I just wanted to say the word 'zip'. It was most pleasing to the mouth.

Eventually I caught on to the cargo-shorted man's desire to fidget away from me, which given the circumstances was completely understandable. Having no idea of whether I'd been fiddling for one minute or ten, I felt the first hot wave of paranoia flush over me. Fortunately it didn't take hold. I was sidetracked before I'd even had the chance to acknowledge it. My distraction came in the form of a lit candle on the table in front of me. That shimmying golden seductress held me captivated until I realised something was wrong. My eyes, man, they were so dry.

A wave of paranoid questions sprung to mind:

How close had I just been sitting to that candle?
Was it too close? Weirdly close? Had people seen?

Are eyeballs even allowed to be this dehydrated?
I blew out the candle.

STAGE THREE – A LONE EXPEDITION OF INDETERMINATE LENGTH

With annoyance, it dawned on me I needed the toilet. Despite only being located a maximum of ten steps away, this expedition felt like a gigantic nuisance. I looked at Rachel and Alana. They both looked lovely. I started to tell them where I was going but failed – my mouth was too dry. Instead I just flung a floppy arm out in the direction of the toilet to indicate my plan, and bravely set out alone.

I successfully completed the ten steps to the bamboo hut housing the toilet without incident. I examined my face in the mirror above the communal sink without blinking for several minutes before realising that the toilet was unoccupied. I pulled open the saloon doors and peered inside with trepidation. The bare bulb hanging from the ceiling did little to illuminate the shadowy corners of the cubicle where god knows what was lurking. I took my seat cautiously, and quickly got lost in the eyes of the hand-painted mural on the toilet door. I couldn't work out what it was but I got the distinct impression it did not like me. Not one bit.

Fortunately, at that moment a rap song I liked came on. I tore my attention away from the mean cartoon staring at me from underneath a fiery rainbow to commence my performance. I gave that toilet cubicle what will probably be its best-ever hip hop recital, complete with head nodding, 'rap hands' and a lot of inaccurate lip syncing. Of all my past impromptu toilet performances, this was certainly up there in terms of panache.

After a brief period of self-congratulation and nods to the imaginary crowd (who were losing their minds FYI), I realised there was a chance that an *actual* crowd could have formed while I was role playing being a badass. Fortunately, when I managed to work out how to open the toilet door (by putting my face as close to the locking mechanism as possible), I found no queue. This was a huge relief given the fact that I felt incapable of making eye contact, or using my mouth to form a word. As I made my advance from the cubicle I realised that in the time I'd been sitting there, all feeling in my legs and feet had vanished. Now, they just tingled. Although that felt positively lovely, I had places to be and dogs to giggle at. Alas, trying to walk on sand when you've no grasp of the force required to propel yourself forwards is mighty tricky. I established that my best bet for successful forward motion was to place two hands on the wall, get my body as close to it as possible and take careful steps while maintaining a very slight bend at the knee. *Just as a nervous mime may have begun life*, I thought to myself, silent tears of mirth rolling down my cheeks. My moving style may have appeared unconventional, but it did the trick at helping me reach my destination, plus, I was having a whale of a time.

STAGE FOUR – A SUDDEN NOSE DIVE

I returned to base to find that, in my absence, Alana had taken a turn for the worse. For a woman who'd spent eight hours a day for the past week sunbathing, she was a shade akin to tracing paper, only more translucent. All signs pointed to a whitey – the unfortunate result of ingesting too much weed, which results in faintness, nausea and a whole lot of sweating. Alana was queasy, her eyes were sunken and all blood seemed to have evacuated her capillaries and fucked off to who knows where. Fearing she may turn invisible we helped her up as subtly as two droopy, giggling girls could, and led her by her moist hand back to our dorm room. When I say 'dorm' I mean wooden hut housing two small four-bed rooms. It was closer to the beach, and far enough away from the communal area to feel like it gave us a bit of breathing space. It was certainly preferable to being surrounded by people using their eyes to look at us, but as there were no lights leading the way there, and only one small light illuminating our room, the fact that our porch area and its surroundings were completely pitch black made me gulp as we approached.

'This doesn't feel okay,' Alana said, crawling into her bunk bed.

Rachel and I perched on the bed opposite and offered the best reassurances we could muster given we too were feeling the effects of the brownies:

AMY: 'Drink some water, babes.'

RACHEL: 'Lie down and close your eyes.'

AMY: 'You'll be fine in five minutes. Just sit up, and drink this.'

RACHEL: 'Focus on the horizon. Keep your eyes on that door handle.'

AMY: 'Do you want me to pat your head?'

RACHEL: 'Drink this. Lie down.'

ALANA: 'I think I'm going to be sick.'

STAGE FIVE – UNREASONABLE PARANOIA

Although outwardly calm, my guts felt like one of those balls constructed entirely from elastic bands (which ordinarily I'm a huge fan of). I was very worried. Alana looked awfully clammy. She was covered in an all-over sheen of something unsettling. She also appeared to have shrunk a little in size. I blinked a few times to clear away any weed residue, and tried sizing her up from the corners of my eyes, but she was definitely smaller. Definitely. She was also shivering despite it being 75 degrees, and the dreary hue of watery grey she'd become looked like it was spreading to her blonde hair. It was as though she was turning to stone right in front of my dilated pupils.

Now I thought about it, I didn't feel too great either. I felt hot and tingly, and as though the top of my head might concertina in like a foldable mug. My right eyebrow was twitching and sweat was forming on my brow. Was I okay? Was Rachel okay? Was it only going to be a matter of time before we too began shrinking and turning grey? Oh, the guilt! I'd invited these two women who I love dearly to come and join me on my holidays, and now we were all going to die.

Fortunately, my negative thoughts were interrupted by Alana taking a deep breath, peeling herself off the bed and going to the toilet. Phew – she must have a little time left. The second the bathroom door was closed, Rachel and I turned to each other and began conversing in panicked whispers. We made sure to pepper our conversation with loud statements about anything that came to mind, too – we couldn't have our weak buddy sitting on the loo catching on to the fact that we were freaking out about the imminence of her expiration.

RACHEL: *(Worried whisper)* 'I'm really worried about her. Didn't you say the guy said he selected them "specially" for us?'
(Out loud) 'Your feet look so tanned, dude.'

AMY: *(Worried whisper)* 'He did say that, *and* he picked them from different corners of the box.'
(Out loud) 'They do, don't they!' *(Genuinely pleased with myself)*

RACHEL: *(Worried whisper)* 'Do you think anyone else is feeling like this? Should one of us go and look? Maybe we should tell someone? I really don't want to go out there.'
(Out loud) 'Or… are they maybe just dirty?'

AMY: *(Worried whisper)* 'Me neither. And who would we even tell? They could be in on it too.'
(Out loud) 'This light is weird. I can't tell.'

RACHEL: *(Out loud)* 'You should lick 'em.'

AMY: *(Out loud)* 'Hahahahahahaha. Okay sure.'

Heaven knows why I didn't just lick my finger and wipe it on my foot to gauge my filth levels. Licking just seemed like the most efficient option. Sadly, investigations revealed my feet were not tanned, they were just filthy, and now so was my tongue. Initial disgust soon dissolved into giggles, and, then realising I'd completely forgotten the outcome of my preliminary investigations, like some kind of germ-loving simpleton I elected to lick my foot again. It was still dirty.

At that point, Alana emerged from the toilet. Rachel and I ceased laughing and simultaneously tilted our heads in concern.

'I'm SO pale.'

'No you're not!' I exclaimed. 'You sparkle! Like Edward Cullen!'

I was lying of course. She looked as though she'd been born in a cave, and had never left.

Perplexed by my out-of-character *Twilight*-based compliment, Alana lay carefully back down. 'Guys, I'm serious, this really doesn't feel like weed. My heart's racing. Feel my heart.'

We both felt her heart, and gravely nodded in agreement that it was indeed beating fast.

Struggling to speak with her dry mouth, Alana asked, 'Do you think it's normal to be this hot?'

I put my hand to her brow, and then Rachel's as a means of comparison.

'I'm not sure. You both feel really hot. But that could be my hands. They feel like they've got shit loads of blood in them right now.'

Rachel muscled in on some of Alana's forehead space, and put her hand up to mine too.

'You're really not much hotter than us, mate,' Rachel reassured. 'Have a feel.'

Alana shakily lifted both hands up and put them to our foreheads. We closed our eyes in deep concentration as though attempting to read each other's thoughts. Sadly moist hands on sticky foreheads didn't equal an innermost-thought conductor (which would have been cool). Instead, the only thing we succeeded in creating was the world's least accurate thermometer.

'I think Colombia's just hot, mate,' I concluded. 'Hold this beer on your neck. It'll cool the blood flow.'

Alana did as she was told, and we sat in contemplative silence for several minutes, willing our friend to cool down. I blew on her a few times, and waved a book in her general direction. At one point I looked down to discover an empty packet of crackers in my hand that I didn't recall buying, or eating. I stared at an adapter plug on the bedside table for a while too. It had attachments.

Alana's condition didn't seem to be improving. As she lay there shivering and taking shallow breaths, my paranoid thoughts were really getting ahead of themselves. I could hear the concerned words of friends and colleagues whirring around in my brain. It was obvious we'd stumbled into something untoward here. Were they in fact going to cut our tits off, as a colleague had suggested back in London? What could they possibly want with them?! Our brownies had clearly been spiked. But by whom? And what were their intentions? Murder? Were they after our possessions, or was this something more sinister? Had one of those torture hostels relocated from Eastern Europe to somewhere no one would ever expect to find them? Perhaps sex traffickers had branched out into different markets, and were now targeting women in their early thirties? It seemed viable. Were there other women here we needed to warn? Maybe if we banded together our collective strength would be enough to derail this kidnap plot, or at least land a few well-timed kicks to the balls of our would-be captors. I was determined to thwart this international terrorist group if it was the last thing I did. Only… I'd have to do it from inside our room because I swear I just heard a noise outside, and I imagine the beach goblins native to this corner of Colombia to be particularly vicious.

'Are you okay in there?' a familiar yet unrecognisable voice asked from outside.

'YEAH,' I shouted, exchanging panicked looks with Rachel. 'Just… err… just hanging out.'

'Okay cool. Are you sure you're okay? You don't need anything?'

Who was this person with their faux-jovial tone, and what the hell did they want with us?

'No thanks, we're fine and dandy in here!' I squawked.

We remained completely silent until we heard whoever it was walk away.

'Who the fuck was that?' I hissed at Rachel and Alana. They shook their heads.

'Do you think it was the dude who sold us the brownies?' Alana asked, reading our minds. 'I saw him watch us walk away.'

'He watched us? Really? Why would he do that?' Rachel asked.

We all just looked at each other with our mouths slightly open. No one had anything resembling an answer.

'I don't know,' I stood and walked to the door, 'but it feels like something's going on here.' I flung open the door with dramatic abandon. No one was there. 'ALL CLEAR!' I reported in a mock old-fashioned-gentleman tone, before saluting the air and beginning to peel a nearby banana.

To calm ourselves down we decided to start listing all the people who could have it in for us. We didn't have many. Everyone who worked at the hostel seemed really nice, but as none of us were accustomed to hanging out with sex traffickers who were we to think we could spot them? We just weren't equipped for the level of critical thinking that sex-criminal spotting required.

Just then a rustling under Alana's bed distracted us. What the hell?! Were 'they' launching an attack from below? This didn't seem feasible. Nevertheless, Rachel and I pulled out our phones to use as torches and adopted different angles around Alana trying to establish the origin of the scratching. Rachel may have been looking for jungle critters but that thought didn't even enter my head – I was looking for signs of floorboard tampering. You know, a trapdoor, a bunk-bed-sized hole, that kind of thing. All I found was a pair of bikini bottoms. What did this mean? Was it some kind of sign? Had these skimpy briefs once belonged to a past victim? Judging by how small they were, she can't have gone for much at the human meat market!

I left the bikini bottoms where they were so as not to alert Rach and Alana to their menacing connotations and took to pacing.

My feet had regained some feeling and walking felt lovely, plus I wanted to think things through and pacing really got things going. I also wanted to be alert… agile… ready to pounce or drop kick anyone that should barge in with a weapon. I couldn't shake the feeling that someone was out there listening in, and I wanted to be the one to catch the sneaky buggers in the act. These people were clearly heartless; lulling us into a false sense of security with their dishevelled, dashing appearances. Blinding us with biceps, homemade hummus and adorable puppies. How could we have been so trusting? How many other women had fallen for this surf-bum guise only to never be seen again? Well whatever happened, I wasn't going to go down without a fight. I'd brought two of my absolute favourite people here and I'd introduced them to our kidnappers, ergo I was responsible for their well-being and their lives. If needs be, I would sacrifice myself. I've got more meat on my bones; I'd go further.

As Rachel and Alana were discussing what could have been in those brownies in place of weed, I padded around listening in different corners of the room for who knows what. Their list was extensive… ketamine… speed… Xanax… poison specifically for humans. None of these made any real sense, but all of them were worrying.

When the feeling someone was just outside became too overbearing, I flung the door open for another look.

THERE HE WAS! THE BROWNIE MAKER! Walking past OUR porch. We made eye contact and I slammed the door.

'Fuck. He's out there!' I stage-whispered.

Alana and Rachel looked back at me in sheer panic.

'What was he doing?' Rachel asked.

'WALKING PAST!' I exclaimed.

'Oh my god!' Alana exhaled from her position on the bed, clutching her hands to her chest.

'Why would he be loitering around here?' I asked. 'Do you think he was looking for you, Alana? Maybe he saw you take a turn for the worse and thought we'd leave you here alone. That's really the only possible explanation!'

'Oh my goodness! I knew it. I told you he was watching me!'

'Guys… he… err… he does work here, remember?' Rachel pointed out. *Woah now, who's side was she on?*

'Yeah… I suppose, Rach. It just seems odd.' I took another stealth-peek out of the door but he was no longer in sight.

Alana sat up and took a shaky glug of beer.

'Don't worry, mate,' Rachel reassured Alana, 'whatever happens, we won't leave you for a second.'

Alana smiled gratefully and I stopped suspecting Rach of collusion.

We still had a problem though. This guy was creepy, and we'd willingly taken drugs from him that made our ankles unsteady. Someone had intended to incapacitate us, we were too scared to leave our room and Alana looked like she was five points from death. The only problem with our problem was that we couldn't concentrate on it for more than 20 seconds before becoming completely distracted.

One minute I'd be trying not to stare too intently at Alana, thinking she looked as though all her blood had been replaced with Tippex, the next I'd find myself over by the windows, marvelling at the sound the shutters made as I repeatedly opened and closed them.

One minute Rachel and I would be discussing an escape plan:

RACHEL: 'I think we should leave at first light.'
AMY: 'Agreed. I trust no one.'
RACHEL: 'Let's leave some money though, yeah? That dinner was delicious.'

AMY: 'Oh, absolutely. That hummus was sensational.'

The next minute we'd be performing an impromptu Irish jig in time with Alana's involuntarily spasming legs, complete with enthusiastic clapping, singing and faux fiddle playing.

One minute I'd be staring at a sign on the wall that read, 'God is watching you', getting creeped out, thinking, *I hope he's the only one.* The next, Rachel and I would be holding each other's elbows, wobbling them about, while thoroughly enjoying how wonderfully floppy our arms and hands felt.

In-between these extreme highs and lows I kept diligent sentry at the only possible entry or exit point. For additional protection, I decided it was wise to shut all the room's doors and windows and to hang up a couple of sarongs over the windows to ensure no would-be peepers would be able to get a view of us panicking. I wanted them to think we were in here readying ourselves for their attack, rather than just becoming increasingly sleepy and dehydrated.

After five minutes I realised the lack of air was doing nothing for Alana, or any of us. We needed a burst of fresh air. I strode purposefully towards the door, steeling myself for whatever may greet me. A battering ram? A human-sized net? Four men wearing balaclavas and wielding tasers?

I took a deep breath and pulled the door wide open, and THERE HE WAS AGAIN. Walking past, carrying a bucket! A bucket!

'ARRGGGGHHHHHH!' I screamed. He started, dropped his bucket and looked at me like I'd lost my mind. Perhaps some kind of bid to throw me off the scent of his imminent bucket-based attack...

We eyeballed each other for a few seconds and then, realising I needed to explain myself, I shouted, 'GO AWAY NOW PLEASE.'

'Amy?' He looked very confused. 'What's going on? Are you girls okay?'

'NO! I MEAN YES... WE'RE EXCELLENT.' I was still shouting.

'O-okay,' he replied, unsure, reaching for his bucket in the flowerbed.

'SORRY ABOUT YOUR BUCKET!' I slammed the door, and turned to see Alana and Rachel looking at me with amusement.

'Well, I think that told him!' Alana joked weakly. Someone had perked up! Come to think of it, she was sitting up and no longer looked like the niece of Voldemort, which was significant progress.

With Alana looking like she might in fact have a bit more time on earth, we made a team decision to go to bed. The intense worry and the fact that our room was as hot as a wood-fired oven had taken its toll and we were all starting to doze off. We were leaving first thing so a good night's shut-eye would be essential. Plus, we needed all our strength in case we needed to run.

I had one final problem: my bed was in the neighbouring dorm. It was only five metres away, but if I wanted to sleep in my own bed I'd have to venture out into the open. I really didn't want to be in a room on my own when that dude was out there carrying a bucket. I may well have managed to scare him away with voice volume and unusual behaviour but that didn't mean I wanted to expose myself to other potential night-time dangers. I was way too embarrassed to admit that, of course, and instead I just shuffled around by the door hoping one of them would clock on. Alana eventually did.

'It's cool, get in with me,' she said, pulling up her mosquito net so I could climb in.

As I lay there in that tiny, sweaty bunk, trying and failing to avoid any skin-on-skin contact with Alana, I decided to sneak a peek at the time. It had to be well after midnight; it felt like we'd been in that room for hours.

It was 9.30 p.m.

What had felt like one of the longest nights of my life had been only an hour and a half. I felt like I'd aged considerably. They'd been right – the brownies were strong.

Just as I was starting to drop off, in stumbled our two roommates, chuckling as enthusiastically as we'd been only a short while ago.

'Blimey! It's fucking hot in here,' said an English male backpacker, flinging open all the window shutters.

'What the…?' he said, tearing down one of the sarong curtains I'd hung. 'Weird.' Clearly he didn't approve of the new decor.

The other roommate didn't even notice. He was far too busy noisily trying to clamber his way into the top bunk.

'SAM! SAM, I CAN'T GET IN!' he declared to his mate. 'I've encountered some kind of impenetrable surface hindering my passage,' he stated, dissolving into giggles.

'That's your mosquito net, you bellend. Look for the corners,' Sam responded helpfully.

As I lay there listening to their nonsense, I allowed myself to relax. If one guy couldn't even get into his bed without assistance, we clearly weren't the only super-high people in this surf camp. What a relief.

Just moments later a voice broke the silence.

'Sam? Are you still awake?'

'Yes Harry. What's up?'

'I… I… I feel really scared.'

You're not the only one, mate.

WINNER = *THE EXPERT*

'Here's the key to understanding risk:
it's largely a matter of opinion.'
Howard Marks

Although I elect Howard the winner in this scenario, it was a very close call. The NHS nurse is of course correct to some extent. Should someone I've never met before come along offering jazzy fruit cocktails and loaded glass pipes, I'd opt to back away slowly. However, as the majority of people I was acquiring things from were strangers, I chose not to suspect everyone of foul play or I'd never have been able to eat or drink, and let's face it, that would've been bloody miserable. I chose to be mindful of who I got things from, especially when those things are known to make me act a little erratically.

In this instance, Howard's advice resonated more. Despite it being highly, highly unlikely that we were going to be kidnapped by surfer dudes, we formed the opinion that we were in grave danger when really the risk was low, especially as they were most likely stoned too. Of course, no one was out to get us. While we were cowering away in our tiny, sweaty room, thinking they were debating how much each of us would get at auction, these guys were just going about their business, trying to make sure that their patrons were having a good time, and that they were safe. I shouldn't have looked for problems where they didn't exist – I shouldn't have tried to find significance in buckets. While I knew I should never be overly trusting or turn a blind eye to warning signs, I knew that I was going to have a better time if I assessed risk with a rational head rather than convincing myself that everyone and their mother was out to ruin my future.

LESSONS LEARNT

It's safe to say those edibles were a lot stronger than we anticipated. We smelt chocolate combined with weed and wanted in. I could say I wouldn't do the same again, but that would be a big ol' porky pie: those brownies were delicious, and they were too damn gooey to be ingested at a sensible pace.

That night I was fortunate. I had my two mates there; I had people on-hand to be weird and paranoid with. I had someone to venture through the shadows with to collect water. I had people to construct elaborately thought-out escape plans with while we speed-ate cheesy biscuits. It's a tried and tested stoner strategy — safety in numbers and all that.

That's not to say that never getting high alone should be a hard and fast rule… I gauge each individual situation using common sense. Arguably one of my favourite days of my travels was spent alone on a beach in Montañita in Ecuador. After realising I'd forgotten my book, rather than head back up the way-too-steep hill to retrieve it, I opted to tuck in to one, then two, of the 'magic brownies' a smiley passer-by was selling. That afternoon, while lazing in the sun watching a group of young Brazilian men frolic in the surf, I reached some important musical conclusions: I listened to NSYNC's *Greatest Hits* and then Backstreet Boys' *Greatest Hits*, and decided once and for all who I prefer (Backstreet Boys, JUST, although I appreciate NSYNC wholeheartedly… especially their choreography). Time well spent, I think you'll agree. This was just another wonderful step on that journey to self-discovery, and it came via the medium of edible weed. I didn't want to rule out finding similar kinds of answers to important life questions with too many rules.

As I was alone, I didn't scoff down the whole lot at once. I took it slowly and was fine. Although I strongly believe that most chocolate things should be eaten as quickly as possible to avoid the wandering hands of anyone wanting to share, those packed with enough weed to fuel Snoop Dogg and his mates for a week should be handled with care. As it's impossible to tell, I always proceed with caution, allowing it a little time to kick in before I declare it isn't working and decide to double up. If unwanted paranoia still strikes, I just try my best to keep positive and ride it out… of course that mural on the toilet door with the red dragon eyes isn't alive and hating me. It's just a cartoon dude, holding a surfboard, under a palm tree. Chill out for Christ's sake.

AN UNFORTUNATE RUN-IN WITH COLOMBIAN DRUG BARONS

FRIENDLY ADVICE:

'Trust no one.'

Jenny Baker, my darling mother

EXPERT ADVICE:

'Listen, smile, agree, and then do whatever the fuck you were gonna do anyway.'

Robert Downey Jr
(No stranger to a drug deal)

I'll admit that over my years on the planet there have been a number of times where I've met my own bloodshot eyes in the mirror and had to shake my head at what I've just done. Where I've pointed a finger at my reflection and had a few harsh words with myself about my continual refusal to engage my brain. Some of them happened in South America, while I was still in the process of figuring stuff out, or more accurately, in this instance – when I cockily thought I'd already done so.

It was my first night in Cartagena on Colombia's northern coastline, a town best known for *Love in the Time of Cholera*, colonial architecture and its charming UNESCO heritage-listed Old Town – a walled city that took over two centuries to complete due to storm damage and pirate attacks. Nowadays, it's admired for its churches, monasteries, swanky palaces and enviable mansions, and many a plaza just perfect for enjoying a coffee or something stronger in the Caribbean heat. There is just one downside: horse and carts are still highly popular, and therefore piles of manure are so abundant that exploring its cobbled streets might as well be called 'High-Stakes Hopscotch'.

I was in town with one thing in mind: partying. Colombia's version of Rio Carnival was set to commence the following morning in Barranquilla, just an hour or so away. This meant the streets and hostels of Cartagena, a city known as a party destination, were jam-packed full of excitable backpackers, each with an abundance of excess energy and very little inclination to wait until the following day to begin expelling it.

I was hanging out with two buddies that I'd met earlier on my journey at a hostel in Medellín: Leanne, a streetwise brunette from the mean streets of Jersey, and Matt, a lovely Aussie dude with the same physique and taste for cycling as Sir Bradley Wiggins. Excited about the festivities starting the next day, we were in the market for 'party favours'… and by that, of course, I mean cocaine.

The usual method of acquisition is tried and tested. You just set up shop in an open-fronted bar along the main backpacker drag and await the arrival of a 'Chiclet Man'. These chaps have earnt themselves this nickname because of the brand of chewing gum (Chiclets) that they flog as a cover for the real sweet treats they're peddling, aka an array of 'sherbet' ideal for snorting. You'll know who they are as they'll lean over the threshold of the bars and cry 'chiclet, chiclet', while wielding a cardboard box seemingly full of nothing more than chewing gum, lollipops, and ciggies.

Despite knowing full well that the Chiclet Men could provide us with all we desired, Leanne was convinced it was possible to find something better. Although I kind of just wanted the free lollipop the Chiclet Men hand out as fun added extras, Leanne had met someone who'd promised her the 'best of the best', and when a promise of that nature is dangled in front of you, you quickly forget the allure of your usual lollipop, even if it does come with a bubblegum centre.

So Leanne, Matt and I set off on our quest to meet Ivan, the young, handsome local Leanne had got chatting to earlier that evening in a nearby bar. Although constantly congested with traffic, Cartagena is an undeniably pretty city. Every building is painted a different colour – bright oranges, mustardy yellows, rose pinks – and the balconies seem to be deliberately decorated to clash as much as possible. From these balconies flow overhanging plants and flowers, and palm trees dot the main squares. Team the colour, the buzz, the greenery and the heat, and you're very much aware that you've reached Colombia's Caribbean coastline.

Bang on time we arrived at the meeting point on Calle 9 just around the corner from our hostel, and there was Ivan, waiting on the pavement opposite, talking on his phone. He was in his early twenties, wore his black hair short and neat and was dressed casually in jeans and a white T-shirt. He grinned, revealing an impressive set of teeth, quickly wrapped up his conversation and greeted us warmly.

'You made it!' he said, kissing Leanne and I on both cheeks and shaking Matt's hand energetically. 'I'm Ivan. It's a pleasure to meet two friends of Leanne.'

'Lovely to meet you too, Ivan,' Matt and I echoed.

'Have I got a treat for you?' he chuckled, leaning in and wiggling his thick eyebrows at us. 'Follow me.' We crossed Calle 9 and headed north, away from the bar.

'Where are we off to, Ivan?' Leanne asked. 'I thought we were just going to hang out back at the bar.'

'We have to meet my friend. He has the stuff. Come, come, it's not far. I'll give you a walking tour of Cartagena!'

The three of us exchanged mildly concerned looks but our respective shrugs indicated a willingness to follow, at least for now. He seemed nice enough.

'So, you guys are from England! Do you live in London?' Ivan enquired.

'I'm actually Australian but I live in Stoke Newington. Amy's in Brixton,' Matt replied, stealing a glance back over his shoulder at the way we came.

'I lived in Elephant Castle for five years. Do you know Elephant Castle?'

'Of course!' I exclaimed, pleased to have something in common with this drug-peddling stranger. 'It's just down the road from me. You must have heard of Brixton?' It didn't appear Ivan had – he just looked back at me blankly. 'At the end of the Victoria line, just past Stockwell? No?' That seemed a bit odd – maybe he was more of a bus man.

We hung a right and continued on. This street was a lot quieter, and markedly darker than the roads near our hostel.

'Okay, well I'm surprised you don't know it,' I continued, filling the slightly awkward silence with chit-chat. 'It's just down the road and it's a cool spot. If you ever go back, you should definitely visit. How come you decided to move home?'

'I missed Colombia! How could I not? The people, the heat, the music. This is heaven right here. Cartagena is my home.

The people are good. In London, people frown all the time,' he wrinkled his forehead to illustrate his point, and to ensure we fully understood he was directly insulting us. 'Here, we smile. Plus, I have a beautiful daughter.'

Ivan pulled his phone from his pocket, and started scrolling through pictures of an adorable toddler. There she was holding a yellow teddy, there playing in the sea, sitting on the back of a large dog...

'Her name is Tatiana. She's two and a half.'

While Leanne leaned in to take a closer look, I seized the opportunity to whisper my growing concerns to Matt.

'Dude... where do you suppose we're being taken?'

'No idea. No idea.' Matt rubbed a worried hand over his shaven head and looked around. There wasn't much to identify the street by – the colourful, flower-covered houses were gone, and instead we were surrounded by nondescript office buildings and the odd bank.

As Ivan was deep in animated conversation with Leanne about Tatiana, it felt rude to interrupt, so we just carried on following them.

'Don't worry, mate, we'll be all right. I'm a fast runner,' Matt joked. 'If anyone points a gun at us, I'll run and get help. I promise I'll *definitely* come back.'

Humour... yes... this felt better than suspicion and fear.

I retaliated, 'You won't see me for dust, mate. You can call me Usain Baker if you want. People do already.'

I was lying, of course. Realistically the only thing I have in common with Usain Bolt is my love of chicken nuggets. I really hoped we wouldn't be made to run. It was hot, I was wearing a dress and my flip-flops facilitated very little purchase on Cartagena's slippery cobbled streets. Besides, I'd only ever participated in games of the High-Stakes Hopscotch I mentioned earlier at a walking pace, and in daylight – I had no desire whatsoever to up the ante.

After maybe 15 more minutes of walking, we arrived at our destination: a first-floor bar with a huge open window overlooking the street. It was accessible via one narrow, poorly lit, rickety staircase, which ordinarily I'd never have risked even the tip of my toe on. However, as it was a public space, and not an alleyway, it seemed a preferable choice at this point in time. I could see people. I could hear merriment. At least if death were imminent there would be witnesses to our demise. Perhaps they'd find it in their hearts to explain to my parents that in my final seconds I looked very, very sorry for my stupidity.

The bar we walked into was not the fun, safer environment we'd been hoping for. We stood out, like badgers in a cattery, and no one looked happy to see us. Smiling and waving didn't help matters either. I clocked some eye rolls from the crowd of perhaps ten patrons. I saw people lean in and whisper things to their drinking buddies. A couple of ladies made a point of looking us up and down before rolling their eyes and turning their backs. There were a few too many pointed glances being exchanged for my liking. Even the barmen nudged each other and shook their heads in thinly veiled disgust before indicating that we should sit in a booth in the far corner, which was only accessible by wading through a sea of tightly packed metal chairs. They seemed most keen to tuck us away, and to hinder any escape attempts.

We noisily and ungracefully negotiated our way through the chair fortress to our corner booth while Ivan went to the bar to acquire us some beers. As soon as we sat down, I seized the opportunity to demonstrate that I was the biggest scaredy-cat in our group.

'Guys, I don't feel a hundred per cent comfortable right now. Do you? This feels really fucking dodgy, plus it's pretty obvious that everyone in here knows what's going on and absolutely hates us.'

'I know,' Leanne said, nervously looking around. 'It does feel off. But… you know, Ivan seems nice, and a couple of my mates told me that they got great stuff through a guy they met on the street.'

'I'm sure it's fine,' Matt reassured us. 'We're here now. Let's just get it, get out and forget we were ever this brainless. How much is it, by the way?'

'Good point; I'm not actually sure. All I know is that we're meeting his mate here.' Leanne clocked Ivan coming back, and asked him the same question.

'Oh, don't worry about that. My friend, he has all the answers and he'll be five minutes. Relax! Enjoy the music.'

It was hard not to. Whether or not it was in protest at our arrival, the already loud reggaeton music had just been cranked up so much it felt like the DJ had set up his decks in my skull. Perhaps it was his attempt to kick-start our clearly sluggish brains into realising that what we were doing was downright reckless.

We leaned back and took synchronised glugs on our beers to relieve our nervous, dry mouths. I commenced a silent mantra of, *'we'll be fine, we'll be fine, of course we'll be fine,'* while biting off what was left of my fingernails. With any luck this would be over soon so we could hotfoot it back to where all the non-threatening, too-drunk-to-inflict-violence people were. I certainly knew the way. I'd fear-mapped it in my brain. Running through it was helping distract me from an elaborately gruesome daydream in which we were all frog-marched to a dark corner of Cartagena's port, before being shot at point-blank range.

Ivan was proving to be quite the chatty Cathy. He'd clocked our hushed whispers and shifty eyes, and was doing his very best to fill our terror-laden silence with chat about his love for his family. And he left no family member uncovered. Once he'd talked us through every picture of Tatiana, he moved on to speaking about his sisters, his brother, his six-year-old nephew. Matt tried to ask him about his life in Elephant and Castle, but every time he did Ivan would just say, 'Yes, Elephant Castle,' and then return to telling us things we didn't care about, which bizarrely included his mum's favourite day of the week (Thursday). This saddened me because I realised I didn't know my mum's favourite day of the week. Friday? Tuesday? I didn't know! Would I ever see her again to ask the question?

Just as I got swept away on a fantasy of my lovely, kind mother materialising to rush me away from this nightmare scenario, the booth went black. Blocking the only rays of light were three enormous men standing in V-formation. At the front was who I assumed was Ivan's mate, an overweight bald man perhaps in his late thirties, with a pink Ralph Lauren T-shirt, a huge watch and a fat neck. The two men flanking him were older and unsmiling. Fat Neck sat down in front of us, and his two mates took up sentry at the exit to the booth, thus rendering it inescapable, unless you went through them. Given their frowny faces and enormous, gnarled hands that would have been no cuddle party. These guys looked mean. Like they'd bully small business owners, steal people's food as they ate and key strangers' cars for thrills.

Fat Neck barely nodded at Ivan, he was too busy slowly and obviously sizing each of us up. We were an odd party of seven: two English chicks, an Aussie, a suddenly nervous-looking local, two retired football hooligans and a man who resembled the rapper, Fat Joe. His pink T-shirt and menacing smile were doing little to quell my fears. He could have eaten me in a human-sized baguette and still have room for ice cream.

'Welcome to Cartagena, amigos. I hear you're looking for the good stuff.'

We all nodded and forced smiles.

'How much for five grams?' Leanne enquired.

'Oh, don't you worry. You try first and then we'll talk money.'

'Could you please just tell us now?' I asked.

'No, no,' he smiled. 'You're our guests. You must try it first.'

Fat Neck pressed a cling-filmed package into Leanne's hand, and nodded towards a bathroom, which was diagonally opposite our secluded corner, via the sea of metal chairs, all the disapproving customers and the bar. For some reason rather than point out that it might be more subtle to do it where we sat, in the shadows of the booth, Leanne and I did exactly as he said. Probably because he had murder in his cold, black eyes. Everyone in the bar turned to look at us as we moved through the chair assault course en route to the one bathroom stall. This was pure idiocy. Anyone with even half a brain would be able to work out what two Western women sharing a drink with three frightening men might be doing in a bathroom together in a location known for rowdy backpackers. However, rather than risk tipping the boat or coming across as impolite, we chose to say nothing and do exactly as this terrifying specimen commanded. It was as though his deep voice had lured us into some kind of buffoon trance. When we were in the stall, I again voiced my concern that we were acting like complete simpletons.

'I know, mate,' Leanne replied. 'I completely agree, but let's just try this, pay the man and get the fuck out of here.'

Goods tested, we headed back to the booth via the site of what must have once been Colombia's biggest musical-chairs competition. We squeezed our way past the two bruisers flanking the booth. I smiled at them, but they were not at all interested in eye contact or pleasantries. They were too busy looking simultaneously sleepy and mean.

'Well?' Fat Neck asked, arms folded across his bulbous stomach.

'It seems fine. We just need to know how much it is,' I answered.

Fat Neck paused, contemplating the question.

'Five million.'

'Pardon?' Leanne exclaimed.

'Five million,' he repeated, his smile nowhere to be seen.

Five grams of coke from the Chiclet Man would have cost us £40. Fat Neck was insisting on around £1,500.

We laughed nervously and looked to Ivan to clear this matter up. His hands were in his lap, his head hanging low.

'No way, man,' Matt exclaimed. 'That can't be right. That's a lot of money.'

'If I say it's right, it's right.'

My legs chose that moment to start shaking.

'But we don't have five million!' I said.

'Then you go get it.' Fat Neck was not messing around.

'But that's a crazy amount. We've never paid that much,' Leanne argued.

'Well you've never bought from me.' He leaned back on his stool, tilted his head and curled his lip. He was doing a jolly good job at being menacing. I wanted to speak up, but I was fighting an urgent need to put my head between my knees. My vision was blurry, my whole body was stiff and my mouth was so dry that even if I had have had something productive to say, I don't think I'd have been able to prise it open.

'We haven't got that much money. Not on us, *or* in our accounts!' Matt was quick to stress.

'Ha… I don't believe you.' He paused before leaning towards us, and speaking slowly: 'Listen my friends, the fact is, you sampled my produce, and now you must pay.'

'Come on, man. Give us a break,' Matt persisted.

My knees were full-on knocking now. I could see my mum's beautiful face in my head mouthing the words, 'Why, Amy? Why would you do this to us? To your family!'

'Hold on. I do not give "breaks". Do you not know who I am?'

We looked at him, at each other, at Ivan, hoping for some answers. We shook our heads to indicate we had no bloody clue who he was, and that we were keen for him to enlighten us. *And then, hopefully, release us, because we hadn't been in possession of all the facts and that was obviously unfair.*

'I'm from the Medellín Cartel.'

Having gone on the Pablo Escobar tour back in Medellín, I knew instantly that this was not good news. Not good news at all. In fact, it seemed we were royally fucked. In my mind 'cartel' was the word for a collective of bad people with a penchant for firing bullets at the backs of people's heads. *Oh god – this could really be it.*

'You sample the merchandise, you pay… or someone else has to pay.' He sneered at Ivan ominously, who looked at us in panic and then back down to his hands.

'Listen,' Leanne began, bravely. 'We don't have that money, and we can't get it. We can give you a bit less. Would you accept less? How about one and a half million?'

That's still a rather pricey £390, but it was far more reasonable – I'd gladly pay it to get as far away from here as possible.

'Five million is the price. I know you have the money. You don't want the Medellín Cartel to know where you're staying, do you?' he said, leaning towards me and pointing his finger in my face, about five centimetres from my nose. 'Like I do.'

The upper-lip sweat chose that moment to show up.

'How do you…' I started but soon trailed off when I saw he was looking at my neon orange wristband, which was emblazoned with the name of my hostel. It was even glowing obnoxiously under the booth's shitty neon light.

I looked to Matt and Leanne in panic. They weren't staying in the same place but they both looked suitably horrified on my behalf. If I got out of this alive, who's to say that in a couple of hours I wouldn't be dragged from my bed by balaclava-wearing heavies who'd force me to kneel on my whitewashed balcony before shooting me execution-style as a warning to other tourists.

Head in hands, I looked at the floor. The faces of my devastated parents greeted me. Think of the things I'd never get to do, the things I'd never get to say, the babies I'd never get to grow! I'd never eaten lobster, for Christ's sake! I'd never been to Hawaii!

While I got increasingly hysterical looking down at the orange wristband that had doomed me, Leanne and Matt apparently still possessed the wherewithal to keep negotiating. I just wasn't able to hear them over the sound of all my body's blood rushing to my ears. When I eventually snapped back to it, Leanne was proving quite the badass.

'We can't pay you. We won't pay you. Ivan, why did you bring us here? Why have you done this? We thought you were our friend.'

Matt appeared generally affronted. 'You showed us pictures of your daughter, man. What the fuck? You set us up!'

Fat Neck glared at Ivan. He didn't seem happy with him either, and was getting increasingly agitated as he rejected counter-offer after counter-offer.

'Look, the absolute most we can give you is two million. That's a lot more than we would pay elsewhere. That's all we have. Please!' Leanne persisted.

'How many times do I have to tell you before I have to hurt you?'

Ivan chose that moment to look up and start appealing: 'Please. If you don't pay, they'll hurt you, they'll hurt me. They'll hurt my family. Please… remember Tatiana.'

Fat Neck was really fidgeting in his seat now, balling his fists and getting redder and redder.

He pointed at Matt. 'If you don't pay, we fight.'

'Fine by me!' Matt declared, throwing his hands in the air. 'If it means this can be over, let's go outside right now.' Leanne and I looked at our brave friend with pure love. I did not fancy his chances.

Fat Neck seemed a little thrown. It was clear he hadn't been expecting Matt to be so up for a rumble.

'I… I don't want to make a scene. We just want our money. You know, the Cali Cartel don't take kindly to non-payment.'

At that Matt and Leanne perked up. 'The what cartel?' Leanne asked. 'I thought you said Medellín Cartel.'

'Yes, Medellín Cartel.'

'You just said Cali, dude,' Leanne said with a valiant dose of sass I'd never have chanced.

Surely that's the coke kicking in, making her braver, I thought to myself as I clenched and unclenched my jaw, and took my own pulse. *A cartel's a cartel; who cares where it's located?* I held my beer to my jugular to try to cool my temperature. *I hope my heart doesn't explode. It feels like it's going to explode.*

'Well?' Leanne challenged. 'Which one is it?'

'I didn't say that,' Fat Neck answered, looking surprisingly shaken. He and Ivan exchanged a quick look, and with that everything became clear – these jokers were having us on! This was nothing more than a blatant attempt at daylight robbery. The work of opportunists. Forgetful opportunists who, now you come to mention it, were *terrible* at acting. *Elephant Castle! How can you live in Elephant and Castle and not know Brixton? That's a complete impossibility! He must have said it because he knows a lot of Colombians live there.* The penny was slowly dropping.

'I... I... I want my money, or you and I outside,' he jabbed his finger at Matt's face, before turning to Ivan. 'You! You sort this, okay!' and then he stood up suddenly, turned around and went outside. The two sleepy heavies sighed resignedly and followed behind. Now I was emerging from my fear trance, the family resemblance with Fat Neck was startling – these heavies were probably uncles or dads dragged away from the TV by the promise of a few bob from their cocky son and his mate.

We were left alone with Ivan, who was once again avoiding eye contact by staring at the ground.

'Please just pay,' he pleaded.

Matt shook his head. 'No way! We're onto you. We know these guys aren't part of any cartel. You're just saying that to scare us into paying you!'

Ivan shook his head. As did I... but more in a bid to get my brain working fully again. *Surely we should pay them something, even if it's just to avoid any chance of violent repercussions? That seemed worth it to me! Did I still need to move hostels? Surely I should still move hostels – I hope I can find a new hostel at this time of night!*

'Please, my family, he'll hurt me, he'll hurt all of us. I beg you.'

'Give it up, Ivan. We know you're lying,' challenged Matt. This time, rather than denying it, Ivan raised his hands in defeat, shrugged and gave us a defeated smile.

We all balked at his revelation like he'd been a close friend. The fact was we'd known this guy for 40 minutes – why we were so hurt that he'd try to take us for a ride, I have no idea.

'Ivan! We'll pay you for the beers, but we're leaving immediately,' Leanne stood up, threw some cash on the table, and then grabbed my shaky hand and hauled me to my feet. 'Come on, Amy!'

There was only one exit, down the rickety stairs, and I was still panicking. They might not be from any cartel, but they were still criminals, and there was a good chance they'd be blocking our path. Maybe they'd gone to get their weapons?

'Just keep moving,' she said as we raced down the empty stairwell, and broke into a run across the street. Fortunately there was no oncoming traffic. Fat Neck and his dads, who were smoking cigarettes just to the right of the bar entrance, started shouting at us as we dashed into the night – we didn't turn around to ask them to enunciate.

After a few wrong turns we found ourselves rejoining a bustling street rammed full of laughing tourists who hadn't yet had the fear of god put into them by faux-gangsters.

'Leanne!' we heard an approaching guy shout. It was one of Leanne's friends from her hostel. As they stopped to chat, Matt and I took the opportunity to hug each other, and swear a lot. What we overheard was most interesting.

'I've been looking for you everywhere. Did you go and meet that random local? I wanted to warn you... a guy at my hostel just told me he got robbed of nearly a thousand dollars last night by some chancers who claimed to be from the Cali Cartel. He saw the very same dude working in a shoe shop today! The receptionist at his hostel told him Cartagena's famous for this kind of scam. Are you okay?'

Leanne spun around to look at us wide-eyed.
I still moved hostels.

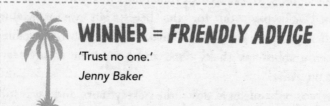

WINNER = *FRIENDLY ADVICE*

'Trust no one.'
Jenny Baker

RDJ, I followed your words to the letter, and things did not go well for me. I listened, smiled, agreed, did what I wanted, and the place I ended up in was bloody scary.

Jennifer Baker, you wise angel. Although I'll admit I thought these words a tad overzealous at the time, your advice to trust no one proved most shrewd in this instance. Not once in my life have I considered recent acquaintances met on street corners to be viable businessmen, or good sorts, so I have no idea why I chose that balmy night in Cartagena to start. I was stupid. I'm sorry. I've learnt my lesson. I won't ever do it again.

LESSONS LEARNT

At this stage, I'd been away for five and a half months. I'd made my way through five countries with absolutely no trouble. I felt confident and at home, and I foolishly thought that everything would be okay. I let my guard down and allowed myself to become cocky. So cocky that I completely ignored my instincts, which, for the record, were freaking out, kicking me in the shins and pinching the backs of my arms, yet I still didn't take any sensible action to remove myself from the situation. If this were a horror film, the whole cinema would have been hurling popcorn at the screen and screaming at us to not go any further.

I chose to continue being in a situation that made me incredibly uncomfortable from start to finish, mostly because I was in a group of people, and I naively thought that because everything on my trip had gone pretty much to plan so far, that it would in this *highly* dubious situation too. Leanne and Matt were aware of how suspicious it was – we all were – but we went along with it up until the point where it actually felt dangerous. Maybe it was because two thirds of us were British, people for whom politeness all too often seems to trump good sense. Whatever the reason, rather than acknowledging all the signs that something was up while we were out in the open, we let ourselves be led into deeper trouble, like tanned, scruffy, silly little lemmings.

This taught me that learning to listen to myself is going to be an ongoing process that will involve repeated mistakes and new realisations. I hadn't miraculously figured out the right ways to behave in every situation just because I'd got myself as far as Colombia. I learnt that realistically, I'm never going to be too far away from another fuck up. Although frightening, this served as an important reminder to not walk around in a dream thinking that everyone wants to give me kittens and baskets of cash. Being consciously aware of what I'm doing in order to make correct decisions takes practice.

I am well aware that we were LUCKY. Things could have gone horribly, horribly wrong, and we'd only have had ourselves to blame. Fortunately these guys weren't dangerous… or at least as dangerous as they were making out. Fortunately we (and by 'we', I mean Leanne and Matt) saw through it. Had I been alone, I would have undoubtedly given them my entire life savings.

To not mention cocaine or to pretend that it isn't everywhere in South America would be to provide a dishonest account of how things are. The problem is that as it's so rife in pretty much every country I visited, and so many people are doing it, it's easy to forget that it's illegal, that it has caused untold amounts of suffering and that it's dangerous to acquire. We were naive and ignorant that night, and well and truly deserved the fright we got in return. I'm not going to preach about not indulging in illegal things – it's the choice of each individual. What I will say is that it's important to consider the realistic side of buying and doing drugs. The offended faces of the people in the bar who knew what we were up to stick with me far more than those of Fat Neck and Ivan. As I'd failed to give the situation the thought it deserved, I ended up being disrespectful and that's not a mistake I'll make again.

HOW NOT TO BEHAVE AROUND MEN

FRIENDLY ADVICE:

'Go break some hearts, babes!'

Tamsin, favourite colleague

EXPERT ADVICE:

'Keeping your emotions all locked up is something that's unfair to you. When you clearly know how you feel, you should say it.'

Taylor Swift

(Lots of romantic experience)

I met Lucas at Costeño Beach, the same spot where Rachel, Alana and I dined upon the weed brownies that almost ate our souls. In fact, he was the dude whose cargo shorts I had a good old fiddle with when I discovered an intense passion for zips. Clearly, demonstrating nimble finger work right off the bat is alluring to the opposite sex, because it didn't put him off – in fact, it served to entice. It only took me a week or so to stop being paranoid that he thought me odd before I noticed that his choice of shorts each day seemed to feature an increasing number of zips and attachments. Was it a seduction tactic? Probably not. Did I take it as an invitation to show interest in his bottom half? Yes, I did.

Lucas was Swedish, long-haired, subtly muscly and, most importantly, shirtless 98 per cent of the time (such is the wonder of hot countries). In other news, he spent a lot of time making sure his ponytail was 'just so', was impeccably colour-coordinated and was constantly smoking the strongest of joints. He also had a good walk; kinda flouncy.

Lucas wasn't a talker so it was difficult to gauge what he was thinking, and I wasn't trying. That's why what happened between us came as a bit of a surprise – a surprise I found myself going along with. One day we were sharing a joint; the next he started stroking my back seemingly out of nowhere; a couple of days later we hooked up; and then BLAMMO – I had a boyfriend. It moved that fast. On one hand it was nice – it was like having sex with Thor (before he got ripped lumping that massive hammer around). On the other, it soon became apparent that he felt the need to keep one hand upon my person at all times, and didn't like it much when I spoke to other dudes. Ideally, I would have liked him to have taken it down between five and eight notches. Hopefully that leap would've meant I was once again able to breathe my own air. Despite the tendency towards clinginess, Lucas was hot. So hot that I was happy to excuse the fact that we didn't have much to say to each other. So hot that I managed to successfully forget I was trying to make more reasoned, thought-out decisions about how to proceed. And so hot that on the day of the unprovoked stroking, I was so delighted, I happily lay there, just letting it happen, knowing full well I was getting sunburnt. I didn't regret it – the burnt bits were totally worth it.

After Rachel and Alana went home I was faced with having to accept that my days of travelling were numbered. I had three weeks left in Colombia before I had to be in Bogotá for a flight home, and that realisation did not please me. It was around this stage that I started getting a little hot around the collar – and that had nothing to do with the 30-degree heat, and all to do with the fact that so far I hadn't cracked all of life's big codes. Up until now, I had felt like time was on my side. I'd had an age to start clocking up the articles I'd envisioned myself writing the whole way round, I'd had loads of places left on my 'to-visit' list, I still had cash, and I had my mates coming to visit me. Now they were gone, my bank balance was in decline and it was becoming more of a challenge to ignore the fact that I was on the home stretch.

I knew from day one that Lucas was a fling, but as he was more enjoyable than confronting my reality, I found myself dedicating more time to him than I should have. Rather than sensibly plan my next three weeks to get the most from every day, I chose to lie back, ignore it and instead focus on how good he looked emerging from the waves, all wet. I chose to bury my head in the sand, which was easy because I was at a beach, and there were a lot of great people to party with. I'd made some good friends at Costeño, and was utterly enamoured of the life that the two owners, Canadian brothers Brian and Colm, had built for themselves here on Colombia's Caribbean coast. The fact that they were so successful and at the same time living such an idyllic life in a beautiful location made me reconsider how I defined success. Maybe success actually meant finding a location you're happy in, rather than a career? Perhaps all the advice I'd received over the years hadn't worked because none of it had pointed me towards life on a Caribbean beach?

As well as the owners, there were a lot of people hanging around that stretch of coastline that had interesting outlooks on life – outlooks that said 'fuck it' to more traditional ways of living, and 'hell yeah' to finding the exact niche that allowed them to live the life they wanted. I was hanging out a lot with an American girl called Mandolin, who was in the process of setting up her own eco-adventure yoga retreats. She was in town getting things in place for her first retreat, which she had people jetting in from the USA for in a couple of weeks' time.

I'd also got to know an Aussie called Chris – the barman at La Brisa Loca, a hostel in Santa Marta. Chris was midway through an epic journey: he'd bought himself a van over a year before in Vancouver, named it Walter, and headed south. Although he was currently enjoying a money-saving pit stop in Colombia, his final destination was Ushuaia, the southernmost city in South America, aptly dubbed 'The End of the World'.

I warmed to Chris instantly because of his smiley face, and the fact that he was so easy to talk to. There were a number of times I was attempting to drag conversation out of Lucas, and Chris would bowl up and the chat would instantly flow. I was also amused by the fact that I'd never before encountered a man so Australian… and I'd lived there for three years. I believe wholeheartedly if everyone the world over was asked to draw a cartoon Australian, Chris would be the real-life equivalent of 99 per cent of people's renderings. Shove a cork hat over his long blond curls and a can of Foster's in his hand and it'd be only seconds before he was crowned national mascot of Australia. Fuck the kangaroo, he's had his day.

'So, I leave tomorrow,' Lucas reminded me as we swung in adjacent hammocks, me reading, he listening to some European techno music I couldn't bring myself to form an opinion on.

'Yeah, yeah. I know. Ah, man.'

'You could always come too?'

'Hmm. Maybe. We'll see. First, I'm going to go to Casa Elemento with Mandolin. I need to take a bit of time to figure out what I'm doing.'

'Okay, sure.' He shrugged, lay back, and lit his joint. And thus concluded one of our longest chats.

The next day, Lucas rolled out of Costeño and I resumed my horizontal position on the beach.

'Hey, Aimz.' Mandolin wandered over, fresh from teaching a yoga class, and joined me on the sun lounger. 'You bummed out about Lucas?'

'Nah, I'm fine.'

'Well, I've got an idea that might appeal: you don't want to go home, right? So why don't you change your flight, and come on my yoga retreat? Changing the flight won't cost much, I'd love to have you there and if you write about it I'll cut you a sweet deal.'

In the blink of an eye I had a plan! I could delay my flight a little, and take some real time to figure out what my next steps would be. A retreat would be the perfect environment. We'd be in the mountains, hiking, doing yoga, eating well – it was a complete no-brainer. It was just what I needed at this important time.

Confident that I was taking productive action, I immediately turned around and took a giant backwards step. Lucas had left to head south from Santa Marta to Medellín with a group of our mates, and I should have left it there. I should have stood waving my hanky forlornly as my moody Nordic prince sped off into the night, dried my tears (*if* they were even there) and merrily pranced on to pastures new. Now I had some time to kill before I went on Mandolin's yoga retreat. But rather than spend it addressing some of the things I needed to address – you know, where I'd live, how I'd earn money, how I was going to ensure this trip hadn't just been a five-month jolly – I decided to go and ignore it a little longer, by putting myself in the company of a dude I knew wasn't right for me, despite vowing every step of the way not to do such a thing. I'd been adamant I wouldn't waste time on guys when I could have been spending essential time with myself. Yet here I was googling how much a return plane ticket to Medellín would cost me. Only £30 as it turned out… the same as a ticket to Thorpe Park… only with a guarantee of way more rides! It seemed like money well spent to me. Plus, did it really matter that I wasn't that into it if we were both having a good time? I was on holiday after all; a holiday that wasn't going to last for that much longer. Fuck sitting down and formulating a strategy, the number one thing holidays are supposed to provide is pleasure. I ummed and ahhed for oh, I don't know, eight minutes, and then splashed the cash for a dirty long weekend in Medellín. I had a week to kill before the retreat – why not spend a bit of it boning He-Man's leaner brother?

▲▲▲▲▲▲▲▲

'Yo, Aimz,' Chris greeted me as I sat down at the bar in La Brisa Loca. He turned around to grab me a beer and I found myself absent-mindedly clocking how broad his shoulders were. 'Where's the boyfriend?' he grinned, placing my beer in front of me.

'Lucas? Oh, he left. He's heading to Medellín.'

'Kept you on a tight leash, that one, eh?'

I chuckled, 'So you noticed too?'

'It was impossible not to, mate.'

'Well, you know, we hooked up and then he instantly wanted to be my boyfriend. It's happened before, it'll no doubt happen again. He is but human, Christopher. Powerless to these charms.' I pointed both my thumbs at my joking face, and treated him to a wink.

'Is that right?'

I shrugged faux-smugly, and toasted his glass.

Chris laughed, 'Well he's onto something I reckon.' And with
that he turned away to serve someone else.

Oh!

Wait, what?

Hmmm…

Interesting.

▲▲▲▲▲▲▲

A day or so later I was on a hike with Mandolin and Sean, one of
Chris's fellow barmen and passenger on Walter for the past couple
of months. Over the course of our hike, Chris and the list of his
wide-ranging attributes became the hot topic of conversation.
Although I'd secretly enjoyed a couple of sexy thoughts about
him, this chat just sealed the deal. My nipples were fully erect and
pointing in his direction. Surprising myself, I came right out and
asked Sean whether he thought Chris might be into 'it' if I were
to express my desire to see him shortless.

Sean laughed and pointed a finger at me. 'I knew it. I bloody
knew it! Sure, Aimz, I reckon it'd be a definite yes, but there's only
one way to find out!'

I nodded. 'Cool.'

'Well, are you gonna ask him?' he urged. 'I think you should.'

'Yeah, yeah,' I said nonchalantly, already strategising my
approach, 'I probably will.'

This decision to be upfront was quite the change from the norm
for me. Usually when I identify someone I fancy I dilly-dally
around a little bit making eyes (read: getting too drunk in front of
them), and then either decide to bite the bullet or miss my chance.
I didn't have the patience for that now. I wanted to know. From
what I knew of Chris, he seemed like he'd handle it well, whether

the answer were 'yay' or 'nay'. I couldn't picture him yelling it from the rooftops or doing a lap of honour around the hostel pool before shouting 'NO' in my face. If he said yes, it was go time. If he said no, I knew I could moonwalk away from the situation with my pride still very much intact. I'd sleep easy, safe in the knowledge I'd taken the matter into my own hands. This assertive approach felt refreshing, and far preferable to my usual tactic of sitting around, twiddling my thumbs, hoping he might.

Aside from the niggly bigger questions about my future, my confidence was through the roof at the time as a result of successfully getting myself where I needed to be, meeting great people to socialise with and discovering a corner of the country where I felt happy. I felt empowered and in control – like I could take on anything. It was far easier to pursue fun when I felt this good, than to let myself get bummed out by thoughts of my future.

When the time came to approach Chris, my wholly unoriginal, 'So… umm… hey… what time do you… err… knock off?' was well-received.

▲▲▲▲▲▲▲

Having spent the night with Chris, I awoke early to catch my flight to Medellín.

Yes, I know, I was heading to see Lucas that very day.

Yes, I know, this would be frowned upon in many a circle of those with sticks wedged firmly up their bottoms.

And yet I didn't care.

I felt comfortable with my decision. These were two fine-looking young men, and I… well I was clearly a sexual sorceress sent back from the future with the sole task of seducing long-locked hunks. If only I'd remembered to pack my cape. As I lay down to catch some much-needed sleep on the backseat of the minibus transporting me to the airport, I congratulated myself for finally working out how to keep emotions out of romantic encounters. Chris was great, had stuff to say and made me laugh, yet I wasn't daydreaming about an imagined future, as I had with Daniel. And Lucas – well, I knew he wasn't for me, but I also knew we were physically compatible and that was all I wanted from this trip to Medellín. Perhaps at last I'd learnt to keep a rational head in affairs of the heart.

This self-conviction diminished somewhat as I drew nearer to Medellín, where Lucas was waiting.

'Amy!' Lucas shouted from a table outside a coffee house across the street. The minute I saw him the realisation that I shouldn't have gone slapped me in the face. I didn't feel anything resembling happiness – instead I was reminded of the hard work involved in trying to get to know him.

We were meeting at a hostel in El Poblado; an area in the south of Medellín known for its cool, healthy eateries, smoothie bars and coffee shops, and for being the location of the majority of the city's hostels.

'So, how was your flight?'

'Yeah, fine! How are you liking Medellín? Have you seen much of it yet?'

'Not really. I've just been hanging out – haven't done much yet.'

'Cool. How are the gang?'

'Fine.'

'Great. I'm looking forward to seeing them.'

After our initial catch up was over, we walked along the street towards the hostel in complete silence. This lack of conversation hadn't been so noticeable when we'd been in a peaceful place by the beach, but now that we were in a busy city the quiet between us felt deafening. I couldn't think of anything to say – and after a night with Chris where we couldn't stop talking, my incompatibility with Lucas was blatant. I quickly shook thoughts of Chris from my head. I knew that thinking about someone else when I'd just flown to see Lucas was shitty behaviour – it was the exact opposite of how I'd wish to be treated.

To begin with, Lucas did sweet things, like buy me coffee every morning and wear an England baseball cap in my honour (I was backpacking – I was easily pleased).

Then he started to do irritating things, like neglect to pass on messages from our mates so that they'd leave for the day without me knowing, and we wouldn't get to hang out. It pissed me off. I'd come to see him for night-time fun, but he was travelling with a group of our friends from Costeño Beach and I wanted to hang out with them too.

The morning before I was due to leave, Lucas and I were out on our sunny balcony. We were sitting in silence, drinking coffee and eating Portuguese custard tarts when he chose that moment to be the most vocal he had been since we'd met.

'Amy? Tell me, I want to know, do you want a baby?'

I stopped mid-bite. Seeing as he'd only asked me ten or so questions in the whole time I had known him, his intense question and hostile tone of voice set warning bells a-clangin'.

'What do you mean, Lucas? Do you mean in the future?'

'Not in the future. Now. Is that what you want? Is that what you want from me?'

His tone was unmistakeably accusatory, like he'd been thinking this for some time.

'What?! No! That's ridiculous. We barely know each other.'

'I feel like that's what you want.'

'Well I assure you that a baby is as far from my mind as it's possible to be.'

'You know some girls, that's all they want. A man like me, to pay for things.'

'Are you kidding me?' I was furious at him. How could he think that I had some kind of cunning plan to entrap him? How long had he been thinking this?

'Some girls… they want to keep men, so they get pregnant. Is that why this is happening?'

I shook my head at him and fought the urge to throw my tart at his stupid face.

'I'm not that girl, Lucas. I don't want *anything* from you, especially not your fucking baby.'

He looked at me, and I could feel him wrestling over whether or not to believe me.

'But… if you did get pregnant?'

I stood up and made for the door. 'I don't want your baby.'

'Tell me what you'd do.'

I slammed the door behind me.

This aggressive line of questioning was a glaring turn-off that obviously brought all nudity to an end once and for all. The morning I left Medellín my mind was well and truly made up: I did not want to see Lucas again. Ever. I was angry I'd wasted time and money on someone like him. I'd assumed he was just quiet, but there must have been a lot going on in his head the whole time that he didn't voice. Although defiant, I instantly felt the impact of this enormous insult take a huge chunk out of my confidence. I'd felt great, and as though I'd finally managed to conquer my tendency to care too much about what people think about me – and then, in two minutes, I learnt that someone I'd thought liked me actually had an incredibly low opinion of me. If he thought that of me, what did other people think? If he got such a wildly incorrect impression of me, what impression had I been making on other people?

▲▲▲▲▲▲▲

I returned to Santa Marta on the eve of the yoga retreat, determined to remove all thoughts of Lucas from my head. I was sitting at the hostel bar, chatting away to Chris, three beers fizzing in my stomach, when the rest of the yoga gang arrived, having just flown in from the USA. First impressions revealed them to be immaculate. Whereas the vast majority of earthlings resemble the walking dead after a six-hour flight, these yogis were shimmering visions of perfection. Glistening from a refreshing dip in the hostel pool, they strutted around the hostel in their swimmers, safe in the knowledge that there wasn't an area of flesh not tightly tucked exactly where it was supposed to be.

The group included Corey — a successful yoga-teacher-cum-lifestyle-guru, who had flown in especially to be Mandolin's co-lead for the retreat. Everyone on the retreat was there because they were Corey's pupils and friends back in the USA, and it wasn't hard to see why people looked to him for guidance, inspiration and body motivation: here was a man with the fullest lips and most symmetrical face I'd ever seen. Corey's looks were so perfect he could have made it in Hollywood without uttering one word... or moving a muscle. When he did talk, however, his words were like melted butter (the only part of him with a high fat content). His teeth were straight enough to cut cling film, and when I inadvertently brushed against his torso, it was so smooth and muscly it felt like running my hands over a cashmere blanket draped across eight jam jars (yes, eight). I envisaged Corey posing by fireplaces in catalogues named *Chunky Knits for Hunks*, full of similar specimens who should be made to go naked at all times. In fact, should he be made to go naked at all times it could potentially bring about world peace. I really should tweet the UN.

Next there was Lois – the most muscular, purple-Lycra-clad 5 ft 1 woman I've ever met. Purple Lycra was to Lois as pantaloons are to genies, i.e. worn with the same regularity and amount of belly button exposure. Despite my having nine inches and six stone on Lois, I wouldn't have taken her on willingly in a fight, not even a thumb war. She would have broken my hand and potentially the wrist as well, because just one glance at her told you all you needed to know – she was 95 per cent muscle.

Finally, there was Monica – a blonde ponytailed married mother of one with a set of abs that looked likely to shatter your shoulder were you to attempt a takedown. Monica was a staunch Christian, and made sure everyone knew the strength of her beliefs within three minutes of shaking her hand.

As my tipsy eyes scanned the paragons I'd be spending the next few days with, I sucked in my tummy, and my cheeks a bit too, and resolved to drink nothing but mineral water and dine on nothing but undressed lettuce leaves for the entire retreat.

▲▲▲▲▲▲▲▲

The plan for our first evening together was to head out for some dinner to get to know each other. I suspected I might return hungry.

Santa Marta is a busy, steaming hot city, where during the daytime every inch of pavement seems to be dominated by market stalls selling anything and everything. There were stalls selling just remote controls, pornography or sunglasses, and others cramped with racks of bejewelled denim items, or extensive collections of baseball caps. We were dining at a restaurant tucked away in the quainter corner of the city — a criss-cross of narrow cobbled streets just around the corner from the hostel on Carrera 3, where there are a number of cute bars and restaurants tucked away in the shadows. Our chosen health-food restaurant was small, with maybe eight tables, and its glass roof gave it the feel of a family friend's conservatory. From our table we could peek into the kitchen to watch our nutritious dinner being prepared.

I looked on bemused as my dinner companions started deconstructing the menu and requesting lemon slices, edible flowers and other such nonsense. I convinced myself I wanted the chicken salad, but passed on mineral water in favour of red wine when it became obvious I was going to need it (around the minute I heard the phrase 'edible flower'). The others were keen to kick-start (or probably continue) the healthy living right off the bat. I wasn't aware people drank fruit juice with their dinner when they were over the age of seven, but evidently I had a lot to learn about maximising my daily vitamin intake.

Half an hour, and some getting-to-know-you chit-chat later, our meals arrived but, just as I raised my eating weapons, Mandolin decided to delay proceedings with a little idea...

'Guys, I thought it could be kind of cool to go around the table to share any concerns you might have, and what you're feeling grateful for right now.'

If you ever need to mess with someone's Zen levels, place freshly prepared food within nibbling distance when they're starving hungry and forbid them to touch it; you'll have them burning their yin-yang-branded pillowcases within seconds. As I had no intention of coming across as rude, I had no choice but to wait until a gang of Americans listed everything that scared them about being in South America before I could start…

'It's the guns that worry me.'

Seems a bit rich.

'My university lecturer told me kidnappers target Americans.'

Everyone targets Americans.

'I just want to come home in one piece.'

You'll be fine, love – you're clearly strong enough to defend the whole city from harm.

'I hear that Colombians deep-fry everything!'

Yes, they do, and it's delicious.

Once all the team's fears were out in the open, we started talking gratitude. Whereas Mandolin's continued postponement of our meal had me sighing and staring at the ceiling, the others were apparently delighted – they even clapped. Sharing was clearly up there on their list of favourite things (alongside unusual nut butters and hydrated chia-seed desserts), and it was glaringly apparent this wasn't their first sharing rodeo – their honed responses gave me cause to suspect they'd prepared in advance.

I sat in silence, somewhat baffled by the sincerity radiating from their pore-less faces. To be discussing 'feelings' without a shred of irony was a first for me. Where was the self-deprecation, and the sarcasm I was used to being around? These guys clearly didn't think there was anything funny about discussing one's feelings. No hesitation, no hedging, no guarded caveats. They just got straight in there, offloading those muscular chests and presenting the whole table with a clear view of their cholesterol-free hearts. They had nothing to hide – they were perfect, inside and out! I felt the familiar tingling of inadequacy prickling in my fingers and toes. Not only were these guys physically perfect, but they were all so self-assured. What must they think of me downing wine and shaking at the mere idea of letting them know what was going on in my head?

Mandolin took the lead: 'I'm just so grateful for the chance to show you the Colombia I love. I can't wait to share it with each and every one of you. And to get to know your power, and to share mine with you.'

Oh god, what am I going to say I'm grateful for? All I can think of is Michael Fassbender, which although completely accurate is hardly appropriate at a time like this.

Next up was Corey: 'I'm grateful to be here in Colombia with each of you, new friends and old.' He flashed me his Hollywood smile. 'I'm excited to see what I can learn, and what change and growth will come over all of us during our time together.'

I swear this table is actually vibrating with the positive vibes.

Then Monica: 'I'm grateful for my husband, and my son, whom I love deeply. And, for those of you who don't know, I'm Christian. This means I'm grateful for all god's creations, and for the Lord Jesus Christ giving me the strength to get on that plane today.'

Why do I feel so incredibly uncomfortable?

As much as I urged Monica's Lord Jesus Christ to slow down the rotation of the earth, my turn rolled around…

'Oh great, my go!' I took a glug of wine. 'I'm… well… I'm grateful for this food,' I gestured to my now-shrivelled chicken, 'and for it being so hot in this restaurant that it's unlikely to be getting cold as we speak! Haha… ha?' *Silence.* 'Errm… okay.' I searched for something, anything. 'MANDOLIN! YES!' I clicked my fingers. 'Mate, I'm very grateful for you inviting me along on this retreat. Thank you for… err… bringing us all together, and… err… thank you to you guys… for… being *so*… American!' *Oh no*. 'We'd never dream of sharing like this in England. It's a real novelty! Cheers!'

Safe to say I fucked that up.

While I chewed on my cold chicken, I started dwelling on my behaviour. I'd been arrogant to think I'd learnt so much about myself on this trip. Clearly, looking around this table, I was still a million miles away from where these guys were. Not just in terms of physical perfection, but in being honest about who I am, and how I'm feeling. These yogis not only seemed to know and understand themselves in great depth, but they were also very clearly not ashamed to speak about their feelings. I was miles behind. I stopped chewing, sat back and felt another crack form in that confidence that'd been so high just one short week ago.

▲▲▲▲▲▲▲▲

When we returned to the hostel, I was delighted to be back in the company of others exhibiting more regular sincerity levels. It felt good to joke, to quip, to not have four sets of eyes probing into the depths of my soul. Chris had news.

'Hey, Aimz… guess who's coming on the retreat?' he said, grinning with excitement, dancing around, wiggling the beer I'd ordered in front of me.

'Please tell me it's you?' I said, head in hands. 'I need all the help I can get.'

'No shit, babe. That chick in all the purple turned her nose up at her free beer! I've never seen anything like it!'

'So, you're coming?'

'Sure am.'

'Brilliant!' I let out a big sigh. 'Thank fucking god.'

That night Chris and I didn't sleep. Instead we got down to it, and then spoke about the kinds of things you speak about when the majority of other people are asleep.

We touched on a mutual relentless desire to see as much of the world as possible, as soon as possible. We idealistically listed the places we wanted to go (everywhere), the things we wanted to experience (everything), and the idea of ever feeling we'd seen enough (nah).

It was clear that we both had similar motivations for coming away. I explained to him how bombarded I'd felt, how the steps I'd taken in life so far hadn't brought me the satisfaction I craved and how I wanted to feel like I was living rather than just existing.

'I came away for the same reason,' Chris nodded. 'Because I wanted some experiences that didn't revolve around work. I worked in the mines so hard and for so long, and it's such a small world up there, it's easy to get stuck. I knew it wasn't what I wanted long-term, but I didn't know what was, so I figured I'd best go look for it, eh?'

Everything Chris was saying felt familiar, as if in a different conversation with a different person the same thoughts and feelings could have been coming out of my mouth.

He continued, 'I was so aware of all the things I should be doing, but none of them filled me with the same excitement that the idea of this road trip did. It's cool we both made that choice – to do the thing we knew would make us the happiest.'

It seemed we had similar motivations. Having faced the realisation over dinner that I was rubbish at talking about my feelings, it was a relief to see how easy it could be when you're speaking to someone who gets you. That was another thing I liked about Chris – he put everyone around him at ease.

'So, do you reckon you know what it is yet? Have you found the thing that will make you happy?' he asked.

'I'm not sure I've found any one answer – but I've definitely gained more understanding of myself, and I suppose that's a start.'

'I think I know now that my focus is on trying to live the best life I can. I want to see as much as possible and experience as much as I can. Work hard, be successful, sure. But most importantly, try to just enjoy myself. I just think it's that simple.'

It felt good to hear that he was also in pursuit of that one simple thing – happiness – and the way he broke it down made it seem like it shouldn't be overcomplicated, or too difficult to find. I'd often felt alienated from other people with clearer ambitions and aims because they had such deliberate plans, but hearing how simple he made it sound, I could see that surely most people are motivated by happiness alone. That desire wasn't unique to me. I was the one choosing to think my aims isolated me from others.

'And are you looking for a boyfriend, Aimz, or what do you reckon? Do you want the hubbie, the house, the car, the kids?'

'Hmm. I suppose I do, eventually. But I want to be happy on my own first. If I'm not even sure what I want, I don't know how I can be in a relationship. I'd rather be alone while I'm figuring that out than with the wrong person.'

Lucas had only served to reconfirm that I didn't want to waste time being with guys just for something to do.

'Yeah, there are so many people that seem to view a relationship as the only thing that matters, and I just think I have too much going on that I want and need to experience at the moment, I don't have the time for it. I want it, if it's right…'

I cut in, 'But if not, you can take it or leave it? Me too.'

'All that stuff everyone thinks they want, relationships, high-powered jobs, it isn't the be-all and end-all to me either.' He paused. 'We think about things the same, hey Aimz?'

I grinned at him. 'Certainly seems like it, beaut.'

DAY ONE

The next morning things were different. Despite every truth that'd tumbled out of my mouth the night before about romance not being my major focus, I now found myself pretty darn set on romance… which was fucking irritating. After Daniel, I'd successfully managed to avoid developing real feelings for any hunk I'd encountered on my way. Then, in the last month, I'd wasted precious time on Lucas, and now I felt the first stirrings of a full-on crush, and it was not welcome in the pit of my stomach at all.

Our plan was to head to Minca for breakfast. While most of the yogis piled into Chris's van, I travelled there in a cab with Mandolin. With every passing minute of that journey up into the mountains, the realisation was dawning that I actually *liked* Chris. I couldn't concentrate on the conversation going on in my cab; my mind was completely on him. 'Normal' Amy Baker had seemingly panic-packed her backpack and headed for the hills.

We were having breakfast at a lovely restaurant in the heart of Minca run by an Irish chap who'd moved to the town permanently a number of years before. Our breakfast table was positioned so that we could gaze out of the open-sided building into the overgrown ravine it overlooked, and down to the fast-flowing river below. Birds buzzed in the trees and butterflies fluttered in beams of sunlight cutting through the trees. As other people fawned over the homemade jam and fresh juice, and buttered slices of toast for each other, I was acutely aware that I seemed to have completely forgotten how to function. I sat beside Chris, trying to appear bright and breezy, but I no longer seemed capable of positioning my hands appropriately, or moving my face like a normal person. I could feel the weight of my body, and was critical of every movement and wobble. I was irrationally uneasy about having something in my teeth, up my nose or around my mouth. I perched on things I'd never normally perch on, and laughed too heartily at things I'd never normally laugh at. I'd entered some dazed state, where I was constantly thinking about what he was thinking about what I was saying or doing.

After breakfast we hiked for a couple of hours up to a waterfall, where we would spend the afternoon rappelling and enjoying a swim. I realised quickly that with how I was feeling, day one of this retreat was doomed to become a huge, warty, moron-athon of ill-thought-out guesswork about what he would want me to do, say and be, influenced entirely by my raging pheromones.

As we hiked, and those around me chatted, I found myself uncharacteristically lost for words and realised that in place of my sense of humour, I now had jealousy and the inability to focus fully on anything that wasn't Chris-shaped.

Halfway through our walk, a final addition to the yoga crew arrived: yet another gorgeous woman by the name of Amber who cruised up to meet us on the back of a motorcycle. She was rocking hot pants and the most banging body I'd seen in a long while (and I'd been hanging out with these yogis for 24 hours). Much to my annoyance, rather than thinking, 'Woohoo – a new friend!' (as I would have done prior to my brain melting into a gloopy love puddle), new Weird-Amy thought, 'More competition, goddammit! I must assess everything they say to each other to ensure I'm safe.'

This made me see that now in place of critical thinking I had irrationality and suspicion…

I was dedicating way too much time to wondering whether any of the other girls found Chris as attractive as I did. I was like a 5 ft 10 tanned Gollum, who, instead of being obsessed with a ring, was obsessed with ringlets.

Just a week ago, my confidence had lounged around appreciating its own excellence in a handheld mirror, but now I had anxiety and self-doubt crinkling my brow and making me feel sick. I was not performing well.

We spent the afternoon taking turns to rappel down the 50-m tropical waterfall. It was great fun – once you got over the initial fear of leaning backwards out into the abyss to take your first slippery steps, that is. After we'd all finished we were splashing around in the pool below to cool off. I couldn't help but shoot sideways glances at the perfect bodies of the women on the retreat who were currently bending themselves into all kinds of poses my wide hips and belly fat wouldn't allow. In that moment, I actually felt what remained of my self-confidence trickling away with the current. I couldn't help but compare myself.

Before I'd come away, my biggest problem had been exactly this – my complete preoccupation with what other people had, what they were doing and what they thought of me. I'd said yes to delaying my flight and coming on this retreat in order to focus on myself. Now, I found myself completely and utterly distracted by this group of seemingly perfect human beings, who made me startlingly aware of how much better I could be. I could feel myself sliding all too easily back into my usual, unhealthy patterns of comparison, and it did not feel good.

▲▲▲▲▲▲▲

That night at dinner, I was on high alert. I was waiting for someone to chirp up and suggest we share our deepest, darkest secrets, or the age at which we'd first got our periods. Thankfully no such question came. The evening was far from surprise-free though… when our food had been cleared away, we were informed we'd be partaking in a sweat lodge ceremony, and we were instructed to go foraging around the garden of our hostel to collect flowers to decorate the altar.

At the word 'altar', Monica started to visibly panic. Sensing a terse exchange was about to kick off, we all quickly busied ourselves clearing away plates while pretending not to listen.

'I thought I'd been clear about not doing anything that contradicts my Christian beliefs.'

'My love, this isn't a religious ceremony of any sort,' Mandolin reassured her. 'It's a purification ceremony designed to help us all connect, and to cleanse our bodies, minds and souls. There are no religious connotations whatsoever.'

Monica tilted her head to one side, and opened her eyes a little wider. 'I need to know that for certain, Mandolin!'

'This ceremony is designed to bring us all together, nothing more. Why don't you come in, and if you start to feel uncomfortable at any stage you can leave.'

Monica looked sceptical. 'Fine! But there's absolutely no way I'll be collecting anything to offer at the altar of anyone other than my Lord Jesus Christ!'

She spun around to address the rest of us: 'EVERYONE! I'm sorry for my outburst, it's just the one thing I'm unprepared to compromise on is my beliefs. My family and I have made a commitment to demonstrate our love for the Lord through every single action we take, every… single… day. I won't do anything to jeopardise or belittle that just because I'm on holiday.' We nodded.

Once our food had gone down we headed down to the sweat lodge; a dome-shaped structure fashioned from branches, leaves, towels and blankets. Outside the lodge a fire burned brightly, and on that fire was a collection of rocks on their way to being red hot.

Our fully clothed group stood around looking unsure while Mandolin and Corey handed out percussion instruments. I was handed some maracas. Others were handed tambourines, bongos, sticks to bang together and a fun-looking knuckleduster made out of bells. A quick scan confirmed there was no rain-stick option, which was a relief. I didn't want another reason to be resentful of anyone. I already had enough envy fruit piled up on my jealousy platter.

'Okay,' Mandolin addressed the group, 'let's get started. Time to strip down though – it's hot in there!'

I loitered at the back of the queue as everyone began to de-robe and crawl into the lodge. Thank goodness it was pitch black – sitting cross-legged in a bikini might lead Monica to believe we'd lured her into a confined, sweaty space with Buddha himself, and I don't think she'd like that.

I crawled in, took a seat on the floor and wiggled around, sweeping away as many of the sharp stones and twigs as I could from my immediate vicinity. It didn't take long to start sweating. It felt like I was being slithered upon by a family of slow-moving Colombian jungle leeches, who were making a beeline for the moist safety of my bum crack.

Mandolin explained that it was our responsibility as a group to instruct the lady manning the fire outside when we were in need of more rocks. To do so, we'd have to repeat the same statement, 'Open the door, and let in the light.' Upon hearing our cry, the door (blanket) would be pulled aside and a burning hot rock would be pushed across the floor into the pit in the centre of our circle.

Our next instruction concerned the 'talking stick', which in our case was a purple ball. The ball was to be passed from person to person, and you were only allowed to talk when it was in your possession. For the rest of the time we were told to stay completely silent to ensure it remained a safe environment that facilitated sharing. Here was my second chance to try to open up a little bit around the yogis. It was also an opportunity to refocus my mind on what was important to me in that moment, rather than wondering about their perceptions, or whether Chris seemed interested.

'Does anyone have any questions? Good. Now let's begin. All together now…'

'OPEN THE DOOR AND LET IN THE LIGHT.'

The blanket was pulled aside and the first stone was pushed into the pit. Mandolin doused the rocks with some lavender water, which sizzled and gave off a batch of thick, fragrant steam.

'Mother Nature!' Mandolin began, 'I call upon you tonight to bless us with your presence in this sweat lodge. I call upon you, with your healing power and wisdom, to help us open up to one another, to create a place of spiritual refuge, and of physical and emotional healing. MOTHER NATURE, JOIN US!'

Monica shuffled in her seat and cleared her throat sternly. I did a little shuffling too. I was 30 per cent sure I was sitting on an ant's nest.

The questions started:

What in this world is most important to you?
'Family and friends.'
'Experiences.'

'Love.'
'The Lord Jesus Christ.'

What do you dream of achieving?
'Happiness.'
'Business success.'
'True love.'
'Seeing my children grow up embracing their faith in the Lord.'

What scares you, and holds you back from actively pursuing that dream?
'Self-doubt.'
'The fear of failure.'
'Laziness.'
'Eternal damnation.'

After 15 or so minutes, Monica made her excuses and vacated the sweat lodge.

We continued, passing the ball and taking our turns to answer questions in detail for another half an hour before it looked as though the ceremony might draw to a close. I was happy with myself: I'd managed to discuss my thoughts and feelings, even if I had had to wait until I was in a pitch-black environment to do so.

Mandolin had just one more request.

'Does anyone have any sounds they'd like to share with the group?'

Did she just say 'sounds'?

It dawned on me what she meant... the time had come to sing. We were going to group sing. Oh dear, just when I was pleased at my progress, I was asked to step it up another embarrassing notch. *Please don't let it be 'Kum Ba Yah', please don't let it be 'Kum Ba Yah'.*

No one made a sound.

'I can't believe you guys are being shy now!' Mandolin exclaimed. 'I'll just have to start then.' She gave a little cough before quietly beginning to sing the Disney classic, 'Bare Necessities'.

After a couple of lines, Mandolin paused, giving us the chance to join in.

No takers. She continued singing.

Then Corey chimed in.

Now Chris.

Amber came in on the bongos.

My maracas started going.

The rest of the sweat lodge came alive.

Once we'd started singing, there was no stopping us. That pitch-black sweat lodge transformed into cramped centre stage for the greatest Disney film reimagination Colombia has ever witnessed. *No lion is going to be sleeping in THIS jungle tonight*, I laughed to myself, waving my maracas in big, enthusiastic circles like a human Chinook helicopter. *Not when there were people impersonating Sebastian the crab, Ariel was singing about 'thingamabobs' and Jasmine and Aladdin were falling in love all over again, only this time under a blanket rather than on top of one.* Our triumphant medley drew to a close with a 'Hakuna Matata'/'I Just Can't Wait to Be King'/'Can You Feel the Love Tonight?' mega mix. I even capitalised upon my British accent to provide an accurate voice for the character of Zazu, demonstrating total commitment to the authenticity of the performance.

And we weren't finished. For the first few seconds of silence following the stunning crescendo of 'Can You Feel the Love Tonight?' no noise was made apart from our sweaty choir drawing ragged breath. Then, out of nowhere, Lois started rapping...

Everyone sat in awed silence as Lois rapped a word-perfect rendition of Arrested Development's classic hit, 'Mr Wendal'. The sweaty crowd went wild.

'Thanks, guys! It's a personal fave. Now, how about one we all know?'

Lois started belting out Backstreet Boys' seminal number, 'I Want It That Way', and this time no one was being shy.

My eyes were closed, I didn't know where I was or what was happening, but I was having the time of my life. There may have been a distinct lack of lasers, but I felt as though I was on *Top of the Pops*. For one glorious second I even forgot I was in self-imposed imaginary competition for the affections of Chris. If he'd been judging us on harmonising ability and near-perfect impersonations of each of the Backstreet Boys, we'd have been fully naked by now.

▲▲▲▲▲▲▲

Incidentally, that night was the first night Chris and I slept in the same bed and nothing happened. It was annoying, because I obviously wanted it to (and my 'Nick Carter' had been bang on), plus, embarrassingly, I tried to casually instigate a kiss a couple of times, but his closed lips clearly conveyed he wasn't up for it. I left it – I wasn't going to send whatever we had spiralling head first into unsalvageable territory by attempting to dry-hump his arm.

Despite my come-on attempt, we managed to ignore the awkwardness and chatted well into the night. Chris's thoughts on the day made me realise I'd been overthinking things to a ridiculous degree. I just needed to relax, enjoy myself and seize back control of my emotions. I resolved to try my best to start to enjoy the retreat and get to know the people we were there with.

Before we knew it, it was 2 a.m., fretting had been replaced with chuckling, and I felt like normal Amy again.

DAY TWO

I awoke seemingly restored to my relaxed former glory – my heart rate wasn't elevated, I wasn't sweating too profusely, my face didn't look a creepy combination of shocked and worried. I was back in the game.

We had a big day of hiking ahead of us today. Our plan was to hike through jungle up to a hostel high in the mountains, and to visit a coffee farm, where we'd enjoy a tasty dinner and wonderful views. I vowed not to let myself get in my head and be all doom and gloom. For someone who neglects to think things through, I'm very adept at overthinking when I decide to. I was hoping that getting the blood pumping and enjoying some beautiful scenery would be enough to distract me from all the insecurities that had been following me around the previous day.

The morning started with us weaving single file along moist jungle paths lined with banana trees, which we stopped to forage. We paused to admire flowers, to listen out for monkeys, and to all get a good glimpse at the processions of ants making their way who knows where, laden with materials to plump their nests.

It was good to be walking, and for a second I almost thought I'd be able to avoid the previous day's concrete mixer of emotions spluttering into life at all. But then I started getting paranoid that I was walking alone or only having quick conversations with people before they set their sights on Chris:

'Chris! Chris! Come and do a handstand on this tree stump/ giant rock/log with me!'

'Chris! Chris! Catch my banana in your mouth!'

'Chris! Chris! Let's climb into this moss cave together!'

'Chris! Chris! Let's take pictures of us acting like dragons!'

That one I actually liked the sound of.

Despite having no interest in climbing into a moss cave that surely had to be a hiding place for giant snakes, I did start to ponder why people wanted to hang out with him more. So now I'd entered even more dangerous overthinking territory – reaching the conclusion that not only did these yogis prefer Chris, but that they also didn't like me.

In my cloudy head, it made total sense. When they directed their eyes at Chris, they saw a relaxed person just doing what he does. When they managed to tear themselves away from the colourful fun park that was Chris, they had me: the crumpled shell of Amy Baker, a person currently perma-agitated by jealous thoughts of their perfect breasts, defined (but not muscly) upper arms and their distinct lack of seated rolls. I mean – who doesn't have at least one seated roll? Have they not heard that people mix chocolate and peanut butter nowadays? Do they not know that when melted, cheese can make you sing involuntarily because it's *that* good? The irrational rejection I felt, teamed with my internal battle to stop being such an overanalytical idiot made me pull a face that did nothing to improve my likeability. I looked like I was smelling off milk.

We arrived at our mountain hostel, which was by far the prettiest accommodation I'd ever had the pleasure of staying in. The building was painted bright white, which made the surrounding flower bushes of every colour pop even more. The large terracotta patio area was criss-crossed by welcoming purple hammocks and cushioned chairs, and dozens of hummingbirds were buzzing around the trees. The view from our balcony not only took in the colourful gardens, but also various mountain peaks and a sweeping valley leading down towards Santa Marta.

We enjoyed a quick yoga session in the gardens in the shade of the trees, and then began the steep hike up to the coffee farm where we'd be enjoying dinner. As we walked, Monica fell into step beside me.

'Oh my goodness, Amy. Chris is just so great! I love him. Don't you?'

'Yeah, he's great isn't he?' I smiled.

'So, anyway, about that… you and him?' She waggled a manicured finger between me and where Chris was. 'You're not *together* together, right?'

'No, no, not at all!' I protested. 'We're just friends.'

'Oh, honey, I knew it,' she grinned. 'I didn't think so. I just had to ask because it didn't make any sense to me. ANY sense!'

I pursed my lips, and nodded, looking everywhere but at her face so she wouldn't see the flush of emotions I'd just experienced cloud my face. I felt the unbearable heat of jealousy surge up my whole body from the tips of my toes to my hair follicles. I felt anger at her for thinking I wasn't good enough for him, and for making sure that I knew that she thought that. And I felt sad — because the people I was battling the urge to compare myself to didn't think that I was good enough for the dude I had feelings for. I couldn't think of any conversation that wouldn't immediately betray all these thoughts, so I just fell silent, and she went to talk to someone else.

I was quiet over dinner, and let the rest of the group chat away as we devoured couscous and vegetables that the owner of the coffee farm had grown in his allotment. After dinner, just as I was melting into a hammock and attempting to lure the resident kitten in for a cuddle (I was hungry for affection), Corey suggested we go around the circle and say what the best thing about the retreat had been so far.

'I'll start,' Corey said. 'Mandolin, I'm overawed by what you've done here. What an incredible businesswoman and beautiful soul. You've made this possible and that is *so* awesome. I also just want to say, I've known most of you a while, but Chris, my brother, it feels great getting to know you. Thank you for being something special, and for honestly and openly showing us the funny, inspiring person you are.'

Cries of 'here, here' filled the air. How nice. The kitten jumped out of my arms, and wandered over to Chris. The circle was complete.

Amber was next to chip in with enthusiastic agreement. 'Oh for sure – thanks to all of you for blessing us with your inner beauty, but especially you, Chris!' she said, high fiving him. 'And Colombia: what a country. Exploring these ecosystems with you guys has been truly incredible.'

More cheers.

'Me next,' Lois spoke up. 'I want you all to know I've loved the last couple of days hiking with you. The yoga has been incredible and I really enjoyed the chance to let loose in the sweat lodge last night, it was *so* cleansing. And Chris… I have to mention you! I'm just *so* pleased you were persuaded to come along last minute – what would we have done without you?'

I hid my face and tried not to let my bottom lip quiver. I knew all too well that I was acting like a baby. It didn't even matter that Chris was their favourite. Just because they liked him, didn't mean they didn't like me. I knew that in the only rational corner of my brain that appeared to still be working, but that didn't mean the chemicals in my body wanted me to believe it. Where on earth had my sense of humour fucked off to?

Monica was next up, so I steeled myself for a low blow. 'I'm also so happy to be here in Colombia. I feel *so* grateful to Mandolin, and to Corey, and of course, to the Lord Jesus Christ for making this possible.' She paused and looked to the heavens for a silent moment before continuing. 'And oh… my… goodness, Christopher! I am just so pleased to meet you,' she gushed. 'You've been like a breath of fresh air,' she giggled and leaned towards him, 'a big, strong breath of fresh air.'

I shook my head in disbelief. I was pretty sure the Lord Jesus Christ wouldn't approve of that level of flirting given the fact that she's a MARRIED WOMAN and has a CHILD! Not that I could express that sentiment out loud. Instead I slumped lower into my shadowy hammock of shame, hoping to make myself as small as I was allowing myself to feel.

When all eyes turned to me, I tried my darndest to appear nonchalant towards their openly expressed preferences. It was hard though, given the fact that my ego had been completely trampled by their comments. I didn't cry, though, which was a small victory at that stage. Instead I muttered something utterly uncharismatic and impersonal along the lines of being grateful for the unique experience, and then promptly shut up.

Once he realised that was all I had to offer, Corey clapped his hands. 'So, just to clarify, we're all in agreement that Chris has been our favourite thing about the retreat so far?' *Come on, Amy!*

I shouted at myself. *You can laugh at this – normally this would crack you up!*

Everyone cheered in agreement, and laughed merrily. Nope, I couldn't laugh it off. *Fuck you all.*

'I suppose that only leaves us to hear from the Man of the Hour! Chris – our hero – what's been your favourite thing?'

Five faces placed chins in upturned palms and gazed at their new favourite human across the fire.

'Well, thanks guys! I feel honoured. You've all been incredible. It's *all* been incredible. Mando – thanks for inviting me, and showing us how beautiful these mountains are. It's been great getting to know all of ya's, but...' He paused, and everyone lent forwards with anticipation. 'I reckon the best thing so far was last night, staying awake chatting with Aimz.' They all whirled around and looked at me with sincere smiles on their faces. 'We just laugh so much when we're together. It was a lot of fun!' He gave me a thumbs up. 'Cheers, Aimz.'

I smiled. I knew full well he wouldn't have said that if the other comments hadn't so blatantly favoured him. He was a perceptive guy, and he could see I was finding it tough to be everyone's second – scratch that – *last* choice, and was trying to cheer me up.

As the group continued to chat, I swung in my hammock analysing why I was allowing myself to get so worked up. They were allowed to like whoever they wanted to like. I was fully aware of how ridiculous I was being, but I just couldn't get a hold on it.

The fact was, it was easier for me to channel all my emotions into anger for the yogis, and to laugh at how they operated, rather than to acknowledge how being around them made me feel about myself. It was easier to dub them weird for being so honest and in touch with their feelings, than to accept that I needed to get better at doing the same.

I had thought I'd come such a long way, but, swinging here, I could see that I still had a long way to go to accepting myself, and not caring what other people thought. This retreat had morphed from a chance to relax and process my trip, into a brutal reality check screaming at me that the opinions of others still mattered to me way too much.

▲▲▲▲▲▲▲

After we'd trudged back through the pitch-black jungle to our mountainside hostel, I was standing on the veranda with Corey. We were having a chat about how he discovered his love of yoga when my eyes were drawn to what he was standing in front of… a gigantic branch of the most perfect, most fresh, most sparkly weed I'd ever seen. It was beautiful. So beautiful it made Corey, a perfect specimen, dull in comparison.

I floated towards it with my arm outstretched. When Corey realised I wasn't reaching for his jugular, he turned around and saw what I was gaping at.

'Woah,' we both said in amazed unison.

'We have to smoke some of this,' I correctly pointed out, reaching out and plucking off a sizeable bud.

Much to my surprise, the yogis agreed wholeheartedly. Maybe they thought it was spirulina?

Skip to 40 minutes later and we were all happily feeling the effects of the Colombian homegrown. It had chilled everyone out, bar me it seemed. No surprises there.

In-between giggling at the puppet shows Chris was performing for the laughing group, I was being annoyingly paranoid. The overthinking came in waves. One minute I felt relaxed, staring up at the starry sky; the next I was wondering what it was about me that these people didn't like. I became paranoid about being paranoid about them not liking me. They'd done absolutely nothing to indicate they didn't like me, yet I was completely convinced that as they preferred Chris, they didn't like me. I'd got so carried away comparing myself to them, and overanalysing every single comment made by anyone I was with, that I'd stopped being myself entirely.

The reason I'd come to South America was to escape how the actions of others made me feel. I could see now that it hadn't been the people offering the advice or opinions that had been causing the problems: it was me.

Me – overthinking and taking people's actions and comments to heart.

Me – who chose to see judgement in their statements.

Me – who was responsible for how bad I felt.

I'd missed all the positive things that the words of people here and back home communicated – concern, love, wanting to help me be happy – and I'd chosen to interpret them in a hostile way, and to take offence. How many caring interactions had I been completely oblivious to in my life because I'd convinced myself that the people offering them just wanted to tell me what to do, or press their opinion upon me. Yes, there were exceptions to this rule, but I needed to learn to distinguish between those that came from a good place, and those that came from a bad. I couldn't carry on assuming they were all bad, otherwise I'd just continue being offended.

How many sweet moments had I missed with Chris, and other people, because I was preoccupied with comparing myself to others? How many instants in my life had I missed like this, because I was obsessing in my head rather than being present in the moment? After six months spent making what I considered significant progress towards being fully happy with who I am, I'd been catapulted back to the beginning. I took a toke on my joint and sighed, majorly bummed out by that revelation.

DAY THREE

Our last day in the mountains was upon us. It was the point at which we stopped walking, and started drinking. Before we headed to the beach for the next stage of the retreat, we had a party planned at Casa Elemento — a hostel on the top of a mountain in the Sierra Nevada de Santa Marta mountain range. As alcohol was going to be involved, the thought obviously popped into my head that if I had any chance of anything happening with Chris again, it would be tonight. There it was... that miniscule glimmer of pathetic hope clinging on by bitten fingernails that makes us all do things we regret.

The party was great. Someone rolled a joint that looked like a spaceship and, as a result, I completely forgot about any kind of Chris seduction plan. When I lethargically remembered I should probably have a bash, I wandered down to the hostel's 20-man hammock to look for him. To my dismay, I found him and Monica having a cuddle. Despite that being decidedly PG, I still felt bitter rejection. I quickly vacated the area... and then I did what some girls do when they feel rejected and desperate to regain control over a situation: I didn't say anything to him, waited until he was asleep and then snogged someone else — the ultimate cleansing act! So what if he didn't want me? Someone else with long curly hair, tattoos and a big grin did — and he just called me beautiful. Ha!

So much for not seeking validation in male attention. It made me feel better for all of 20 minutes.

POST YOGA RETREAT

The next day, Chris returned to work at La Brisa Loca, and the rest of us made for the beach. With him gone, at least the only emotions I had to battle were inadequacy rather than rejection. My last interaction with Monica came at Costeño Beach. She was heading back to the USA that night, via Chris's hostel. When I realised she'd be seeing him, I for some reason felt compelled to 'joke' she'd better 'keep her hands off'. Rather than protest, Monica said, 'I can't promise you that, I'm afraid'. She teamed her statement with an appreciative squeeze of my arm, which I assume she was envisioning as his bicep judging by her throaty 'ooh' noise and sexy lip-bite.

If it hadn't been dark she would have seen my face go purple and steam come out of my ears. Despite myself, I felt the fury of a thousand pissed-off super-fans who've just seen pictures of their dreamboat walking hand-in-hand through Central Park with Taylor Swift. I was either going to use this anger to fuel some creepy fan art produced only from my bodily fluids, or I was going to yank out her entire ponytail by the roots and start parading it up and down the beach to the sound of my own manic trumpet impressions and incredibly aggressive can-can kicks. I'd clap and fist pump and wave her dismembered ponytail in the air for no other reason than to flaunt it in her face. I'd make my victory all the more dignified by patting myself on the back repeatedly with one hand, while flipping her the bird with the other. And then, as a grand finale I'd strut down to the water's edge, click my heels in the air like Dick van Dyke and hand-deliver the ponytail into the

T his is an invented story, containing an account of a true one. The 1939 lifeboat disaster at St Ives, Cornwall, really happened. William and Margaret Freeman and John Stevens are or were real people. The great kindness to me of Mrs Margaret Freeman, who told me her story, and of Barry Cockcroft who lent me a copy of his film *Take a Lifejacket* has made it possible to enter the real people into the story almost entirely in their own words. Anyone who would like to read a non-fiction account of the 1939 lifeboat disaster will find the story well told in Barry Cockcroft's recent *The Call of the Running Tide* (Hodder & Stoughton).

Apart from the passing mentions of established artists and lifeboat men, all the other people in this story, including Thomas Tremorvah and Stella Harmaker, are imaginary. They have been conjured out of thin air and bear no resemblance to any real person living or dead.

I would like to thank John Rowe Townsend, Peter Davison and Bill Scott-Kerr, who know best what help they gave; Mr Graham Care for introducing me to Margaret Freeman; Mr Philip Moran for information on the current organization of the St Ives lifeboat; David Bass, Gillian, Brendan and Aidan McClure for playing me

Alice's music; and finally the people of St Ives, among whom, although I am a stranger and they are much beset by strangers, I have found only friendship and kindness all my life.

mouth of a passing hair-eating porpoise... who would high five me with his fin... because *he* understands.

Breathe.

That was how it might have gone if I'd allowed my feelings to betray me. But I was very aware I had not a leg to stand on, and that I needed to stop letting flippant comments from people affect me so profoundly. Monica had done nothing wrong other than appreciate a handsome man. A handsome man who I was dedicating too much time to thinking about when my thoughts should have been directed in more important places. I wanted more time. I couldn't go back to the UK now, feeling like I did.

▲▲▲▲▲▲▲

A couple of days later, I bumped into Mandolin in Santa Marta, and she had news about who Chris was hooking up with now. I knew it was coming – there's nothing quite like the intuition of a lady flogging a long-dead horse – but I hadn't expected it to be someone that I knew: a girl named Catalina who worked at Costeño Beach, who I'd hung out with a lot back when Lucas was around.

I cringed at the revelation. Immediately after the yoga retreat, I'd updated Catalina on everything that had happened with Lucas in gruesome detail, and confessed everything that had happened with Chris blow-by-blow. How I liked him, but knew it wasn't going to happen, and how I was gutted because he was great – etc., etc. – as hearts poured out of my eyes like some kind of sex-crazed Care Bear.

I felt like an idiot, because come to think of it, when I'd said it she *had* looked incredibly sheepish, and *had* quickly taken her leave having muttered something along the lines of, 'Well I like Chris, and I like you, so I hope it works out for you.'

The same day I heard this news, as I moped around feeling embarrassed for pouring my heart out to the one person I shouldn't have, and jealous that Catalina had won him over with South American sex moves I couldn't reasonably be expected to know, I made a terrible Lucas-shaped mistake. Remember him – the handsome, stroppy Swede from a fair few pages back? Well, he'd been contacting me on a regular basis asking whether he could come and visit me. I'd been ignoring his messages because justifiably I was still furious at how he'd spoken to me.

I wish I could tell you I said, 'HELL NO', explained I wasn't into the idea, or him, and that his money would be better spent visiting somewhere else. Instead, I stood staring at the message for about 15 minutes...

And then...

Because I felt rejected by Chris...

Because I was humiliated by how uncool I'd been over the course of the retreat...

Because I was gutted that the sexy Colombian had beaten me in the sex appeal stakes...

I said yes.

This was an utterly idiotic decision, because no part of me wanted him to come. The idea of spending time with him didn't appeal to me, and there was zero chance of us hooking up again after how he'd spoken to me. I should have been upfront about that, and then we could have moved on with our lives, and perhaps retained a couple of memories of the positive parts of our interactions before they took a sour turn. Instead, I set up a situation where things were only going to get progressively worse just because I was lacking the attention of the real object of my affections.

I ended up sticking around in Colombia for another six weeks (more about that later). In that time, I returned to the land of the sane and ended up planning a trip to the desert with Chris, Mandolin, and group of friends from Costeño Beach. There was one problem: the day Lucas had arranged to fly in, I would be heading out, and it wouldn't only be me leaving town…

I'd be going with all his mates from the area that technically he'd known first.

Shit.

If only I'd said 'no' all those weeks back when he honestly asked me whether I wanted to see him again. 'No' wouldn't have been so hard to say back when we had the distance between us, and when he hadn't altered his travel plans specifically to come and see me.

I had no choice… I had to tell him that I wouldn't be there.

I chose to tell him as quickly (and as carelessly) as possible by breaking the news to him via Facebook Messenger, in a couple of poorly considered sentences about how what was going on with us was casual, that I didn't want to miss out on this opportunity to visit that corner of the country, and that no, he wasn't invited. Lucas had acted badly, but it was my choice to use his behaviour as an excuse to act like a dick in return.

I felt dreadful, of course, but the one saving grace was that because I wouldn't have to see him, I could pretend it never happened. That was of course how it was supposed to go down – we'd be miles out of town by the time his plane came in to land in Santa Marta. Karma wasn't having any of that, though…

The morning we were supposed to depart, Chris's van decided to throw a wobbly and refused to go anywhere. We sat around in La Brisa Loca for hours with bags at our feet. I was jumpy. Every time someone new arrived, I panicked it might be Lucas. And suddenly, inevitably, there he was. Frowning at me.

Everyone stood up to greet him. They all knew the story, and had been pretty vocal about their opinions on how I could have handled it better. He hugged everyone and when he eventually got round to me, he whispered in my ear, 'You're a fucking bitch.' Ever the charmer! Lucas was far from blameless, but I was solely responsible for manufacturing this situation, where I allowed him to speak to me like this again. Rather than standing up for myself, I screwed up my face, nodded in agreement and managed to squeak out a 'sorry', before removing myself from his line of sight to chain-smoke on the balcony.

The day that should have been spent listening to Bon Jovi and cruising north was instead spent awkwardly hanging out with Lucas while we awaited news of Walter's health.

This was clearly the universe providing me with an opportunity to step up and act like the adult I hoped I'd become during my time away. All I needed to do was deal with this situation in an open and honest way that communicated to Lucas why I was so prepared to act badly towards him. Then he would have known how terrible his comments were, and I would have felt better, because I'd have effectively communicated how I felt.

Instead I squirmed in my seat, avoided eye contact and justified my behaviour to myself by thinking about the five or six super-shitty things he'd said and done.

When the time came for him to leave, rather than seize my final opportunity to make the best of a shit situation, I shouted 'sorry' at his departing back, and then grimaced at the faces of my disappointed mates.

'A group shout-out, Amy? Really?' Mandolin fairly pointed out, clearly echoing the sentiments of the entire group. 'Not cool, man.'

I nodded in agreement. Talk about another backwards step.

WINNER = *THE EXPERT*

'Keeping your emotions all locked up is something that's unfair to you. When you clearly know how you feel, you should say it.'
Taylor Swift

I like to imagine Taylor imparting her wisdom on me in her New York penthouse, as we nibble upon her home-baked cookies and play with her cats, maybe discussing the appendages of various rock stars and boy band members as the evening progresses... Maybe not; that's a little presumptuous of me...

Yes, Lucas did some stuff that was unacceptable, but I should have spoken to him about that rather than using his poor behaviour as an excuse to act immaturely myself. Not speaking my mind and letting that resentment grow resulted in me behaving in a way I wasn't proud of. If, as Taylor advises, I'd acknowledged the truth about how Lucas made me feel, I could have avoided a whole lot of hassle. I'd been so annoyed at myself back in Bolivia when I met Daniel, for not being as open and honest as I wanted to be in interactions. As a result, as I travelled, I'd made a concerted effort to be honest with men and new friends, and it had paid off. I was disappointed to discover how quickly and easily I could revert to how I'd been before I travelled if I didn't actually try to behave differently.

> When it came to Chris, rather than letting my suppressed feelings overwhelm me, I should have voiced them. Maybe then I wouldn't have mutated into a frenzied ball of hormones prone to jealously, exasperation and rubbish jokes.

LESSONS LEARNT

Prior to leaving the UK, I'd been so preoccupied with other people's thoughts and opinions that I'd indiscriminately shunned everything. I hadn't wanted to listen to or acknowledge anything. By this point in my journey I'd mistakenly thought I had figured out pretty much everything. What transpired as a result of a couple of knocks to my confidence, at a time when I was feeling unsure and a little vulnerable, was a glaring, uncomfortable reminder of how easy it is to revert to old behaviour, which only served to make me feel dreadful.

I quickly regressed to old patterns of pointless comparison that not only made me feel sick and act bizarrely, but prevented me from making the most of my opportunities to grow. It highlighted to me how hung up I allow myself to get on other people. I assume that everyone is observing and judging me – and the only possible outcome of this unhealthy way of thinking is hindering myself, and making myself unhappy.

I could have enjoyed that retreat a whole lot more if, rather than being defensive as I always was, I'd opened myself up to other ways of thinking and expressing myself, and concentrated on friendship. Instead I fell into old traps of placing too much emphasis on relationships, and paying too much mind to what other people think.

This clusterfuck of mistakes and poor interactions with all kinds of good and bad humans finally confirmed what I already suspected to be true, and what I'd been slowly figuring out travelling alone – that I needed to focus on myself, what I think, and what makes me happy. When placed in a group with people I perceived to be more successful than me, I became fixated on my status amongst them. Happiness doesn't come from someone else; it comes from within – and clearly, I was still looking for it in other people's validation, and in romance. I wasn't where I wanted to be yet, but I was determined to salvage this.

LIFE ABOVE THE CLOUDS

FRIENDLY ADVICE:

'Don't you go getting holed up anywhere with a bunch of hippies. You know what happens in places like that? I do... Orgies.'

Mikey, post room

EXPERT ADVICE:

'The less I needed, the better I felt.'

Charles Bukowski
('The prophet of the under-employed')

Post yoga retreat, I was being a gigantic baby about leaving Colombia and heading back to the UK. I didn't want to go home. I was having the time of my life in the Caribbean sunshine, sharing nightly beers around fires with people I liked talking to; I got to lie down a lot; Colombia is beautiful and captivating, as are the people that live there; and there was definite room for improvement with my tan – which we all know is a huge priority when returning from anywhere.

I needed to formulate a plan that would mean I could stay longer. I took a couple of glugs of rum for Dutch courage, and marched to the nearest cash machine, determined to finally face up to the reality of my dwindling bank balance. It was an enormous relief to discover that if I ate as little as possible and could source free accommodation, it would be entirely possible to eke out six more weeks in this glorious country.

Aside from all these surface-level reasons I repeated to my friends and parents to justify prolonging my stay, there were a few slightly more serious, more underlying stomach-cramping reasons why I didn't want to go home. Actual real concerns that made getting into a little bit of debt a far favourable option to being on that plane in ten days' time.

Firstly, the end of this trip had come upon me all of a sudden, just as I felt I was getting to the nitty gritty of the learning opportunities it presented. I'd spent the first month or so completely overwhelmed by every experience, the next couple growing cocky, thinking I knew everything there was to know about travelling and life, and then having that reality come crashing down on a busy street in Peru, in a dimly lit bar in Cartagena and on a yoga retreat in the Colombian mountains. The last month or so had seen me finally face up to the importance of looking after my safety, learning to make the right decisions, how to deal (or not deal) with members of the opposite sex and, most recently, and probably most importantly, how detrimental it is to fall into a pointless void of comparing myself to others, and speculating about how they perceive me. I'd been waylaid in a big way, forced to challenge my outlooks on everything, and now I was left with one huge question – the question that I'd actually come away to answer: how was I going to find the satisfaction I'd been seeking?

By now, I'd realised my error in being so quick to blame others for why I wasn't happy. I'd deemed all advice 'bad', and blamed it for distracting me from what I wanted to do – even though I didn't really know what that was. Slowly, and through considerable trial and error, I'd learnt to listen to the right advice, and to interpret it subjectively. As a result, the realisation also dawned on me that I couldn't blame other people for why I wasn't where I wanted to be – I needed to start taking responsibility for myself. I had to take control. I could clearly do it. I'd nearly completed my journey, and I was alive. I'd used the knowledge I acquired to figure out how to travel. Now I needed to use this new knowledge of myself to work out a plan for the future.

If I were to go home now, I risked reverting to old patterns and allowing all the lessons I'd learnt over the course of my trip to disintegrate into thin air somewhere over the Atlantic Ocean. I needed to make the time to focus on finding the solution to the conundrum I'd set out to solve. When I'd decided to skedaddle five months ago, my aim had been to return with an overabundance of experiences to write about, a list of 'next-steps' and an address book oozing new contacts I'd have made from having articles published as I travelled. The experiences were there – I'd diligently noted them all down in notebooks – but the ideas, and the prospects? They were non-existent. My intentions had been golden, but then I got completely carried away looking around rather than down at the page and neglected my main reason for booking the flight in the first place. My tail was well and truly between my legs and the words of my boss rung loudly in my ears…

Amy, I know you'll come to regret this… mark my words.

The thought that John might end up being right was too much to face up to, especially in the Colombian heat.

I was desperate to have something significant to show from this time away, other than just tales of fun and games. I couldn't let what I'd hoped would be a life-defining trip become nothing more than fond memories.

I knew what I needed to do. I needed to go somewhere where I could get some peace and quiet. Somewhere where it would be impossible to get sucked into monitoring what people in my life were up to via their various carefully curated social media channels. Where I could dodge well-meaning questions from loved ones back home that might make me panic, about where I'd be living and working. I'd go where there was no internet or phone signal. Up into the Sierra Nevada de Santa Marta mountains, the highest coastal mountain range in the world at that, to Casa Elemento, where if I offered to help out, they might just let me have a free bed.

▲▲▲▲▲▲▲▲

Luckily, I had a friend on the inside. Mandolin had been the first person to let me in on the relative secret of the hostel before my doomed trip to see Lucas, and before I'd reverted to pre-South America Amy on her retreat. We'd been lying in the sun at Costeño Beach when she rolled over, her trucker cap pulled low over her blonde hair and blue eyes, which were looking at me conspiratorially…

'Hey, you wanna go somewhere new with me?'

I put down *Game of Thrones*.

'Tell me more.'

'I know this beautiful place in the mountains that I think you'll like. It could be just the spot for you right now. How about it?'

'When do we leave?'

A day later we set out for Minca. From there we embarked on a sweaty three-hour hike up the jungle road leading to Casa

Elemento. The road is constantly changing as you climb higher. At the start the way is dusty and you have to hug the edges to avoid walking in the glaring sunshine. As you progress 30 minutes, 40 minutes, things take a tropical turn, and you walk alongside a bubbling river flowing down the mountain, criss-crossed above by vines and bordered by flower-filled bushes, past enormous bamboo trees fanning up and out into the sky higher than houses. Temperatures fall as you reach pine forests where the vibe takes a turn for the moody and you find yourself walking through thick patches of clouds, before emerging the other side into brilliant sunshine. It may be just one track, but you journey through a number of eco-systems en route to 'that bunch of hippies living on the mountain', as the empanada seller in Minca called them as he bagged up our snacks for the trip.

When we arrived, sweaty and parched, I wasn't disappointed. The view of snowy mountain peaks and dense jungle, the urban sprawl of Santa Marta and the Caribbean Sea twinkling in the distance, was undeniably spectacular, but it was the refreshments that really got my blood pumping...

'Can I get you a cup of tea?' Jean, one of the four owners of the hostel, hollered in a thick Scottish accent from over by the bar.

At this, my ears pricked up. *Tea, you say? Prove it.*

South America's tea will never set the world on fire. Argentinian *mate* is one thing, but when it's breakfast time and you're parched, there's only one thing a true Brit craves with an intensity akin to Batman pursuing, well, *anything* – a good cup of tea.

It took just two days on the continent for me to realise the error I'd made not cramming a sandwich bag full of English Breakfast and stashing it alongside my socks. While almost every other experience brought some semblance of joy, every cup of tea I sipped brought nothing but bitter exasperation – how could a teabag this weak even exist? How has Lipton tea survived so many years when it's this SHIT?

Despite constantly being proven right, I kept on truckin', hoping that any given day I'd discover a cup of tea that bore even a slight resemblance to Tetley, or... *be still my beating heart...* PG tips. I made a concerted effort not to complain about it, to scowl too visibly at the boxes of 'black tea' or to fling full-to-the-brim mugs into the nearest bin in disgust. I double- and triple-bagged. I played around with my milk quantities. I tried to compensate for lack of flavour by piling in sugar after sugar while fighting back frustrated tears. Nothing made it drinkable, and I missed it... so much so that every time I met anyone from Yorkshire I'd ask their opinion, and then we'd hold each other as we both sobbed.

'What kind do you have?'

Jean reached under the bar and, with the wide grin of a game-show hostess, she produced a miracle... a box of PG tips.

Sweet tears of happiness stung my eyes. Not only was I on top of a mountain, I was on top of the world.

As Jean placed that long overdue steaming cup of heaven into my hands, I knew that it was love. Love for this beautiful Scottish thirst quencher, for this hostel, for the finest beverage that'd passed my lips in five months – the tea-to-milk ratio was bang on, the brew time 100 per cent accurate. It had been more than worth the wait. It tasted like liquid sunbeams.

In addition to its prize beverage, Casa Elemento seemed the perfect option for a lady trying to figure out what to do next. Firstly, it had all the staples required by adults who aren't fully committed to the notion of 'growing up': a tree house, slack line, camp fire, six dogs, two cats and a ruddy bloody swimming pool. More importantly, its total isolation from the outside world afforded me the peace and quiet I needed to finally focus on myself – to process where I'd been and what I'd done and, fingers crossed, to formulate that all-important game plan.

But first I needed to see if they'd take me.

▲▲▲▲▲▲▲▲

'Mandoliiiin…' I sidled up beside her as she sat eating papaya in La Brisa Loca the morning after the yoga retreat, 'reckon Casa Elemento could do with an extra pair of very helpful, very capable hands?' I wiggled my fingers at her, flaunting my impressive finger length.

'Sure thing, bud. Let me call them.' Mando whipped out her phone and started to dial.

'Hey, Jeany. It's Mandolin. Can Amy come work with you guys? Uh huh, sure thing, let me ask…' She covered the mouthpiece and looked at me. 'Aimz, can you cook?'

'Cakes!'

I heard loud cheering from the other end of the phone.

'You're in!'

BOOM.

▲▲▲▲▲▲▲▲

Life at Casa Elemento was bloody lovely. The hostel sits on a hill, hugged on three sides by a deep jungle valley. It's like a moat of every shade of green, and you're the King of the Castle. The tiered-sides leading down to the communal hammock are dotted with trees and vegetable patches that are fiercely guarded and maintained by Andrew, another of the four owners, who hails from Toronto and rises early to tend to the veggies and answer emails over a pint or two of coffee. I know I've already harped on about the view, but it is really something. To be greeted with all the best the world has to offer (jungle, mountains, ocean) every time you exit the building really takes it out of you. I definitely exhausted the average human's quota of the word 'woah'. I also did a lot of open-mouthed pointing. This was because despite the view remaining the same (which would have been enough to satisfy me), something cool and weather-y was always happening, which gave you something new to look at – whether that was thunderclouds wreaking havoc over the towns and jungle below; such clear weather we could see onto the roof of La Brisa Loca through a telescope (which I *hadn't* bought to spy on Chris just FYI); or the clouds coming so high you were either walking within them, or upon them.

As is always the job of the new fresh-faced recruits, I was appointed Coffee Captain, which sounds only slightly cooler than it was. Essentially it meant waking up well before the rest of the hostel to ensure there was a huge vat of coffee ready to rock at the sign of the first riser. I didn't mind my assignment at all, especially because coffee and sunny early mornings are a favourite combo of mine and this was potentially the world's best spot to marry the two. After I'd got the coffee brewing, I'd sit back with a mug of PG heaven and enjoy the sights and sounds of the jungle. You could hear howler monkeys hooting and hollering, making a racket akin to a fleet of helicopters as they made their way through the surrounding trees. There was a toucan that would come and perch at the end of the bar and just watch me from the side of his face. He wasn't one for conversation but we hung out in respectful silence at least twice a week. Parakeets liked to dive-bomb the pool, or me, as I challenged myself to carry all the hostel's mugs in one go from the kitchen to the bar. The only native that didn't like me, or anyone for that matter, was Biscuit – the world's meanest jungle cat. I've never seen evil eyes like it, or heard a miaow that cut to my core like his – this kitty was mean in the extreme. I'm talking scratching-eyeballs-out-of-other-cats'-heads, attacking-dogs-twice-his-size kitty. There may have been spiders, snakes and maybe even the odd scorpion lurking out of sight, but it was this cat that made me live in fear of being cornered. Although at first there was a lot of staring and hissing first thing in the morning (from him, mostly), over my time there we gradually learnt to co-exist... but I never turned my back on him. Not once. I treasure my eyeballs, as we well know.

When the coffee was poured and bellies were full from breakfast, my tasks would vary. I'd paint stuff. Bake cakes using fruit foraged from the jungle. Change beds. Do laundry. Rake up leaves. Wash up. Make granola. Invent games to entertain guests. Fetch beers for Ed and Jack, the two remaining owners, who were always building something, chopping something, or strategising the next thing on their building agenda – a climbing wall, a zip line, snazzy new bungalows. But when I wasn't doing that, I'd just chat to people, and keep them hydrated. It was simple work, and hardly ground-breaking, but it was a pleasure to feel useful after five months of pleasing myself.

One of my major aims post retreat, was to take a leaf out of the yogis' books and try to be more present in my interactions rather than so in my head. I needed to try to combat my inherent tendency to overanalyse. If I was going to work out what made me happy, I needed to pay attention to how things affected me, rather than wasting time wondering what effect they were having on other people. The retreat had forced me to acknowledge how awful it is to be preoccupied with what other people are thinking and doing. I'd wasted enough precious time worrying and wondering – I wasn't going to make that same mistake here.

One of my favourite things about Casa Elemento was that you never knew who was going to arrive. There were guests from all over the world. Some came for days, some stayed for weeks, some were just passing by for one night. Some had travelled here on the same motorbikes that had transported them all around South America. Some were fresh off volunteering assignments at nearby hospitals or schools. Some were heading home with new business ideas, plans to relocate or with dreams for onward travel. Some days, no one would come at all, and then a group would arrive on foot having hiked through the jungle specifically to watch the sunset from our impressive vantage point. Everyone that visited Casa Elemento had been somewhere, done something and was going through the same process as me – taking some time out to work things out.

In my first week or two on top of that mountain, my predominant train of thought was, 'Blimey, I think I could bloody live 'ere!' I wandered around in a daydream, high on the thought of finding a Colombian utopia of my own to afford me this life of total relaxation. Like a shirty teenager refusing to go shopping with their mother, I shuddered every time anyone mentioned London, and allowed myself to get carried away comparing life on top of this mountain with life back home. The relaxed pace of life, the wonderful simplicity of my day-to-day tasks, the fact that from all the way up here I was constantly aware I was on earth, which made it far easier not to get wrapped up in inconsequential things. I genuinely thought I was onto something. I felt happy. Maybe mountain life was the life for me? I could stay forever, and then I'd never have to worry about getting a 'respectable' job or wearing clothes that weren't elasticated. I could give up brushing my hair altogether, forgo make-up in favour of an all-over golden body tan and spend my life prancing around barefoot. Lovely jubbly. Maybe rather than looking for answers to the life I had back home, I'd stumbled upon a new answer – a new kind of life altogether…

▲▲▲▲▲▲▲

'So, Miss Baker, I hear you're a writer?' Ed asked me, sizing me up through cigarette smoke.

It was the end of my second week and it was the first time since I'd arrived that all the guests were in bed, and we had the chance to enjoy a peaceful team beer.

'Yeah, I'm trying!'

'What kind of stuff do you write?' Jean enquired.

'I suppose you could call it "travel humour"?' I squirmed.

'Cool, man!' they all commented in relaxed semi-unison.

'So you must have written loads while you've been away?' asked Jack as he pulled another five beers from the fridge.

'Hmm… not so much. That was the plan, but I definitely could have done A LOT more.'

'But you've got shitloads of notebooks?' He smirked, gesturing at the small pile I'd left on the side of the bar. 'This one even says, "My First Book" on it!'

I laughed, 'My mate Lindsey gave me that as a going-away gift – it wasn't me that wrote that! I know it looks like there's loads but they're just full of pointless bits and pieces that don't really mean anything. I've only had a couple of things published while I've been here. I've been lazy.'

'Can we read some?'

'Sure, Jean, if you really want to? Let me dig you out something that I'm not completely embarrassed by tomorrow.'

'Woah, man,' Ed cut in, 'what's with the negativity? You're funny: I'm sure it's great.'

'Yeah, maybe. I'm just a bit pissed off at myself at the moment for not being more proactive, and now I'm pretty much at the end of my trip, so I've run out of time to salvage it.'

'Not if you decide to stay!' Jack interjected.

'Ha… sure. But even so, it's nearly time and I feel guilty that I haven't achieved what I initially set out to.'

'I wouldn't worry about it. Surely it's not all about getting published?' Ed asked, taking a swig of his beer.

'Yeah,' I half-agreed, 'but can I really call myself a "writer" if I'm not putting work out there for people to read?'

Andrew, who up until this point had been just smiling his encouragement, cut in. 'You know what I think?' he said, pointing his cigarette at me. 'Maybe these notebooks are just your way of figuring out what you *want* to get published… did you think of that?'

They all turned from Andrew to me and nodded.

'Maybe this time wasn't about getting published… maybe it was about research?'

'Huh! Well, that's an interesting way of looking at it.'

▲▲▲▲▲▲▲

The next morning while the rest of the hostel were still snoozing, I took my notebooks down to the giant hammock and, for the first time, had a real read through of everything I'd recorded. They were a mess: memories noted out of order, sentences highlighted, circled or underlined enthusiastically, later reflections scribbled in margins. There were notes about locations, dudes, friends, mistakes. There were a couple of book ideas. I'd scribbled the names of those whose advice had ended up being relevant at the tops of pages where I'd recalled how I'd messed up, and how it'd made me feel. In-between these descriptions and records of funny and resonant things people had said to me, there were all the lessons I'd been learning as I went:

If a man's not suitable, they aren't suitable – don't make them suitable out of boredom.
This had been a big one for me – from Daniel to Lucas and Chris. Maybe I'd finally addressed my tendency to crave male attention, even when it came from the wrong sources, or when friendship would have been the better outcome.

Learn to be happy in your own company.
I'd always been good at being alone, but now I also felt confident about it too. I'd learnt a lot about what I actually like and dislike both in terms of the world and my character traits.

You don't have to prove yourself to anyone.
It might have taken me the whole trip, and it may well be a lesson I have to continue learning for years to come but this was the big one – to just let go of what other people think.

I turned to a page where I'd written all about my encounter with Daniel, the handsome Portuguese numerologist. Alongside 'GOOGLE NUMEROLOGY', I'd underlined a couple of the bits that clearly resonated most at the time…
   'You turn and run every time the going gets tough. Some of your most valuable life lessons could be learnt from sticking around, and learning from those situations.'

Well, this was correct. I'd always been one to turn on my heel and Tom Cruise-run away from things the minute I experienced even the slightest bit of boredom… to new cities, new countries, from job-to-job. I hadn't stuck with anything longer than 18 months since university. And I'd graduated eight years ago.

This turn-and-run attitude had definitely been challenged on this trip. I hadn't been able to turn back halfway up Huayna Potosí, which meant I finally saw the benefits of actually achieving something for once. I'd been forced to keep going when normally I'd have adopted any tactic necessary to remove myself as quickly as possible from that challenging situation. I didn't want that mountain to be the only thing I ever conquered. There were challenges that held far more significance for me, and this time, hopefully, I'd be more determined because I now understood the elation of a successful outcome.

The jungle had been full-on, too – but it had taught me that discomfort often leads to experiencing spectacular things. I didn't want to avoid feeling challenged any more just for an easy life.

I'd also been forced to face up to aspects of my personality that I'd managed to ignore up until this point. From searching for US dollars in Argentina, to trusting complete strangers, to letting myself get ill because of my laissez-faire attitude towards what is best for me, I couldn't avoid facing up to my laziness, my naivety, my tendency to worry, overthink situations and take things too personally. Being in situations where my shortcomings were exposed helped me finally accept and understand them. Travelling alone had shown me how much I had to learn, and then taught me those lessons – and then some. Back in London, I hadn't been able to address what I had managed to here. Everything I was told back home felt like instructions rather than suggestions, and because I'm inherently stubborn, I'd refused to hear it.

'You're scared to put yourself out there.'

Perhaps I had been. But now I'd taken this trip, despite the elements of it I feared, and reaped the many benefits of doing so – I certainly wouldn't be scared any more.

Maybe Andrew was right, and this time did count as research after all…

▲▲▲▲▲▲▲▲

'I'm thinking I might write a book,' I announced to Mandolin one day a couple of weeks later.

I'd been considering this idea ever since that morning in the hammock, and in quiet moments I'd been adding to my notes, getting down the stuff I'd neglected to record while in a funk about being a useless, unpublished idiot. I hadn't voiced this idea to anyone, until now…

Mandolin popped up from behind the fridge door with a huge smile on her face.

'Yes! Write a book! That's a fuckin' rad idea. Oh man, that's cool!' Mandolin poured us both some juice, and came and sat beside me at the bar. 'Oooh, maybe this is your "thing".'

I tilted my head. Mandolin smiled knowingly. 'Okay, come on then, shower me with some yogi philosophy,' I said.

'Get ready, girl! If you look closely, Aimz, most people hanging round here have their thing, man. You think everyone's just bumming around, but people are making plans and getting shit done. Just look at who you know here now.'

'You mean the guys that run this place?'

'Yeah – *especially* these guys! These guys work HARD. They barely rest. Jack can hardly move his neck. I worry that they work *too* hard.'

She was right of course. After my initial honeymoon period at Casa Elemento, I'd quickly caught on to the fact that Jack, Jean, Ed and Andrew rarely stopped: they were four impressively driven business owners merely disguised as completely unintimidating scruff bags. Day after day they were up and at 'em, taking care of their jobs, heavy lifting, building, cleaning and keeping the books in order. Even when they were sitting down drinking beers or having a smoke, they weren't making idle chit-chat, they were planning – what they'd do that afternoon, tomorrow, next month, next year… what they could do to make this place bigger, better, and everything they wanted it to be. They were passionate and relentless.

Was I passionate enough about *anything* to work as hard as they did? Was that thing writing? I *thought* so, but could I be sure? If I hadn't been writing all the time on this trip, did that show that I didn't care enough? Shouldn't I be constantly compelled to write if I want to be a writer? Did I actually want it enough to justify all the years I'd already spent doing it without making any real progress, and to keep on trying? By the time I left London, I'd been making a reasonable living as a writer for four years. The work that I'd done had been poorly paid, and at times utterly shit, but I had kept going and kept trying, because it was the one constant I had.

'It's not just them; the guys at Costeño Beach… me, man, I'm trying to make my stuff happen too.'

'You're not *trying* to make it happen, mate, you're doing it! Your retreat was great. Things are going well, aren't they?'

'Sure, I'm doing fine, but I'm just starting out too – things can always go better. Being an entrepreneur is hard; everything's a learning curve. I've put all my eggs in this yoga and wellness-retreat basket. Stuff falls through. People break their word. I mess up a lot because I'm learning. It's tough, dude – making the decision to shun how things usually work, to stop listening to what other people think is best for you and to do something different to what most people do.'

Maybe that had been what I'd been most scared to do – admit to others and myself that I wanted to do something different. Maybe I'd needed to make all the decisions I had this far, and done all the jobs I'd done, just so I could work out they weren't for me.

'Worth it though, surely?'

'Of course! But you've got to want it otherwise you'll get beaten by the person who cares more. You've gotta know that it's the thing you want to do more than anything, the thing you want to build the rest of your world around, because it'll be on your mind *constantly*. Even when you don't think you're thinking about it, you're thinking about it.'

I'd been so frustrated back in London. This meant every suggestion pissed me off because there were so many people making them that I couldn't hear my own. Although ignoring advice had caused me to make mistakes, it had also been helpful: it had afforded me an arena to experience enough, and make enough decisions for myself, that maybe this time round I'd actually learnt my lessons.

'Sounds full-on.'

'It is. But… if it's what speaks to you… if it's the only thing you can think about, or the only thing you want to do… you've gotta heed that call, Aimz. And if you really want it, you won't mind working crazy hard – until you can't move your neck like Jack either, because you're working towards the thing that matters to you. At least, that's what I tell myself.'

'Ah shit – that sounds like a right ball-ache.'
'Then you'd better get to work.'

▲▲▲▲▲▲▲

If I was deciding here and now to go after the one thing I knew I wanted – a successful writing career – I needed to work out a way to do it in London; a place where it's incredibly difficult not to compare yourself to the people around you, being successful in different ways, achieving their own goals. I had to hope that now, having learnt first-hand that living your life to impress others can make you unhappy, I'd behave differently.

Up until this conversation with Mandolin, I'd felt like I could stay at Casa Elemento forever, but now I could see that there was a time limit on how long I could spend there, helping them achieve their dreams, before I needed to go after my own. After all, that's what I'd been doing for far too long now – chasing other people's dreams and ideas rather than my own. I could delay the inevitable, or I could save myself what little money I did have left, actually get on my flight home, and get to work on figuring out how the hell you go about writing a book.

Decision made.

▲▲▲▲▲▲▲

Soon enough, my six weeks were up, and it was time to head to Bogotá for my return flight. Although I was devastated to be leaving the place and the people who'd unknowingly taught me so much, I also felt somewhere, even if it was just in the tips of my toes, that it was the right thing to do. London has so much to offer — maybe I'd just needed to be away for a while to realise that.

Turns out that leaving South America wasn't, as I'd so desperately feared, the end of my journey. It was just the break I needed, to learn the lessons necessary, so that it could finally start.

WINNER = *THE EXPERT*

'The less I needed, the better I felt.'
Charles Bukowski

At first, Casa Elemento felt like a playground: a safe haven away from everything, where I could have fun and escape from having to give any thought to reality. By the time I left, it had become the school attached to the playground: the place where I finally sat up and took notice of the lessons I'd unwittingly learnt along the way.

By putting myself in a location with fewer distractions, and barely any influence from the outside world, I was able to block out all the noise and realise what actually mattered: the one plan that was always there waving at me from behind my computer screen, trying to get me to look up and realise I was unhappy because I was wasting time on other people's dreams rather than giving my own the attention they deserved. There had been constant distractions everywhere in London; so many voices offering different suggestions. And there had been so many people everywhere, both online and in real life, that my world felt crowded with those I perceived as being in my way. Turns out they weren't. I was the only one standing in my way – I just had to put myself on top of a mountain to realise that.

Mikey was wildly wrong – the closest I came to an orgy was a group hug in the giant hammock. Perhaps there were orgies going on down in the jungle valley, but I never caught wind. Bukowski's words ring truer than any of the expert advice I've consulted for this whole book. When I broke it down to what really mattered, I could see that all I wanted and needed, besides my friends and family of course, was to achieve this one goal. Now I knew what my plan was. In every sense, the less I needed, the better I felt.

LESSONS LEARNT

Initially, I thought that the owners of Casa Elemento had an easy life. They were living in a beautiful place, in the sunshine, hanging out with interesting people and making money at the same time – they had it made! It didn't take long for me to notice just how tirelessly they worked, seven days a week. This was their dream and they were working hard to make it happen, no matter how exhausted they were, or how thankless backpackers can be. They had grand plans that they've since made happen. They weren't just lucky – they worked hard for their success.

It was hanging around Jean, Jack, Ed, Andrew, Mandolin, and the dudes at Costeño Beach, that made me appreciate that if you want something badly, you're going to have to put in the work, and take the chances. If you know that you want a certain life, that's the price you pay. Seeing how their hard work had paid off motivated me to go after my own pay-off. From stopping and taking a look at how I'd been living, I could finally see that I was doing the right thing. *My* right thing. And nothing else mattered.

EPILOGUE

MY ADVICE:

Take the time to pay attention.

Amy Baker

A year or so later and I'd managed to successfully bash out three chapters I was finally happy with. The time had come to start schmoozing literary agents so I was skulking around the shelves of Hatchards in Piccadilly, flipping to the backs of books to note down names of agents who'd secured publishing deals. I sensed a man browsing beside me peering over my shoulder to take a look at what I was scribbling down.

'Do you mind if I ask what you're up to young lady?' This chap was in his sixties, very smartly dressed, a posh umbrella with a wooden handle hooked over his wrist.

'No, of course not! I'm writing a book at the moment, so I'm just noting down some agents to approach.'

'Oh you're writing a book! How very ambitious of you!'

'Thank you.' It was ambitious, but that was exciting, because this time I cared. I'd been working hard and was committed to making it happen because I knew I wanted the result. Having finally learnt to listen to myself, I was no longer making wild guesses about what I should do, and what might make me satisfied – this was it.

'You know, it's a tough game. I once fancied myself a budding crime writer.'

'Great! Did you ever have anything published?'

'Oh no, dear! It's an awfully difficult business, let me tell you. I hope you're doggedly determined, or chances are you won't get there. Thousands don't.'

'Yeah, so I understand.' I slotted the book I was holding back into place.

Before my trip, this kind of interaction with a stranger would have made me apoplectic. There's a high chance I would have disregarded his age, seized his fancy umbrella, pointed the steel tip right at his eyeball and then asked him where the hell he got off. Or I would have at least imagined that scenario as I huffed towards Hatchards' wooden spiral staircase, before flipping him the bird from a safe distance, behind the bestsellers table.

I'd been so frustrated about where I was and what I was doing, that it had been far easier to get angry, and shift blame onto others so I didn't have to address the fact that I couldn't quite manage to make the changes I wanted to see in myself. I'd thought back then that I had encyclopedic knowledge of my inner workings – it's safe to say I didn't have a clue. Thank goodness I'd made the choice to pay attention, practice and learn. It meant now I was far less prone to aggressive thoughts and overreactions to normal, everyday encounters with people. Which is a huge relief.

'A friend of mine's son has been trying to get his book published for almost a decade!' the man continued.

'Oh dear.'

'Yes, I believe he's become awfully depressed; just can't seem to move on. I hope that doesn't happen to you, dear, but best you prepare for the worst.'

His tone of voice couldn't have been more reminiscent of some of the advice I received before my trip, from Sally's completely obvious and downright terrifying advice about 'trying' not to be raped, to Mary who told me that, if in doubt, always shoot for the testes. It reminded me of the well-meaning advice of my loving parents, of colleagues who told me to prepare for the worst and look out for those who might try to slit my throat, and of Diane who very rightly warned me off rat. This stranger was doing what all those people had been doing: telling me what they thought they knew about something. Having that information wasn't harmful to me – it was just additional information that I could choose to interpret as I wished.

Fortunately my days of allowing negative comments from complete strangers to nark me are long gone. I've evolved into a human duck. If an opinion doesn't serve me, it pools in my feathers and then I just shake it off as I waddle away. I don't ignore everything of course – ignoring the good advice I'd received over the years had just meant I missed out on chances to learn, and helpful hints about which areas of myself could use some work.

I smiled at this well-meaning stranger. 'I'm going to try to stay positive.'

'Good idea! Takes enormous perseverance to get anywhere in this world, and a little positivity certainly can't hurt.' *Well said.*

I nodded and turned to leave. 'Anyway, have a lovely day. It's nice to meet you.'

And it was nice to meet him – he had a nice face, was awfully polite and, now that I'd done what I needed to do to reach my own conclusions and to become my own expert, I could see that his advice came from a good place, and that it was a waste of time to read anything more into it.

'And you! Best of luck to you!'

'Thanks, and to you!' I laughed to myself as I walked away, and sang Mary's words to myself from all those months ago: *'And I promise to always go for the testes.'*

'What was that, dear?'

'Oh, sorry.' I turned around with a grin. 'I just said, I'll certainly be trying my best-y!'

Because that's what we're all doing, right?

ACKNOWLEDGEMENTS

To my agent Jen Christie – thanks for always laughing at my jokes, and for believing in this book. To everyone at Summersdale, for being so kind and welcoming. Debbie – for your eagle eye, and Abi – for being a complete champion, and pleasure to work with. Thanks for everything, especially the inspirational cat photos.

To every beaut I met in South America. Jean, Jack, Ed and Andrew – my time with you guys at Casa Elemento was so incredible I still think about it daily. To all the dudes at Costeño Beach – such good times with you all. Mandolin – I'm delighted you lent me your hat, and Chris, thanks for being a great human and friend.

Massive love to everyone who read early chapters and said nice things – Tammy Two Skins, Kooks, Conor, Emily, Hooksy, Bonham, Josie, Charlie Boyd, Rosy Edwards, Simmsy, and of course, Stomps, what an inspiration you are. Honoured to be your girl crush – you are 100 per cent mine. Anna and Damo for being first readers, and love inspiration. Thanks to everyone who helped me out, Charlotte, Niki and Rob, Ducky, Nicky Burnham, Rachface, Christine Purkis, and Kate Hudson. Hector – for reading and considering every chapter, for noticing things I didn't notice, and for being a golden god. Surely, now it's time for some mead? L'Rage – what a supportive, generous, and understanding group you champs are. I love you all. You too, Bateman.

Thanks to every hero who let me crash at their house – Anne Legg, you're the best – thank you for flip-flop advice and for birthing Virginia's best human. Richard and Leslie Saltsman, and Carew, Zorro (and Hogan). To Bonks – No1 Brother in the god damn world, thank you for always offering wisdom I actually listen to, and to both you and Katy– thank you for reading my chapters, giving me a place to stay, and for being the most wonderful family I could ask for. Eggman – you legend, and Rich, Henry and Ruth – for showing me the importance of trying, planning, and being a responsible human. Leggers – not a day goes by that I don't thank my lucky stars that you exist. Thanks for the pep talks and for never leaving your leg man. Kinzett – my angel. Thanks for the support, for discussing minute details for far longer than necessary, for giving me a home, and for being such a wonderful friend. Bobby – there are many, many reasons, but mostly thank you for your rational perspective and for always being my hero. Mum and Dad – thank you for your patience and understanding, for letting me keep all my stuff in your garage, and for raising me to seek out adventure and happiness. I love you.

Big love to anyone I might have forgotten and everyone who cared enough to offer me their words of wisdom in the first place. Lastly, to everyone reading this book – thank you for picking it up. I hope it made you laugh.